KU-393-012

THE STRUCTURE OF THE UNITED NATIONS GENERAL ASSEMBLY:

Its Committees, Commissions and Other Organisms

1946-1973

Volume III

by

Blanche Finley

1977
Oceana Publications, Inc.
Dobbs Ferry, New York

Library of Congress Cataloging in Publication Data

Finley, Blanche, 1906-
  The structure of the United Nations General
Assembly, its committees, commissions, and other
organisms, 1946-1973.

  Bibliography: p.
  Includes index.
  1. United Nations. General Assembly.
I. Title: The structure of the United Nations
General Assembly . . .
JX1977.A495F56   341.23'2   77-72373
ISBN 0-379-10240-4 (set)
      0-379-10243-9 (Vol. III)

©Copyright 1977 by Oceana Publications, Inc.

All rights reserved. No part of this publication may be reproduced or transmitted in any form or by any means, electronic or mechanical, including photocopy, recording, xerography, or any information storage and retrieval system, without permission in writing from the publisher.

Manufactured in the United States of America

TABLE OF CONTENTS

Annexes:

Chapter VIII

REVISION AND COMMEMORATION OF THE
CHARTER

United Nations Committee on the Programme
for the Commemoration of the Tenth Anniversary of the Signing of the Charter (1955)

Committee on Arrangements for a Conference
for the Purpose of Reviewing the Charter
(1957-1967)

Preparatory Committee for the Twenty-fifth
Anniversary of the United Nations (1969)

Committee for the Twenty-fifth Anniversary
of the United Nations (1970-1971)

REVISION AND COMMEMORATION OF THE CHARTER

United Nations Committee on the Programme for the Commemoration of the Tenth Anniversary of the Signing of the Charter

Established by Assembly resolution 889 B (IX), of 17 December 1954.

Terms of Reference

The Assembly recommended the acceptance, by the Government of each Member State, of the invitation (GAOR, Sess.IX, Annexes, agenda item 73, A/2864, annex I) of the City of San Francisco to hold a commemorative meeting in that city in 1955; decided to commemorate the tenth anniversary of the signing of the Charter in the City of San Francisco by arranging a seven-day commemoration, including four days of unofficial meetings of the Members of the United Nations, to be held in San Francisco from 20 to 26 June 1955, the unofficial meetings to be presided over by Eelco van Kleffens (Netherlands), President of the ninth session of the General Assembly; requested the Secretary-General, in cooperation with a committee, established by the resolution, and in consultation with the civic authorities of the City of San Francisco, to arrange the program for the commemoration.

Membership

Paragraph 3 designated the members of the Committee as follows:
> Belgium, Canada, China, Czechoslovakia, Ecuador, France, India, Lebanon, Turkey,

USSR, United Kingdom, and United States
of America. On the basis of the decision
taken by the General Assembly at the same
meeting, those Members having permanent
seats on the Security Council were included in the membership of the Committee.

The representatives of members were as follows:
Paul Bihin and Jules Woulbroun (Belgium);
David M. Johnson and J.E. Thibault (Canada); Dr.
Shih-Shun Liu, Chiping H.C. Kiang (China);
Jaroslav Rybar (Czech); Dr. José Vicente Tru-
jillo, Dr. Julio Prado (Ecuador); Pierre Ordon-
neau (France); Arthur S. Lall and Dr. Balachan-
dra Rajan (India); Edward Rizk (Lebanon); Vahap
Asiroglu and Ilhan Akant (Turkey); Georgy F.
Saksin (USSR); A. H. Clough and P.E. Ramsbotham
(UK); James J. Wadsworth, William O. Hall,
Albert F. Bender, Jr. (USA).

Action

The officers of the Committee were: Chairman:
Dag Hammarskjold, Secretary-General; David M.
Johnson (Canada), Vice-Chairman. Andrew W.
Cordier (USA), Executive Assistant to the Secretary-General, was the Committee Secretary. A
report -- Commemoration of the Tenth Anniversary
of the Signing of the United Nations Charter --
(ST/SG/6, Sales no.: 1955.I.26) was published
in December 1955, and contained the program for
the commemoration, the proceedings of the meetings held from 20 to 26 June 1955, and also included the list of members and representatives
of the Committee created by the General Assembly
and the San Francisco Executive Committee for
the United Nations Commemorative Session.

Committee on Arrangements for a Conference for the Purpose of Reviewing the Charter (A/AC.81/-)

Established by Assembly resolution 992 (X), of 21 November 1955, mindful that paragraph 3 of Article 109 of the Charter provides that if a General Conference of the Members of the United Nations for the purpose of reviewing the Charter had not been held before the tenth annual session of the General Assembly, such a conference should be held if so decided by a majority vote of the Members of the General Assembly and by a vote of any seven members of the Security Council.

Terms of Reference

Believing it desirable to review the Charter in the light of experience gained in its operation, and recognizing that such a review should be conducted under auspicious international circumstances, the Assembly decided that a General Conference to review the Charter should be held at an appropriate time, and appointed a Committee consisting of all the Members of the United Nations to consider, in consultation with the Secretary-General, the question of fixing a time and place for the Conference, and its organizations and procedures; and requested the Secretary-General to report to the twelfth session of the Assembly.

Paragraph 4 of the resolution requested the Secretary-General to complete the publication program undertaken pursuant to General Assembly resolution 796 (VIII) of 23 November 1953 and to continue, prior to the twelfth session of the Assembly, to prepare and circulate supplements, as appropriate, to the <u>Repertory of Practice of United Nations Organs</u>.

Membership

The Committee was composed of all Member States of the United Nations.

Action

At meetings held in 1957, 1959, 1961, 1962, 1963, 1965, and 1967, the Committee decided time was not appropriate for a review of the Charter and recommended the fixing of a date for a review conference be postponed.

Reports of the sessions were as follows:

<u>1957</u> -   The Committee met on 3 June. Its officers were: Chairman: Abdul Hamid Aziz (Afghanistan); Vice-Chairman: José Vincente Trujillo (Ecuador); Rapporteur: Franz Matsch (Austria). The report (<u>GAOR</u>, Sess.XII, <u>Annexes</u>, agenda item 22, A/3593), was issued on 19 June 1957.

<u>1959</u> -   The Committee held three meetings in September. Its Chairman: Abdul Rahman Pazhwak (Afghanistan), and Vice-Chairman, Carlos Adrián Perdomo (Honduras), were elected to replace Mr. Aziz and Mr. Trujillo. The report of the session (<u>GAOR,</u> Sess. XIV, <u>Annexes,</u> agenda item 22, A/4199) was issued on 8 September 1959.

<u>1961</u> -   The Committee met on 14 September, electing Enrique Jiménez (Panama) to replace Mr. Perdomo who had left New York. The report (<u>GAOR</u>, Sess. XIV, <u>Annexes</u>, agenda item 18, A/4877) was issued on 18 September 1961.

1962 -   The fourth session, held on 5 September, elected Fernando Volio Jiménez (Costa Rica) to replace Enrique Jiménez (Panama) who was no longer a member of his delegation. The report (GAOR, Sess. XVII, Annexes, agenda item 21, A/5193) was issued on 14 September 1962, and drew attention to a note of the Secretary-General regarding publication of supplements to the Repertory of Practice (A/AC.81/4, mimeographed).

1963 -   The fifth session held meetings from 1 to 10 July, with the same officers presiding: Abdul Rahman Pazhwak (Afghanistan) as Chairman, Fernando Volio Jiménez (Costa Rica) as Vice-Chairman, and Franz Matsch (Austria) as Rapporteur.

During the session, the Committee established a nine-member Sub-Committee, appointed by the Committee Chairman, consisting of Brazil, Guinea, Iran, Liberia, Nepal, Netherlands, Poland, UAR, and Uruguay. Its officers were: Chairman: Mohamed H. El-Zayyat (UAR); Vice-Chairman: Carlos María Velázquez (Uruguay); and Rapporteur: Ram C. Malhotra (Nepal). The Sub-Committee held five meetings from 29 July to 22 August. It sent a letter (A/AC.81/SC.1/1, mimeographed) to all Member States, inviting an expression of their views concerning a recommendation that should be made to the General Assembly. Fifty-one Member States replied, and the report (A/AC.81/7) of 22 August 1967 was annexed to the Committee report.

The Committee's report of its fifth session (GAOR, Sess. XVIII, Annexes, vol.1, agenda item 21, A/5487) was issued on 4 September 1963.

1965 -   The sixth session met on 16 September, with José Luis Redondo Gómez (Costa Rica) as

Vice-Chairman, and Kurt Waldheim (Austria) as
Rapporteur, filling the vacancies left by Mr.
Volio Jiménez and Dr. Matsch. Its report (GAOR,
Sess. XX, Annexes, vol. 2, agenda item 26,
A/5987) was issued on 22 September 1965.

1967 -   The seventh session, held on 11-12
September, elected Luis Demetrio Tinoco (Costa
Rica) to replace a vacancy left by Mr. Redondo
Gómez. Its report (GAOR, Sess.XXII, Annexes,
vol.2, agenda item 26, A/6865) was issued on 18
October 1967.

The following Assembly resolutions called for
the Committee to be continued, and for the work
envisaged in paragraph 4 of resolution 992 (X)
(concerning the publication of supplements to
the Repertory of Practice of United Nations Organs) be continued:

        1136 (XII), 14 October 1957
        1381 (XIV), 20 November 1959
        1670 (XVI), 15 December 1961
        1756 (XVII), 23 October 1962
        1993 (XVIII), 17 December 1963
        2114 (XX), 21 December 1965
        2285 (XXII), 5 December 1967.

Documents - Summary records of the committee
(A/AC.81/SR.1-13) covered meetings held from 3
June 1957 to 16 September 1965. None were issued for the 1967 meeting, and no meetings of
the Committee have been held since that date.
All documents issued under the document series
symbol were in mimeographed form.

Preparatory Committee for the Twenty-Fifth Anniversary of the United Nations (A/AC.139/-, restricted series)

At its 1749th plenary meeting, on 19 December 1968, at the twenty-third session, the General Assembly adopted without objection a recommendation of the General Committee (GAOR, Sess. XXIII, Annexes, agenda item 8, A/7250/Add.5) of 18 December 1968, that the 25th anniversary of the United Nations "should be commemorated in an appropriate manner and that the Assembly should appoint a Preparatory Committee for the twenty-fifth anniversary of the United Nations, consisting of all the Member States represented in the General Committee at the twenty-third session".

Terms of Reference

The Preparatory Committee, the Assembly decided, would be entrusted with the task of preparing recommendations and plans for the anniversary, and would be asked to report to the Assembly in the very early part of the twenty-fourth session.

Membership

In accordance with this decision, the following 24 Member States were appointed:

Austria	Lebanon
Bulgaria	Mauritania
Byelorussia	Peru
Canada	Philippines
China	Somalia
France	Sweden
Ghana	Togo
Guinea	Trinidad and Tobago
Guyana	Uganda
India	USSR
Iran	United Kingdom
Italy	United States of America

Action

The Preparatory Committee met at United Nations
Headquarters from 20 January to 13 October 1969,
and elected Richard M. Akwei (Ghana) as Chair-
man; the Permanent Representatives of Bulgaria,
Guyana and India as Vice-Chairmen; and Mario
Franzi (Italy) as Rapporteur.

The report of the Preparatory Committee (GAOR,
Sess.XXIII, Annexes, agenda item 25, A/7690) of
9 October 1969, dealt, inter alia, with the
theme of the anniversary, programs, and activities at the international level, commemorative
stamps and medallions, awards, youth participation, and public information activities. Assembly resolution 2499 (XXIV), of 31 October
1969, acted on many of the proposals and suggestions of the Preparatory Committee and established a Committee for the Twenty-Fifth Anniversary of the United Nations.

Committee for the Twenty-Fifth Anniversary of the United Nations (A/AC.144/-, restricted series)

Established by Assembly resolution 2499 (XXIV), of 31 October 1969, after consideration of the report of the Preparatory Committee (GAOR, Sess. XXIII, Annexes, agenda item 25, A/7690).

Terms of Reference

The Assembly decided that the theme of the anniversary should be "Peace, justice and progress" and expressed the desire that the year 1970 should mark the beginning of an era of peace; decided also that a commemorative session of the General Assembly should be held during a short period, culminating on 24 October 1970 with the signing and/or adoption of a final document or documents.

In view of the above, the Assembly established a Committee for the Twenty-Fifth Anniversary of the United Nations, to (a) draw up and coordinate plans for the anniversary; (b) organize suitable activities for the anniversary, to be undertaken by the United Nations, in the light of the report of the Preparatory Committee; (c) consider proposals and suggestions, in relation to the anniversary, for increasing the effectiveness of the United Nations; and to prepare, with the assistance of the Secretary-General, a suitable text for a final document or documents to be signed and/or adopted during the commemorative session, for consideration by the General Assembly, during the early part of its twenty-fifth session.

In paragraph 12 of the resolution, the Assembly decided to convene a world youth assembly within the general framework described in the report

of the Preparatory Committee, and invited the
Governments of Member States to consider the
inclusion of representatives of youth in their
delegations to the twenty-fifth session of the
General Assembly.

Membership

Paragraph 5 of the resolution called for a Committee composed of 25 members to be designated
by the President of the General Assembly on the
basis of equitable geographical distribution
and bearing in mind the composition of the Preparatory Committee.

At the 1797th plenary meeting, on 31 October
1969, the President of the General Assembly
designated the following members:

Austria	Italy
Bulgaria	Lebanon
Byelorussia	Mauritania
Canada	Peru
China	Philippines
France	Somalia
Ghana	Sweden
Guatemala	Togo
Guinea	Trinidad and Tobago
Guyana	Uganda
India	USSR
Iran	United Kingdom
	United States of America

Action

The Committee met at United Nations Headquarters
in New York and held 20 meetings from 9 December
1969 to 11 September 1970. Its officers were:
Chairman: Richard M. Akwei (Ghana); Vice-Chairmen: Mrs. E. Gavrilova (Bulgaria), Miss A.

Jardin (Guyana), and S. Sen (India); Rapporteur:
Giovanni Migliuola (Italy). P.A.T. Thompson
(Guyana) later replaced Miss Jardin.

Preliminary reports on organization of the commemorative session (GAOR, Sess.XXV, Annexes,
vol.1, agenda item 21, A/8060 and Add.1) were
issued on 15 September and 9 October 1970. Two
reports on the preparation of the final document
(Ibid., A/8103 and Add.1-2) were issued on 9,
21 and 22 October 1970. On 24 October 1970, the
Secretary-General transmitted to the Assembly
texts of documents relating to the commemoration of the 25th anniversary (A/L.600, offset)
as follows: Program of action for the full implementation of the Declaration on the Granting
of Independence in Colonial Countries and Peoples; Declaration on Principles of International Law concerning Friendly Relations and Cooperation among States in accordance with the Charter of the United Nations; an international
development strategy for the Second United Nations Development Decade; and the Declaration
on the Occasion of the Twenty-fifth Anniversary
of the United Nations.

In resolution 2627 (XXV), of 24 October 1970,
the General Assembly accepted the Declaration
on the Occasion of the Twenty-fifth Anniversary,
text of which was set forth in the resolution.

In compliance with the establishing resolution,
the Committee issued its final report (GAOR,
Sess.XXVI, Suppl.25 (A/8425)) in November 1971.
The report dealt with the commemorative session,
the final declaration, the World Youth Assembly,
commemorative stamps and medals, the celebration
in San Francisco and at the United Nations Office at Geneva, public information activities,

commemoration of the anniversary at the national level and by specialized agencies and other Members of the United Nations system, ratification of, or accession to, international instruments, and suggestions for increasing the effectiveness of the United Nations.

Chapter IX

ORGANIZATION AND PROCEDURES OF THE GENERAL ASSEMBLY

Committee on Procedures and Organization (1947)

Special Committee on Methods and Procedures of the General Assembly (1949)

Special Committee for the Consideration of the Methods and Procedures of the General Assembly for Dealing with Legal and Drafting Questions (1952)

Committee on Special Administrative Questions (1953)

Committee on Control and Limitation of Documentation (1958)

Ad Hoc Committee on the Improvement of Methods of Work of the General Assembly (1962-1963)

Committee on Conferences (1967-1969)

Special Committee on the Rationalization of the Procedures and Organization of the General Assembly (1971)

ORGANIZATION AND PROCEDURES OF THE GENERAL ASSEMBLY

Committee on Procedures and Organization (A/AC.12/-)

Established by Assembly resolution 102 (I), of 15 December 1946.

Terms of Reference

The resolution directed the Secretary-General to make a study of measures to economize the time of the General Assembly, and of the provisional rules of procedure, taking into account:

(1) the memoranda of 2 and 24 October 1946 submitted by the delegation of Canada (GAOR, Sess.I (part 2), General Committee, annex 16, A/92, and Add.1);

(2) suggestions received from Members pursuant to an invitation by the Assembly to forward to the Secretary-General any suggestions they might wish to make regarding measures to economize the time of the Assembly and proposed changes in the provisional rules of procedure;

(3) the views expressed in the Sub-Committee of the General Committee during the consideration of this question (Ibid., annex 16a, A/BUR/71), 12 December 1946; and

(4) the experience acquired and the precedents established during its first session.

The Sub-Committee (paragraph 3) was created by the General Committee at its 25th meeting, on 6 November 1946, composed of representatives of Bulgaria, France, Panama, Syria, Ukraine, USSR, United Kingdom, Uruguay, and Canada (in a consultative capacity), to consider the question of measures to economize the time of the General Assembly. It held two meetings, on 23 November and 6 December, and issued its report on 12 December 1946 (A/BUR/71).

The resolution appointed a Committee on Procedures and Organization, consisting of 15 members to be designated by their Governments, which would meet one week before the opening of the second regular session for the purpose of studying the provisional rules of procedure and internal organization of the General Assembly, and to present a report thereon to the General Assembly at the beginning of the second regular session.

Membership

The 15 members designated in the resolution were:

Argentina, Belgium, Canada, China, Cuba, Denmark, France, Greece, Haiti, Peru, Ukraine, USSR, United Kingdom, United States of America, and Yugoslavia.

Their representatives were as follows: José Arce, Rodolfo Muñoz, Enrique V. Corominas (Argentina); Roland Lebeau (Belgium); Escott Reid (Canada); C.L. Hsia (China); Carlos Blanco (Cuba); William Borberg (Denmark); Pierre Ordonneau (France); Alexis Kyrou (Greece); Max H. Dorsinville (Haiti); Carlos Holguín de Lavalle (Peru); Alexei D. Voina (Ukraine); Alexei A. Krasilnikov (USSR); C.D.W. O'Neill (UK); Paul Taylor (USA); Leo Mattes (Yugoslavia).

Action

The Committee met at Lake Success from 9 September to 8 October 1947. Its elected officers were: Chairman: Escott Reid (Canada); Vice-Chairman: Carlos Holguín de Lavalle (Peru); Rapporteur: William Borberg (Denmark).

The Committee had before it the report of the Secretary-General (A/316 and Corr.1, Add.1-2, mimeographed), issued on 8 July 1947. The report of the Committee (GAOR, Sess.II, Plenary meetings, vol.2, annex 4b, A/388), of 23 September 1947, contained a series of suggestions and a proposed redraft of the provisional rules of procedure, based on the draft rules submitted by the Secretary-General. These were adopted by the General Assembly (resolution 173 (II)) on 17 December 1947.

Special Committee on Methods and Procedures of the General Assembly (A/AC.30/-)

Established by Assembly resolution 271 (III), of 29 April 1949.

Terms of Reference

Mindful of the increasing length of General Assembly sessions, and of the growing tendency towards protracted debates in its plenary meetings and committees, the Assembly decided to create a Special Committee in order to:

(a)   consider methods and procedures which would enable the General Assembly and its Committees to discharge their functions more effectively and expeditiously;

(b)   submit, if possible, a preliminary report to the General Assembly during the second part of its third session; and

(c)   transmit a report to the Secretary-General, not later than 15 August 1949, for circulation to Members and for consideration at the fourth regular session of the General Assembly.

Membership

Paragraph 1 of the resolution designated the following Member States as members of the Special Committee:

> Belgium, Brazil, Canada, China, Czechoslovakia, Egypt, France, India, Iran, Mexico, Sweden, USSR, United Kingdom, United States of America, and Uruguay.

Their representatives were listed in paragraph 2 of the report of the Special Committee (A/937).

Action

The Special Committee held 23 meetings in June,

July and August 1949. Its elected officers
were: Nasrollah Entezam (Iran) Chairman;
Vladimir Houdek (Czech) Vice-Chairman; and
Sven Grafström (Sweden) Rapporteur. After the
departure of Mr. Entezam, Mr. Grafström was
elected Chairman by the application of rule 96
of the rules of procedure, and combined the
functions of Chairman with those of Rapporteur.

During its second meeting, on 10 May, the Special Committee decided, on the proposal of its
Bureau, that because its members were obliged
to attend meetings of other committees it would
be unable to submit a preliminary report before
the end of the second part of the third session.

The report of the Special Committee (GAOR, Sess.
IV, Suppl.12 (A/937)) was issued on 12 August
1949, and published in November 1949. It contained inter alia chapters on recommendations
concerning the establishment of the agenda, relating to the organization of General Assembly
sessions, and to the conduct of debates in
plenary meetings and in committees; the Secretary-General's proposal for an interval of
prayer or meditation in meetings of the General
Assembly, statements of views of individual
delegations. Two annexes contained proposals
submitted to the Special Committee, and a memorandum by the Secretary-General on mechanical
and technical devices.

Assembly resolution 362 (IV), of 22 October
1949, approved the amendments and additions to
its rules of procedure, as set forth in annex I
to the resolution, which would enter into force
on 1 January 1950; and approved the recommendations and suggestions of the Special Committee,
as set forth in annex II of the resolution.

Special Committee for the Consideration of the
Methods and Procedures of the General Assembly
for Dealing with Legal and Drafting Questions
(A/AC.60/-)

Established by Assembly resolution 597 (VI) of
20 December 1951, as the "Special Committee on
Legal and Drafting Questions". At its sixth
meeting, on 4 September 1952, the Committee
changed its title to the "Special Committee for
the Consideration of the Methods and Procedures
of the General Assembly for Dealing with Legal
and Drafting Questions".

Terms of Reference

The resolution requested the Special Committee
to consider the documents, draft resolutions
and amendments submitted to the Sixth Committee,
during the debate on the methods and procedures
for dealing with legal and drafting questions,
as well as the records of its debates, to study
the question further and to report thereon to
the General Assembly at its seventh session.

Membership

Paragraph 1 of the resolution established a
special committee of fifteen members, consisting
of the representatives of each of the following
Member States:

> Belgium, Canada, Chile, Czechoslovakia,
> Egypt, El Salvador, France, Indonesia,
> Iran, Israel, Sweden, USSR, United King-
> dom, United States of America, and
> Venezuela.

Their representatives were listed in paragraph
2 of the Special Committee's report (A/2174).

Action

The Special Committee met at United Nations Headquarters from 27 August to 5 September 1952. Its elected officers were: Chairman: Djalal Abdoh (Iran); Vice-Chairman: Victor M. Pérez Perozo (Venezuela); Rapporteur: A. Raymond Crépault (Canada). Its report (GAOR, Sess. VII, Annexes, vol. 2, agenda item 53, A/2174) was issued on 8 September 1952.

Assembly resolution 684 (VII), of 6 November 1952, endorsed the recommendations of the Special Committee, and directed that the terms of the recommendations as outlined in paragraph 1 of the resolution should be embodied as an annex to the rules of procedure of the General Assembly, and that the said annex should also set out, verbatim, paragraphs 19, 20, 29, 30, 35-39 of the report of the Special Committee.

Committee on Special Administrative Questions
(A/AC.68/-)

Established by Assembly resolution 681 B (VII),
of 21 December 1952.

Terms of Reference

Noting paragraphs 38 to 44 of a memorandum of
the Secretary-General (GAOR, Sess.VII, Annexes,
agenda item 69, A/2214), the Assembly decided
to refer these paragraphs to a Committee to meet
in the interval between the seventh and eighth
sessions of the General Assembly, and to report
to the eighth session. The paragraphs dealt
with certain aspects of the procedure of the
General Assembly and portions of the Statute of
the United Nations Administrative Tribunal. The
report of the Committee was to be circulated,
with the recommendations of the Advisory Committee on Administrative and Budgetary Questions,
to all Members of the United Nations four weeks
before the opening of the Assembly's eighth
session. In his note (A/AC.68/1, mimeographed),
of 29 April 1953, the Secretary-General outlined
the tasks of the Committee as:
(1) the study of paragraphs 38-44 of the
Secretary-General's memorandum on the relationship between the Secretariat and the General Assembly;
(2) the study of paragraphs 154-156 of
the rules of procedure of the General Assembly;
and
(3) the study of the Statute of the
United Nations Administrative Tribunal.

Membership

The resolution established the following membership of eleven:
Australia, Belgium, Brazil, Chile, China,

Dominican Republic, Greece, Iraq, Norway, Pakistan, and Poland.

A list of representatives was published in paragraph 2 of the Committee report (A/2429).

Action

The Committee held two meetings on 4 and 8 May 1953; its elected officers were: Chairman: Viqar Ahmed Hamdani (Pakistan); Vice-Chairman: Luis Bastian-Pinto (Brazil); Rapporteur: K.G. Brennan (Australia). The Committee adopted a resolution deciding to make no recommendations on matters referred to the Committee unless further proposals on those matters were made by the Secretary-General or by the government of a Member State; invited the Secretary-General to report to the Committee any proposals he wished to make or which might be made by the governments of Member States; and, if no such proposals were made, to report that fact to the Assembly. At the outset of the Committee's discussion, the Secretary-General stated that before making any proposal to the Assembly regarding the reorganization of the present administrative structure of the Secretariat, he would have to make a thorough study of the working of the Secretariat, and he was also not prepared to make any proposals on the subjects referred to the Committee by the Assembly.

At its third meeting, on 3 August 1953, in accordance with its resolution, noting no proposals had been received, the Committee decided to make no recommendations to the General Assembly, but to allow Members and the Secretary-General time for further study of the matters in question.

The eighth session of the General Assembly, in
resolution 764 (VIII), of 3 November 1963, took
note of the report of the Committee (<u>GAOR</u>, Sess.
VIII, <u>Annexes</u>, agenda item 49, A/2429), of 3
August 1953.

Committee on Control and Limitation of Documentation (A/AC.92/-, restricted series)

Established pursuant to Assembly resolution 1203 (XII), of 13 December 1957.

Terms of Reference

The resolution (a) requested the Secretary-General to continue his efforts, in cooperation with Member States, to reduce the length and amount of documentation produced during 1958; (b) suggested for this purpose the figure of 25% below the 1957 level for the over-all output of such documentation; (c) established a Committee of nine Member States to consult with and advise the Secretary-General on the most effective means of implementing the resolution, and to report and make recommendations to the General Assembly at its thirteenth session concerning methods of achieving reductions in the over-all output of documentation; (d) invited the Secretary-General to report to the General Assembly, before the opening of the thirteenth session, on the steps taken and on the nature and extent of the reductions achieved.

Membership

Pursuant to paragraph (c) of the terms of reference, establishing a committee of nine, the membership was as follows:

Dr. Raúl Quijano (Argentina), Chairman;
Derek C. Arnould (Canada), Rapporteur;
Yin-Shou Che (China);
Philippe Marandet (France);
Kadhim Khalaf (Iraq);
Eduardo Espinosa y Prieto and Arturo L. de Ortigosa (Mexico);
Niaz Naik (Pakistan);
Vladimir Molchanov (USSR);
A.H.M. Hillis (UK).

Action

The Committee held 17 meetings between 18 March
and 11 July 1958. Its report (<u>GAOR</u>, Sess.XIII,
<u>Annexes</u>, agenda item 51, A/3888) was issued on
19 August 1958. Annex I of the report contained
texts of previous General Assembly resolutions
on the subject, and annex 2 contained statistics
on the volume of documentation reproduced by
mimeograph and offset processes. The report of
the Secretary-General (<u>Ibid</u>., A/3921) on steps
taken and the nature and extent of the reductions achieved, was issued on 19 September 1958.
Assembly resolution 1272 (XIII), of 14 November
1958, commended the Secretary-General's report,
endorsed the Committee's report, and requested
the Secretary-General and the ACABQ to report
on the operation of the present resolution at
the fifteenth session.

Ad Hoc Committee on the Improvement of Methods of Work of the General Assembly (A/AC.111/-)

Established at plenary meeting 1162, on 30 October 1962, when the General Assembly decided to refer an item, proposed by the Tunisian Delegation, on the subject of improvement of the methods of work of the Assembly (GAOR, Sess. XVII, Annexes, vol.3, agenda item 86, A/5165) to a committee of the thirteen Vice-Presidents of the seventeenth session of the General Assembly, plus the past Presidents of the Assembly serving as members of their delegations, as well as Mongi Slim (Tunisia) who had submitted a memorandum on this subject (Ibid., A/5123), as President of the sixteenth General Assembly, to the Secretary-General on 3 May 1962 or, in his absence, the Chairman of the Tunisian Delegation. The President of the seventeenth Assembly was to serve as ex officio Chairman of the Committee.

Terms of Reference

The Committee was requested to study available documentation, including Ambassador Slim's memorandum, together with any other suggestions that might be received.

Membership

Thirteen Vice-Presidents of the seventeenth General Assembly:
> Australia, Belgium, China, Colombia, France, Guinea, Haiti, Jordan, Madagascar, Romania, USSR, United Kingdom, United States of America.

Past Presidents of the Assembly serving as members of their delegations:
    Peru - Dr. Víctor A. Belaunde
    Ireland - Frederick H. Boland
    Mexico - Dr. Luis Padilla Nervo

Tunisian Ambassador or, in his absence, Chairman of the Tunisian Delegation:
    Tunisia - Mongi Slim, or Taieb Slim

President of the seventeenth General Assembly, ex officio Chairman of the Committee:
    Pakistan - Muhammad Zafrulla Khan

Paragraph 5 of the Ad Hoc Committee report (A/5423) listed the representatives and their alternates.

Action

The Committee met on 13 November, 11 and 17 December 1962; its elected officers were: Chairman: Muhammad Zafrulla Khan; Vice-Chairman: Frederick H. Boland (Ireland); Rapporteur: Taieb Slim (Tunisia). A preliminary report (Ibid., A/5370) was issued on 17 December 1962. Assembly resolution 1845 (XVII), of 19 December 1962, continued the Committee with the same membership and terms of reference, requesting it to transmit a report to the Secretary-General by 31 May 1963.

The Committee held nine meetings between 4 February and 1 March, and seven more from 30 April to 27 May 1963. The same officers served, except that Mr. Boland (Ireland), the Vice-Chairman, acted as Chairman in the absence of Mr. Zafrulla Khan (Pakistan). Its report (GAOR, Sess.XVIII, Annexes, vol.2, agenda item 25, A/5423) was issued on 28 May 1963.

Assembly resolution 1898 (XVIII), of 11 November 1963, approved the recommendations in the report, in particular those set forth in sub-paragraphs (a) to (g) of the resolution, covering the functions of the President of the General Assembly, of the Main Committees, the General Committee, and the presiding officers.

Committee on Conferences (A/AC.130/-)

Established by Assembly resolution 2239 (XXI),
of 20 December 1966.

At the twenty-fourth session, in resolution 2609
(XXIV), 16 December 1969, the Assembly decided
to reconsider at its twenty-fifth session the
question of the membership and terms of reference of the Committee on Conferences, and in the
meantime not to reconstitute the membership of
the Committee.

A Committee on Conferences was again established
by resolution 3351 (XXIX), Part II, of 18 December 1974.

Terms of Reference

The Committee was established on an experimental
basis subject to review by the General Assembly
at its twenty-fourth session, and its functions
were defined as follows: (a) to submit to the
General Assembly at each regular session a calendar of meetings and conferences in the following year for the competent organs of the General
Assembly; (b) to undertake such other tasks in
this general field as might be requested by the
General Assembly.

Paragraph 7 of the resolution further defined
the terms of reference, and in paragraph 9, the
Assembly recommended that all competent organs
of the United Nations, including subsidiary organs of the General Assembly, should bear in
mind that proposals involving new meetings and
conferences would be subject to the recommendations of the Committee on Conferences and to
final approval by the Assembly.

Paragraph 13 of resolution 2609 (XXIV), 16 December 1969 requested the Secretary-General to

submit to the General Assembly at its twenty-fifth session a calendar of conferences for 1971 and preliminary calendars for 1972 and 1973. The Secretary-General continued to perform this function, until a new Committee on Conferences was established at the twenty-ninth session of the General Assembly (resolution 3351 (XXIX) on 18 December 1974.

Membership

The resolution called for a membership of fifteen Member States, to be designated by the President of the General Assembly on the basis of broad equitable geographical distribution, to serve on the Committee for three years. Members of the Committee were requested to nominate representatives with wide experience in the work of the United Nations.

On 18 January 1967, (GAOR, Sess. XXI, Annexes, agenda item 74, A/6634), the President informed the Secretary-General that he had designated the following Member States to serve for a period of three years:
> Algeria, Burma, Congo (Democratic Rep. of), Czechoslovakia, France, India, Jamaica, Japan, New Zealand, Spain, USSR, United Kingdom, United States of America, Venezuela, Zambia.

Annexes to each of the reports of the Committee contained a list of representatives of Members.

Action

The Committee on Conferences held ten meetings between 15 September and 14 December 1967, and elected Brian J. Lynch (NZ) as Chairman, and A. S. Gonsalves (India) as Vice-Chairman/Rapporteur. Its report (GAOR, Sess.XXII, Annexes, vol.3,

agenda item 75, A/6991/Rev.1) was issued on 22
December 1967, and contained inter alia chapters
on major special conferences, the 1968 program
of conferences and meetings, and the 1969 calendar of conferences and meetings. Annex II of
the report contained the calendar of conferences
and meetings for 1968 (A/6991/Rev.2, offset, of
2 February 1968, brought this calendar up to
date); annex III contained a list of special
conferences from 1958 to 1968.

In 1968, the Committee held a series of 13 meetings between 1 March and 23 April, and a second
series on 6 September 1968. The reports (GAOR,
Sess.XXIII, Annexes, vol.2, agenda item 75,
A/7361 and Add.1 of December 1968 and January
1969, both issued as separate documents), contained chapters on the pattern of recurrent conferences and meetings for 1969, 1970, and 1971.
Annexes contained (I) evaluation of elements
which might figure in determining that a conference was one of major proportions; (II) bodies
that should be asked to dispense with summary
records; (III) calendar of conferences and meetings for 1969, (IV) for 1970, and (V) for 1971.
The addendum brought information up to date on
annexes III and V.

The Committee held 13 meetings between 6 February and 13 November 1969. Its report (GAOR,
Sess.XXIV, Suppl.26, (A/7626, and Corr.1)), issued in November 1969, included chapters on the
progress made toward reduction in the meetings
programs and volume of documentation; consideration of meetings and documentation questions by
other bodies; and annexes contained calendars of
conferences and meetings for 1970, 1971 and 1972.
The addendum (Ibid., Suppl.26A, A/7626/Add.1)
was issued in January 1970, and reflected the
modifications required by subsequent decisions

of the General Assembly in the calendar of conferences for 1970.

In resolution 2609 (XXIV), of 16 December 1969,
the Assembly decided to reconsider the questions
of the membership and terms of reference of the
Committee on Conferences, and in the meantime
not to reconstitute the membership of the Committee. Paragraph 13 of the resolution requested the Secretary-General to submit to the General Assembly at its twenty-fifth session a calendar of conferences for 1971, and preliminary
calendars of conferences for 1972 and 1973.

Resolution 2693 (XXV), of 11 December 1970, took
note of the report of the Secretary-General
(GAOR, Sess.XXV, Annexes, agenda item 75, A/8138),
of 28 October 1970; and approved an addendum
(A/8138/Add.1, offset), 12 November 1970, on the
calendar of conferences and meetings of the United Nations for 1971, and a preliminary calendar
for 1972 and 1973; a second addendum (A/8138/
Add.2, mimeographed) presented modifications in
the calendar for 1971.

Resolution 2834 (XXVI), of 17 December 1971, approved the Secretary-General's report on the
pattern of conferences (A/8448, and Add.1-2,
offset), issued on 4 October, 23 November, and
20 December 1971.

Resolution 2960 (XXVII), of 13 December 1972,
approved the calendar as set forth in the Secretary-General's report (A/8790, and Corr.1 and
Add.1-3, offset) issued in October, November and
December 1972; and requested the Secretary-General to continue to submit, in close cooperation
with ACABQ, programs of meetings and conferences
to the General Assembly at each session for its
approval.

In a decision at the 219th plenary meeting, on 11 December 1973, at the twenty-eighth session, the General Assembly, on recommendation of the Fifth Committee (GAOR, Sess.XXVIII, Annexes, agenda item 82, A/9427, paragraph 7), approved the calendar for 1974 as set out in the report of the Secretary-General (A/9214, annex I, Add. 1 and Corr.1, offset), of 18 October 1973; and endorsed observations and recommendations in the report of ACABQ (A/9345, offset), of 26 November 1973.

Resolution 3351 (XXIX), of 18 December 1974, approved the calendar for 1975 as set forth in the Secretary-General's report (A/9768 and Corr. 1, and Add.1, offset) of 3 October 1974 and 15 January 1975; and in Part II of the resolution established, on an experimental basis and subject to review at its thirty-second session, a Committee on Conferences composed of 22 Member States (A/AC.172/-).

Documents

Summary records (A/AC.130/SR.1-10) were issued for the first ten meetings of the Committee on Conferences, held from 15 September to 14 December 1967. No further summary records were issued. Other documents issued under the Committee document series symbol (A/AC.130/-) were issued in mimeographed form.

Special Committee on the Rationalization of the Procedures and Organization of the General Assembly (A/AC.149/-)

Established by Assembly resolution 2632 (XXV), of 9 November 1970.

Terms of Reference

The Special Committee was to study ways and means of improving the procedures and organization of the Assembly in accordance with the provisions of the Charter, including the allocation of agenda items, the organization of work, documentation, rules of procedure and related questions, methods and practices, and was to submit a report to the Assembly at its twenty-sixth session.

The Committee was authorized to maintain and circulate summary records of its proceedings.

Membership

The resolution called for a membership of 31 Member States, chosen on the basis of equitable geographical distribution. At the 1933rd plenary meeting, on 17 December 1970, the President of the General Assembly, in pursuance of paragraph c of the resolution, designated the following as members of the Special Committee:

Afghanistan	France	Poland
Austria	Greece	Romania
Barbados	India	Senegal
Bolivia	Japan	Tunisia
Brazil	Lebanon	UAR
Burundi	Liberia	USSR
Cameroon	Netherlands	United Kingdom
Canada	Nigeria	USA
Chile	Pakistan	Venezuela
Denmark	Philippines	Yugoslavia
		Zambia

A list of representatives appeared in annex I
of the report of the Special Committee (A/8426).

Action

The Special Committee held 45 meetings from 2
February to 9 July and 8 to 17 September 1971.
Its elected officers were: Chairman: Otto R.
Borch (Denmark); Vice-Chairmen: Ibrahim Boye
(Senegal); Eugeniusz Kulaga (Poland), Motoo
Ogiso (Japan); Rapporteur: Bernardo Brito
(Brazil), from 2 February to 4 June; Ronaldo M.
Sardenberg (Brazil) from 4 June.

On 22 January 1971, a Secretary-General note
(A/AC.149/L.2, mimeographed), which contained
a synopsis of proposals considered by previous
committees which were not acted upon by the General Assembly, was debated by the Special Committee. The report of the Special Committee
(GAOR, Sess.XXVI, Suppl.26 (A/8426)), issued in
October 1971, included annexes containing statistical data on the General Assembly and the Main
Committees; and an analytical summary of views
and suggestions submitted to the Special Committee by Member States, former Presidents of the
General Assembly, and former Chairmen of Main
Committees.

The twenty-sixth session of the Assembly endorsed
the view of the Special Committee that the existing rules of procedure were generally satisfactory and that most improvements would be achieved
not through changes in the rules of procedure,
but through their better application. Assembly
resolution 2837 (XXVI), of 17 December 1971, did,
however, amend the rules of procedure by incor-
porating some modifications as set forth in annex I of the resolution.

Chapter X

FINANCIAL AND BUDGETARY QUESTIONS

A. General Financial Questions

Working Groups on the Examination of the
Administrative and Budgetary Procedures of
the United Nations (1961 and 1963)

Ad Hoc Committee of Experts to Examine the
Finances of the United Nations and the
Specialized Agencies (1966-1968)

Special Committee on the Financial Situation
of the United Nations (1972--)

Working Group on Currency Instability
(1974--)

B. Specific Financing Problems and Extra-
budgetary Funds

Negotiating Committee on Contributions to
Programs of Relief and Rehabilitation (in
Korea, and Relief and Reintegration of
Palestine Refugees) (1950-1951)

Negotiating Committees for Extra-budgetary
Funds (1952 and 1961)

Special Committee on Peace-keeping Operations (1965--)

Working Group on the Financing of the United
Nations Relief and Works Agency for Palestine Refugees in the Near East (1971--)

C. Financing of Economic Development

Committees of Nine (1953 and 1955)

Ad Hoc Committee on the Question of the Establishment of a Special United Nations Fund for Economic Development (1955-1957)

Committee on a United Nations Capital Development Fund (1961-1966)

United Nations Capital Development Fund (1967--)
Executive Board (1967--)

D. Investment of Funds and Audit of Accounts

Investments Committee (1947--)

Panel of External Auditors (1948--)

FINANCIAL AND BUDGETARY QUESTIONS

A. General Financial Questions

Working Group on the Examination of the Administrative and Budgetary Procedures of the United Nations (A/AC.104/-)

Established by Assembly resolution 1620 (XV), of 21 April 1961, concerning the financing of United Nations peace-keeping operations.

Terms of Reference

To fulfill its obligations under the Charter and recognizing that in order to fulfill these obligations, the United Nations must have at its disposal adequate financial resources and generally recognized procedures for dealing with the financial problems resulting from activities undertaken by the Organization, the Assembly decided to place on the provisional agenda of the sixteenth session, as a matter of prime importance and urgency, the question of the administrative and budgetary procedures of the United Nations, including the following points: (a) methods for covering the cost of peace-keeping operations; and (b) the relationship between such methods and the existing administrative and budgetary procedures of the Organization.

Membership

The resolution requested the President of the General Assembly to appoint a working group composed of 15 Member States -- the permanent members of the Security Council, two States from Africa, two from Asia, two from Latin America, two from Western Europe, one from Eastern

Europe, and one from the Commonwealth.

On 25 May 1961, the President of the General Assembly appointed the following membership:

Brazil, Bulgaria, Canada, China, France, India, Italy, Japan, Mexico, Nigeria, Sweden, USSR, UAR, United Kingdom, and the United States of America.

The Working Group was referred to as the "Working Group of Fifteen."

Action

The report of the Working Group (GAOR, Sess.XVI, Annexes, agenda item 62), was issued on 15 November 1961. Its elected officers were: Chairman: C.S. Jha (India); Vice-Chairman: Assen Georgiev (Bulgaria); Rapporteur: Ahmed El-Messiri (UAR). The Working Group did not present a set of recommendations for study in view of the divergence of opinion of its members, but noted that a majority of the Group favored a request by the General Assembly to the International Court of Justice for an advisory opinion on States Members' financial obligations for peace-keeping operations.

Assembly resolution 1731 (XVI), of 20 December 1961, did authorize such a request of ICJ, and requested the Secretary-General, in accordance with Article 65 of the Statute of ICJ, to transmit the resolution to the Court accompanied by all documents likely to throw light upon the question.

The Secretary-General, in a note of 15 August 1962 (A/5161 and Corr.1, mimeographed), transmitted to Members of the General Assembly the advisory opinion given by the ICJ (<u>Certain expenses of the United Nations</u> (Article 17, paragraph 2, of the Charter), Advisory Opinion of 20 July 1962: ICJ Reports 1962, p.151).

Working Group on the Examination of the Administrative and Budgetary Procedures of the United Nations (A/AC.113/-)

Established by Assembly resolution 1854 (XVII), of 19 December 1962.

Terms of Reference

Having received ICJ's advisory opinion of 20 July 1962, that the expenditures authorized in the Assembly resolutions designated in resolution 1731 (XVI) constitute "expenses of the Organization" within the meaning of Article 17, paragraph 2, of the Charter, the Assembly accepted the opinion of the Court.

The Working Group was reestablished to study, in consultation as appropriate with the Advisory Committee on Administrative and Budgetary Questions (ACABQ) and the Committee on Contributions, special methods for financing peace-keeping operations of the United Nations involving heavy expenditures, such as those for the Congo and Middle East, including a possible special scale of assessments.

It was also requested to take into account in its study the criteria for the sharing of the costs of peace-keeping operations mentioned in past resolutions of the General Assembly, giving particular attention to the following:
    (a) the references to a special financial responsibility of members of the Security Council as indicated in Assembly resolutions 1619 (XV), 21 April 1961, and 1732 (XVI), 20 December 1961;
    (b) such special factors relating to particular peace-keeping operation as might be relevant to a variation in the sharing of the costs of the operation;

(c) the degree of economic development of each Member State and whether or not a developing State was in receipt of technical assistance from the United Nations;

(d) the collective financial responsibility of the Members of the United Nations.

The Working Group was also to take into account any criteria proposed by Member States at the seventeenth session of the Assembly or submitted by them directly to the Working Group; and to study the situation arising from the arrears of some Member States in their payment of contributions for financing peace-keeping operations, and to recommend, within the letter and spirit of the Charter of the United Nations, arrangements designed to bring up to date such payments, having in mind the relative economic positions of such Member States.

The Working Group was requested to meet as soon as possible in 1963, and to submit its report with the least possible delay and in any case not later than 31 March 1963.

Membership

The resolution re-established the Working Group with the same membership as that established by Assembly resolution 1620 (XV), and increased its composition to 21 by the addition of six Member States to be appointed by the President of the Assembly with due regard to geographical distribution.

As a result, the Working Group (referred to as the "Working Group of Twenty-One") was composed of the following members (asterisks indicate the new members):

Argentina*, Australia*, Brazil, Bulgaria,
Cameroons*, Canada, China, France, India,
Italy, Japan, Mexico, Mongolia*, Nether-
lands*, Nigeria, Pakistan*, Sweden, USSR,
UAR, United Kingdom, and United States of
America.

Action

The Working Group held 18 meetings between 29
January and 29 March 1963. The elected officers
were: Chairman: S.O. Adebo (Nigeria); Vice-
Chairman: R. Quijano (Argentina); Rapporteur:
V. A. Hamdani (Pakistan). Its report (GAOR,
Sess. S-IV, Annexes, agenda item 7, A/5407) was
issued on 29 March 1963. A report by the Secretary-General on the United Nations financial
position and prospects (Ibid., A/AC.5/974) was
issued on 14 May 1963. The documents of the
Working Group (A/AC.113/2-27) containing texts
of working papers and statements of members
were reproduced in the Official Records (Ibid.).

On recommendation of the report of the Fifth
Committee (Ibid., A/5438), the Fourth Special
Session adopted a number of resolutions , among
which were the following pertinent to the work
of the Working Group:

Resolution 1874 (S-IV), of 27 June 1963,
on general principles to serve as guidelines for
the sharing of the costs of future peace-keeping
operations involving heavy expenditures, which
noted with appreciation the report of the Working Group;

Resolution 1877 (S-IV), of 27 June 1963,
on payment of arrears in respect of assessed
contributions to the United Nations Emergency
Force Special Account and the Ad Hoc Account for

the United Nations Operation in the Congo, which considered the report of the Working Group;

Resolution 1880 (S-IV), of 27 June 1963, noting that the tasks with which the Working Group was charged had not been completed, decided to continue in being the Working Group with a new mandate to recommend a special method for the equitable sharing of the costs of future peace-keeping operations involving heavy expenditures to the extent not otherwise covered by agreed arrangements; to consider suggestions regarding other sources of financing future peace-keeping operations; to explore ways and means for bringing about the widest possible measure of agreement among all Member States on the question of the financing of all future peace-keeping operations.

The Working Group was never re-established. At the nineteenth session of the General Assembly, resolution 2006 (XIX), of 18 February 1965, under the item "Comprehensive review of the whole question of peace-keeping operations in all their aspects", established a Special Committee on Peace-Keeping Operations.

Ad Hoc Committee of Experts to Examine the
Finances of the United Nations and the Specialized Agencies (A/AC.124/-)

Established by resolution 2049/Rev.1 (XX), of
13 December 1965, to carry out an over-all examination of the budgets of the United Nations
and the specialized agencies. (Known as the
"Committee of Fourteen").

Terms of Reference

The resolution requested the Secretary-General
to
(a) draw up an analysis of the finances of
the United Nations, showing actual expenditure
by type of activity, including the amount of
expenditure committed for the different peace-
keeping operations since their inception, the
resources utilized to meet them and, where applicable, the debts contracted by the United
Nations;
(b) prepare a complete statement of the
financial situation of the Organization as at
30 September 1965;
(c) deliver the document in question to
the members of the Ad Hoc Committee, as soon as
the experts have been appointed, and transmit it
at the same time to other Member States. The
Ad Hoc Committee was requested to examine the
document delivered by the Secretary-General and
to transmit its comments, through the Secretary-
General, to Member States by 11 March 1966, at
the latest.

The Ad Hoc Committee was also to
(a) examine with the assistance of the
Advisory Committee on Administrative and Budgetary Questions (ACABQ), and in liaison with the

Secretary-General and the executive heads of
the specialized agencies and the IAEA, the entire range of the budgetary problems of the United Nations and the organizations brought into
relationship with it, notably their administrative and budgetary procedures, the means of
comparing and, if possible, standardizing their
budgets and the financial aspect of their expansion, with a view to avoiding needless expenditures, particularly expenditure resulting from
duplication;

     (b) submit to the General Assembly at its
21st session, without prejudice to the terms of
reference of the Special Committee on Peace-
Keeping Operations, such recommendations as it
deemed appropriate, in order, on the one hand,
to secure better utilization of the funds available through rationalization and more thorough
coordination of the activities of the organizations and, on the other, to ensure that any expansion of these activities should take into
account both the needs they were intended to
meet and the costs Member States would have to
bear as a result.

Membership

The resolution called for a membership of 14
Member States, which the President of the General Assembly would designate, and which in turn
would appoint such experts as they deemed best
qualified to perform the functions listed in the
terms of reference.

At the 1408th plenary meeting, on 21 December
1965, the President designated the following
countries:
    Argentina, Brazil, Canada, France, Hungary,
    India, Italy, Japan, Nigeria, Senegal, UAR,
     USSR, United Kingdom, and United States of
    America.

Action

The Ad Hoc Committee met in New York from 2 February to 25 March 1966, in closed meetings. Its officers were Mario Majoli (Italy), Chairman; Karoly Csatorday (Hungary), First Vice-Chairman; Mencumbe Sar (Senegal), Second Vice-Chairman. Its report (GAOR, Sess.XXI, Annexes, vol.3, agenda item 80, A/6289, and Add.1), issued on 28 March 1966, contained an analysis of the financial situation of the United Nations, a summary of the short-term (current) financial situation as at 30 September 196 5, and a summary of the long-term financial situation. Its six annexes (A/6289/Add.1) contained a text of the establishing resolution, a list of representatives, explanatory comments of the table contained in paragraph 24 of the report, views of the delegations of the USA and France on the question of surplus accounts, questions and observations on the report of the Secretary-General and replies by the Secretary-General, and text of a letter to the specialized agencies.

A second addendum to the report (Ibid., A/6289/ Add.2) of 31 March 1966, prepared by the Secretary-General in reply to questions by the representatives of the USSR, UAR and Senegal (annex V, Add.1), provided a comparison between the appropriations approved under the regular budget of the United Nations for 1966 and corresponding expenditures in 1954. Annexes to Add.2 included growth in United Nations membership during the period 1954-1966, average increases in Base Salaries and Cost of Living/Post Adjustment Rates at Headquarters and Geneva since 1954, statement showing number of established posts approved in the professional and higher levels, general service and local level categories under Section 3 of the budget for each year from 1954 to 1966.

The Committee's second session was held in Geneva from 19 April to 6 May 1966; its third from 6 June to 19 July 1966 was held in New York. The Committee's report (Ibid., A/6343) was issued on 19 July 1966. Annex I of the report listed the representatives of the 14 countries who attended each of the three sessions.

The second session of the Committee was devoted solely to meetings with specialized agencies. The third session held 43 meetings and its Drafting Committee of the Whole held 20 meetings; it began with an examination of the financial and budgetary problem of the United Nations and concentrated its endeavors on the basic measures needed to ensure greater efficiency and real value for money in the vital work of human, social and economic development.

Resolution 2150 (XXI), of 4 November 1966, requested the Secretary-General to submit a report to the 22nd session of the General Assembly in 1967 on implementation of the recommendations of the Ad Hoc Committee. After consulting the executive heads of other organizations to which the report had been addressed, such as the specialized agencies, the Secretary-General submitted his report (GAOR, Sess.XXII, Annexes, vol.3, agenda item 80, A/6803) on 22 September 1967.

Operative paragraph 4 of resolution 2360 (XXII), of 19 December 1967, invited the Secretary-General, as chief administrator of the United Nations and in his capacity as Chairman of the Administrative Committee on Coordination (ACC), to submit to all Members and to the ACABQ, at the earliest possible date, and in any event not later than 30 April 1968, a report giving fuller information on the implementation by the United Nations, by the individual specialized agencies

and the IAEA, of each of the specific recommendations contained in the report of the Ad Hoc
Committee, indicating "not only their positions
and the action they have taken to date, but also what further action they propose to take and
the timing thereof".

The Secretary-General's report to the 23rd session of the General Assembly (GAOR, Sess.XXIII,
Annexes, vol.2, addendum to agenda item 80,
A/7124, and Add.1) was issued on 16 April and
30 September 1968. Annexes to the report contained a list of 52 recommendations of the Ad
Hoc Committee, and observations of the organizations on each of the recommendations addressed
to them. The addendum to the report (A/7124/
Add.1), presented certain additional information
relating to developments up to 31 August 1968,
since the preparation of the report of 16 April,
specifically concerning the United Nations, the
ILO, FAO, UNESCO, WHO, and WMO.

Special Committee on the Financial Situation of the United Nations (A/AC.155/-)

Established by a decision without objection of the General Assembly at the 2031st meeting of the twenty-sixth session of the Assembly, on 22 December 1971 in view of its recognition that the finances of the United Nations must be placed on a sound footing.

Terms of Reference

The Secretary-General in a statement at the first meeting of the Special Committee on 20 January 1972 (A/AC.155/R.2, mimeographed), noted that the establishment of the Special Committee had its origins in the report made to Secretary-General U Thant in December 1971, by Ambassador Edvard Hambro (Norway) (A/AC.155/R.1, 27 January 1972), in which he suggested, inter alia, that, in order to utilize the time between the twenty-sixth and twenty-seventh sessions and, if possible, to prepare the next session fully for action, delegates might consider establishing an intergovernmental working group; he proposed that it meet between the sessions to study all the facts and new suggestions for a solution to the cash liquidity position of the United Nations and the current deficit situation and consider the possible working out of concrete proposals for the next session of the Assembly. The Assembly accepted the proposal and decided that, in view of the nature of its work, the Committee should hold its meetings in private, with interpretation but without summary records.

Membership

The Assembly decided the Special Committee was to be composed of 15 members as follows:

Brazil, Canada, China, France, Ghana,
India, Japan, Kenya, Mexico, Nigeria,
Norway, Poland, USSR, United Kingdom,
and United States of America.

Action

The Special Committee unanimously elected Ole
Algard (Norway) as Chairman: Joseph Quao Cleland
(Ghana), Eugeniusz Kulaga (Poland), and Toru
Nakagawa (Japan) as Vice-Chairmen; and Juan An-
tonio Merigo Aza (Mexico) as Rapporteur, who
later was succeeded by Alvaro Carranco Ávila
(Mexico).

On 20 January 1972, the Secretary-General convened the first meeting of the Special Committee. No summary records were issued of the
meetings, and the report of the Special Committee does not record how many meetings were held
nor the dates. The report of the Special Committee (GAOR, Sess.XXVII, Suppl.29 (A/8729)) was
issued in November 1972. The annexes included
an analysis of the short-term deficit of the
United Nations as at 31 December 1972; and assessed contributions to the United Nations Regular Budget which remained unpaid, together with
assessed contributions for certain other items
which remained unpaid mainly for reasons of
principle, as at 30 September 1972.

In submitting the report, the Special Committee
noted it had been unable to formulate a common
position on the matter of resolving the financial situation of the United Nations since no
common viewpoint was reached among members of
the Committee, although the report set forth
both proposals having the support of a majority
of its members and proposals and points of view
expressed by other members.

Working Group on Currency Instability
(A/AC.164/-, restricted series)

Adopted by the General Assembly at its 2296th
plenary meeting, on 18 December 1973, on the recommendation of its Fifth Committee (GAOR, Sess.
XXVIII, Annexes, agenda item 79, A/9450/Add.1,
paragraphs 43-48).

Terms of Reference

To consider alternative solutions to the difficulties resulting from the effect of continuing
currency instability and inflation on the budgets of organizations in the United Nations
system. The Working Group should study, inter
alia, the recommendations and proposals contained in the report of the ACABQ on the effect of
continuing currency instability on the budgets
of organizations in the United Nations system
(Ibid., Suppl.8A (A/9008/Add.16)), and the draft
resolution by Cuba and Guinea (Ibid., A/9450/Add.
1, paragraph 43), A/C.5/L.1146/Rev.1), and the
discussions held in the Fifth Committee during
the twenty-eighth session, and report on the results of its work to the Assembly at its twenty-
ninth session.

Membership

At the same meeting, the President designated
the following States as members of the Working
Group:
    Bulgaria, China, Cuba, France, Germany
    (Fed.Rep.), Ghana, India, Japan, Kenya,
    USSR, United Kingdom, United States of
    America, and Venezuela.

Their representatives were listed in a Working
Group document (A/AC.164/R.1) of 22 February
1974.

Action

The report of the Working Group (A/9773, offset)
was issued on 26 September 1974. The Working
Group held 22 meetings between 20 February and
20 September 1974. At its second meeting, on
25 February, the Working Group elected Ambassador N.P. Jain (India) as Chairman, and Dr.
Rudolf Schmidt (Germany, Fed.Rep.) as Vice-
Chairman. Paragraphs 60-81 of the report of the
Fifth Committee (GAOR, Sess. XIX, Annexes,
agenda item 73, A/9960) discussed the report
and recommended measures which the Assembly a-
dopted in its resolution 3360 (XXIX), of 18
December 1974. The resolution noted that the
Working Group found no generally agreed alternatives to policies already being utilized in the
United Nations and related agencies; took particular note of the statement of the representative of the Secretary-General, contained in paragraph 7 of the report of the Working Group,
which stressed that payment by Member States in
accordance with the Financial Regulations of the
United Nations and the elimination of the short-
term deficit of the Organization would resolve
many of the currency problems faced by the United Nations, and, in turn, obviate in large
measure the need for solutions; and requested
the Secretary-General to keep these problems in
view, in consultation with members of the Administrative Committee on Co-ordination (ACC), and
to report to the thirtieth session of the Assembly.

B. Specific Financing Problems and
Extra-Budgetary Funds

Negotiating Committee on Contributions to Programs of Relief and Rehabilitation (in Korea and Relief and Reintegration of Palestine Refugees) (A/AC.41/-)

Established by General Assembly resolutions 410 B, paragraph 1 (V), of 1 December 1950 (for Korea), and 393, paragraph 8 (V), of 2 December 1950 (for Palestine refugees).

The Committee was terminated by Assembly resolution 571 (VI), of 7 December 1951.

Terms of Reference

Both resolutions requested the President of the General Assembly to appoint a Negotiating Committee for the purpose of consulting, as soon as possible during the current session of the General Assembly, with Member and non-Member States as to the amount which governments might be willing to contribute toward financing the program for relief in Korea and for the program of relief and reintegration projects for Palestine refugees.

Both resolutions authorized the Negotiating Committee to adopt procedures best suited to the accomplishment of its task, bearing in mind (a) the need for securing the maximum contributions in cash; (b) the desirability of ensuring that any contributions in kind were of a nature which met the requirements of the contemplated programs; and (c) the degree of assistance which could be rendered by specialized agencies, non-member states and other contributors. Another

clause in resolution 393 (V) asked the Committee
to bear in mind the importance of enabling the
UN Relief and Works Agency for Palestine Re -
fugees in the Near East (UNRWA) to plan its
programs in advance and to carry them out with
funds regularly contributed.

Both resolutions requested that as soon as the
Negotiating Committee had ascertained the extent
to which Member States were willing to make contributions, all delegations be notified accordingly by the Secretary-General in order that
they might consult with their Governments. It
was also decided that, as soon as the Negotiating Committee had completed its work, the Secretary-General should, at the Committee's request, arrange, during the current session of
the General Assembly, an appropriate meeting of
Member and non-Member States at which Members
could commit themselves to their national contributions and the contributions of non-Members
could be made known.

Membership

In accordance with the terms of the resolutions,
the President of the General Assembly, at the
318th plenary meeting, on 4 December 1950, appointed the following seven States as members of
the Committee:

> Canada, Egypt, France, India, United
> Kingdom, United States of America, and
> Uruguay.

Their representatives were: John W. Holmes, Al-
ternate A.R. Crépault (Canada); Mohammed Riad,
Alternate Mostafa Bey (Egypt); Philippe de Seynes
Alternate Jacques Devinat (France); Lt.-Gen. His
Highness Maharaja Jam Shri Digvijayasinhji Saheb,

Alternate A.S. Mehta (India); Lord Crook, G.T. Corley Smith (UK); John J. Sparkman, Alternate William O. Hall (USA); Dr. Emilio N. Oribe, Alternate Enrique Rodriguez Fabregat (Uruguay).

Action

A Negotiating Committee, covering both resolutions on relief in Korea and for the Palestine refugees, was set up and held its first meeting on 6 December 1950. The Maharaja Jam Saheb of Nawanagar (India) was elected Chairman and served from 6 to 14 December. From 20 December 1950, G.T. Corley Smith (UK) served until the Committee ended its work.

The first report of the Negotiating Committee (A/1744, mimeographed) of 15 December 1950, contained a letter from the Chairman of the Committee to the Secretary-General transmitting a statement on the status of the Committee's work and its plans for the future. A second report (A/1769, mimeographed) of 26 January 1951, contained a letter from the Chairman of the Committee to the Secretary-General, to which was attached its report.

The Negotiating Committee held 14 meetings, and with its second report considered it had completed the present stage of its work. Annex I of the report dealt with Korea, and annex II with the Palestine refugees. A third report (A/1801, mimeographed) of 16 May 1951, brought the information on the Committee's work up to date through annex I dealing with Korea, and annex II with the Palestine refugees.

The Committee was superseded by a Negotiating Committee for Extra-budgetary Funds established by Assembly resolution 571 (VI), of 7 December 1951.

A report of the Economic and Social Council
(GAOR, Sess. VI, Suppl. 3 (A/1884, chapter XII,
paragraphs 928-947)) of October 1951, for
ECOSOC involvement in the relief needs of
Korea.

The Committee documents (A/AC.41/-) were issued in mimeographed form and restricted in
distribution.

1. Negotiating Committee for Extra-Budgetary Funds (A/AC.54/-)

Established by resolution 571 B (VI), of 7 December 1951.

Terms of Reference

The Committee was established for the purpose of consulting as soon as possible during the General Assembly session with Member and non-Member States as to the amounts which Governments would contribute on a voluntary basis to programs approved by the Assembly, for which funds were not available through the regular budget of the United Nations and for which the Negotiating Committee was specifically asked by the Assembly to obtain pledges of voluntary contributions from Governments.

Under its terms of reference, the Committee was to obtain voluntary contributions for (1) the United Nations Relief and Works Agency for Palestine Refugees in the Near East (UNWRA); (2) the United Nations High Commissioner's Office for Refugees (UNHCR); (3) the United Nations Korean Reconstruction Agency (UNKRA); (4) the United Nations Children's Fund (UNICEF); (5) the Expanded Programme of Technical Assistance (EPTA).

Membership

The Committee was composed of seven members appointed by the President of the Assembly at plenary meeting 358, on 11 January 1952, as follows:

> Canada, France, Lebanon, Pakistan, United Kingdom, United States of America, and Uruguay. Subsequently, Colombia replaced Uruguay which withdrew as a member.

Action

The Committee elected Philippe de Seynes (France) as Chairman. Its report (GAOR, Sess. VII, Annexes, vol.2, agenda item 43, A/2210, and Corr.1, and Add.1) was issued on 6 and 14 October 1952.

Resolution 607 (VI), of 29 January 1952, authorized the Committee to continue its activities for such period as required after the close of the sixth session of the General Assembly, since it was only on 12 January 1952 that the Assembly in resolution 519 A (VI), requested the Committee to obtain pledges of voluntary contributions from Governments.

2. Negotiating Committee for Extra-budgetary Funds (A/AC.62/-)

Established by resolution 693 (VII), on 25 October 1952, the Negotiating Committee was reconstituted, with the same terms of reference, by General Assembly resolutions 759 (VIII), 5 October 1953; 861 A (IX), 29 October 1954; 958 A (X), 8 November 1955; 1091 B (XI), 27 February 1957; 1197 B (XII), 13 December 1957; 1296 B (XIII), 5 December 1958; 1440 B (XIV), 5 December 1959; 1556 B (XV), 18 December 1960.

Resolution 1728 (XVI), of 20 December 1961, established an ad hoc Committee of the Whole at each session for the purpose of announcing voluntary pledges. The Negotiating Committee for Extra-budgetary Funds, was terminated at its own recommendation in its last report.

Terms of Reference

A Negotiating Committee was reconstituted for the purpose of consulting as soon as possible with Member and non-Member States as to the amounts which Governments might be willing to contribute on a voluntary basis toward the EPTA, the programs of UNWRA, UNKRA, UNICEF, and such other programs as might be approved by the General Assembly for which funds were not available through the regular budget of the United Nations, and for which the Negotiating Committee was specifically requested by the Assembly to obtain pledges of voluntary contributions from Governments.

The Negotiating Committee was to adopt the procedures best suited to the accomplishment of its task, bearing in mind:

(a) the necessity of maintaining the identity and integrity of each program;

(b) the necessity of obtaining pledges and payments of contributions to each program as soon as possible;

(c) the need for securing the widest possible and most equitable participation in the programs;

(d) the desirability of ensuring that any contribution in kind was of a nature which met the requirements of the contemplated programs;

(e) the degree of assistance which could be continued to be rendered by specialized agencies, non-Member States and other contributors.

The Assembly also decided that, as soon as the Negotiating Committee had ascertained the extent to which States were willing to make contributions, the Secretary-General should, if the Committee so requested, arrange an appropriate meeting or meetings of Member and non-Member States at which their pledges might be made known.

Beginning with resolution 1091 (XI), of 27 February 1957, the Assembly decided to convene, during the next session of the Assembly, an ad hoc committee of the whole Assembly, under the chairmanship of the President of the session, where pledges of voluntary contributions for the two refugee programs for the following financial year would be announced, with separate meetings dedicated to each program.

The same ad hoc committee was set up by Assembly resolutions 1197 A (XII), 15 December 1957; 1296 A (XIII), 5 December 1958; 1440 A (XIV), 5 December 1959; 1556 A (XV), 18 December 1960.

Resolution 1729 (XVI), 20 December 1961, decided to establish an ad hoc Committee of the Whole Assembly, under the chairmanship of the President of the session, as soon as practicable after the opening of each regular session of the General Assembly for the purpose of announcing pledges of voluntary contributions to the refugee programs for the following year.

Membership

The resolutions cited above specified that the Committee should be composed of not more than 10 members appointed by the President of the session, and the following were selected at the plenary meetings cited:

At the 393rd plenary meeting, on 11 November 1952: Australia, Canada, Colombia, France, Haiti, Lebanon, Pakistan, United Kingdom, and United States of America.

At the 451st plenary meeting, on 5 October 1953: Australia, Canada, Chile, Colombia, France, Lebanon, Pakistan, United Kingdom, and United States of America.

At the 497th plenary meeting, on 4 November 1954: Australia, Canada, Colombia, France, Lebanon, Pakistan, United Kingdom, United States of America, and Uruguay.

At the 558th plenary meeting, on 16 December 1955: Argentina, Australia, Canada, Chile, France, Lebanon, Pakistan, United Kingdom, and United States of America.

At the 662nd plenary meeting, on 27 February 1957: Argentina, Brazil, Canada, France, Lebanon, New Zealand, Pakistan, United Kingdom, and United States of America.

At the 729th plenary meeting, on 13 December 1957, the 782nd plenary meeting, on 5 December 1958; and the 846th plenary meeting, on 5 December 1959, the same membership was reelected.

Resolution 1556 B (XV), of 18 December 1960, increased the membership to not more than 14 members; and at the 995th plenary meeting, on 21 April 1961, the following were appointed:

Brazil, Canada, France, Ghana, Ireland, Norway, Pakistan, Senegal, United Kingdom, and United States of America.

Chairmen of the Negotiating Committees:

1952 - Philippe de Seynes (France)
1953 - Dr. Karim Askoul (Lebanon)
1954 - Dr. Azkoul reelected, and succeeded by Dr. V.A. Hamdani (Pakistan) when the former left the United Nations.
1955 - Dr. V.A. Hamdani reelected
1956 - T. Wakeham Cutts (Australia)
1957 - Eurico Penteado (Brazil)

1958 - 1959 - D. C. Arnould (Canada)
1960 - D. C. Arnould reelected, but was succeeded by Raul A.J. Quijano (Argentina) when he left the United Nations.
1961 - Brandon T. Nolan (Ireland)

Action

The reports of each session of the Negotiating Committee for Extra-budgetary Funds were:

A/2478 (GAOR, Sess.VIII, Annexes, agenda item 44), 17 September 1953;

A/2730 (GAOR, Sess.IX, Annexes, agenda item 42), 20 September 1954;

A/2945 (GAOR, Sess.X, Annexes, agenda item 40), 30 August 1955;

A/3194 (GAOR, Sess.XI, Annexes, vol.1, agenda item 45), 21 September 1956;

A/3668 and Add.1 (GAOR, Sess.XII, Annexes, agenda item 43), 18 September and 4 December 1957;

A/3944 and Add.1 (GAOR, Sess.XIII, Annexes, agenda item 46), 9 October and 14 November 1958;

A/4267 and Add 1 (GAOR, Sess.XIV, Annexes, agenda item 46), 10 November 1959 and 29 February 1960;

A/4623 (GAOR, Sess.XV, Annexes, agenda item 55), 7 December 1960;

A/5031 (GAOR, Sess.XVI, Annexes, vol.2, agenda item 60), 13 December 1961.

In its report, the Negotiating Committee, noting that its present mandate expired at the close of the 16th session of the General Assembly, felt that the Assembly had sufficient experience in the technique of pledging sessions to justify putting on a regular annual basis the meetings of ad hoc committees of the Assembly to hear pledges to the refugee funds, and therefore the Negotiating Committee for 1961, having

completed its allotted task, did not recommend
that a new Committee be appointed for 1962.

Resolution 1729 (XVI), of 20 December 1961, decided that an ad hoc Committee of the Whole
Assembly, under the chairmanship of the President of the session, should be convened as soon
as possible after the opening of each regular
session of the General Assembly for the purpose
of announcing pledges of voluntary contributions
to the refugee programs for the following year;
and requested the Secretary-General to fix each
year appropriate dates for the meetings of the
Ad Hoc Committee and the Pledging Conference
for the Special Fund and the Expanded Program
of Technical Assistance convened in accordance
with Assembly resolution 1091 A (XI), of 27
February 1957, and to notify the members of
these dates in good time.

Documents issued under the Committee symbol
(A/AC.62/-) were issued in mimeographed form
and restricted in distribution.

Special Committee on Peace-Keeping Operations
(A/AC.121/-)

Established by Assembly resolution 2006 (XIX),
of 23 February 1965. (Referred to as the "Committee of Thirty-three").

Terms of Reference

Under agenda item "Comprehensive review of the
whole question of peace-keeping operations in
all their aspects", the Assembly expressed its
concern at the situation which resulted in a
deadlock at the nineteenth session of the General Assembly, and invited the Secretary-General
and the Assembly President, as a matter of urgency, to make arrangements for, and undertake
appropriate consultations on, the whole question
of peace-keeping operations in all their aspects, including ways of overcoming the then
financial difficulties of the Organization.
The resolution authorized the President of the
Assembly to establish a Special Committee, under
the chairmanship of the President, and with the
collaboration of the Secretary-General, to accomplish these objectives. The Special Committee was requested to report not later than 15
June 1965.

Assembly resolution 2308 (XXII), of 13 December
1967, requested the Special Committee to continue the work assigned to it by paragraph 2 of Assembly resolution 2249 (S-V), of 23 May 1967, to
study the various suggestions made by different
delegations during the Fifth Special Session,
especially those relating to
    (a) methods of financing future peace-
keeping operations in accordance with the Charter, and
    (b) facilities, services and personnel
which Member States might voluntarily provide,

in accordance with the Charter, for the United
Nations peace-keeping operations.

Membership

The President of the General Assembly announced,
on 26 February 1965, the following membership
of 33 (GAOR, Sess.XIX, Annexes, annex no. 21,
A/5900):

Afghanistan	Hungary	Romania
Algeria	India	Sierra Leone
Argentina	Iraq	Spain
Australia	Italy	Sweden
Austria	Japan	Thailand
Brazil	Mauritania	USSR
Canada	Mexico	UAR
Czechoslovakia	Netherlands	United Kingdom
El Salvador	Nigeria	USA
Ethiopia	Pakistan	Venezuela
France	Poland	Yugoslavia

Sweden resigned (GAOR, Sess.XXIV, Annexes,
agenda item 35, A/7632) as of 8 December 1969.
At its 1838th meeting, on 17 December 1969, the
Assembly agreed without objection to appoint
Denmark to replace Sweden.

The representatives of Member States were listed
in documents of 20 April, 6 May, and 24 August
1965 (GAOR, Sess.XIX, Annexes, vol.2, annex no.
21, A/AC.121/INF.1, and Rev.1 and 2).

Action in 1965

The Special Committee met at United Nations
Headquarters in New York, and held 14 meetings
from 26 March to 15 June 1965. The report of
the Special Committee (Ibid., A/5915), of 15
June 1965, noted that the members agreed that

the United Nations should be strengthened
through a cooperative effort and that the General Assembly, when it convened, must conduct
its work according to the normal procedure established by its rules of procedure. An addendum to the report (Ibid., A/5915/Add.1)
of 12 June 1965, contained in two annexes, a
record of the meetings of the Special Committee
(A/AC.121/SR.1-14), and a "Report of the Secretary-General and the President of the General
Assembly" (A/AC.121/4), pursuant to operative
paragraph 1 of the establishing resolution. In
sections I to IV the joint report placed before
the members of the Special Committee an account
of the views and suggestions made both during
the informal consultations and the formal meetings of the Special Committee on the different
aspects of the matter covered by the resolution.
In section I, there was also a short account of
the experience of the United Nations in the
field of peace-keeping operations; and section
V contained some broad conclusions to be drawn
from the views expressed by members.

A second report of the Special Committee (Ibid.,
A/5916/Add.1), of 30 September 1965, contained
summary records of those meetings. At the con-
clusion of the 18th meeting, the Chairman made
a statement which represented the consensus of
the Committee, -- that the Assembly was to carry on its work normally, that the question of
applicability of Article 19 of the Charter
would not be raised with regard to the United
Nations Emergency Force and the United Nations
Operation in the Congo, that the financial difficulties of the Organization should be solved
through voluntary contributions by Member States,
with the highly developed countries making sub-
stantial contributions.

The Assembly, in resolution 2053 (XX), of 15
December 1965, took note of the reports of the
Special Committee and of the replies submitted
by Member States to a request for their views
on the guidelines in regard to future peace-
keeping contained in the joint report of the
Secretary-General and the Assembly President
(A/AC.121/4). The replies were submitted by a
Secretary-General note (A/AC.121/5 and Add.1-3),
5 August 1965 to 25 April 1966.

Action in 1966

On 29 April 1966, at the 20th meeting, the Special Committee decided to constitute itself as a
Working Group which would hold official or semi-
official meetings, without records, rather than
private consultations. The Committee's third
report (GAOR, Sess.XXI, Annexes, agenda item 33,
A/6414), issued on 30 September 1966, covered its
four meetings held between 4 February and 13
September 1966, and the three meetings the Working Group held on 10 and 13 May, and 14 June
1966. Annex I contained the summary records of
the meetings. A list of delegations and representatives was appended to the report.

Action in 1967

At the opening meeting on 16 February 1967, on
recommendation of 11 members, the Special Committee established two Working Groups of the
Whole: Group A which was concerned with the financing of peace-keeping operations; and Group B
which was concerned with matters related to the
facilities, services and personnel which Member
States might voluntarily provide for a United
Nations peace-keeping operation (A/AC.121/L.3
and Add.1), annex I of the report of the Special
Committee.

The Special Committee held four meetings on 3,
12, 15 and 16 May. Its report (GAOR, Sess. S-V,
Annexes, agenda item 8, A/6654), issued on 17
May 1967, contained annexes giving the texts of,
inter alia, a memorandum of 15 March 1963 submitted by seven members of the Working Group on
Administrative and Budgetary Procedures of the
United Nations on "Principles to be considered
in the examination of the method for the financing of future peace-keeping operations"; Assembly resolution 1874 (S-IV), 27 June 1963, on
general principles to serve as guidelines for
the sharing of the costs of future peace-keeping
operations involving heavy expenditures; memorandum submitted by nine members of the Special
Committee on conclusions of the recent meetings
of the Special Committee; and memoranda submitted by France and the United Kingdom stating
their positions on the question of voluntary
contributions.

In response to Assembly resolution 2249 (S-V),
of 23 May 1967, requesting the Special Committee
to report on the progress of its work to the
twenty-second session of the General Assembly,
the Special Committee issued a report (GAOR, Sess.
XXII, Annexes, agenda item 37, A/6815), on 14
September 1967, stating that "owing to the pre-
occupation of the entire membership of the Organization with certain international developments, the Special Committee was unable to undertake the task entrusted to it by the General
Assembly". The report concluded that the Special Committee should continue to carry out its
mandate.

Action in 1968 and 1969

A progress report (GAOR, Sess.XXIII, Annexes, agenda item 32, A/7131) was issued by the Special Committee on 2 July 1968, covering the meetings held between 4 March and 27 June 1968. At its 34th meeting, on 3 April 1968, a Working Group was established composed of representatives of the officers of the Special Committee: Canada, Czechoslovakia, Mexico, and UAR, plus four others, France, USSR, United Kingdom, and the United States of America. Its terms of reference were to prepare working papers for the study the Special Committee was to submit to the General Assembly in accordance with the provisions of operative paragraphs 3 and 4 of Assembly resolution 2308 (XXII) (on matters related to facilities, services and personnel which Member States might provide); and to study the documents submitted by the members of the Special Committee. The Working Group held a series of meetings during April, May and June 1968, and approved as a first model of its program of work a study of the United Nations military observers established or authorized by the Security Council for observation purposes. On 12 September 1968, the Special Committee issued its report on the progress of the study (Ibid., A/7396).

At its 37th meeting, on 14 February 1969, the Chairman of the Special Committee informed the members regarding the progress of the work of the Working Group; an annex of the report (GAOR, Sess.XXIV, Annexes, vol.1, agenda item 35, A/7742), of 3 November 1969, contained the first report of the Working Group (A/AC.121/L.8). The appendix to the report contained the schema of Model I of a standard agreement between the United Nations and the host country on the status of military observer missions.

Action in 1970 and 1971

The Assembly in resolution 2576 (XXIV), of 15
December 1969, authorized the Special Committee
to continue its work on a comprehensive report
on United Nations military observers, and at its
43rd meeting, on 20 March 1970, the Special Committee approved the plan of work for the Working
Group on Models I and II of the study. The
Working Group met from 4 May to 8 September,
and its report (A/AC.121/L.10) appeared as an
annex to the report of the Special Committee
(GAOR, Sess.XXV, Annexes, vol.1, agenda item 36,
A/8081), of 1 October 1970.

The Special Committee held its 49th meeting, the
first of the year, on 1 April 1971, and two more,
on 6 May and 1 September 1971. The report (GAOR,
Sess.XXVI, Annexes, agenda item 39, A/8550), issued on 3 December 1971, contained the third and
fourth reports of the Working Group (A/AC.121/L.
12 and L.13) in annexes I and II. In its third
report, the Working Group noted that it was continuing its work under the rotating and effective chairmanship of the two Vice-Chairmen, but
expressed the hope that it would soon be possible
for the Special Committee to elect a chairman.

Action in 1972

The Special Committee held six meetings between
4 May and 10 November; and the Working Group
held three meetings in October 1972. At the
55th meeting, on 28 June, the Special Committee
endorsed the consensus among the members on
several points concerning its officers, inter
alia, that the representative of Nigeria should
be Chairman of the Special Committee, and Dr. E.
O. Ogbu took the chair; and the Working Group

should include, in addition to the six officers, the representatives of Argentina, France, India, Pakistan, USSR, United Kingdom, and the United States of America.

At its 56th meeting, on 27 September, the Special Committee decided to request the Working Group to continue its work, taking into account Assembly resolution 2835 (XXVI), of 17 December 1971, the views and suggestions submitted by Member States in response to paragraph 4 of the above resolution; letters from the representatives of the USSR (A/8669), the USA (A/8876), and Canada (A/SPC/152); a note of the Secretary-General transmitting views and suggestions of Member States (A/AC.121/L.15, and Add.1-3); as well as statements made by members of the Special Committee in the course of its meetings in 1972.

The documents cited above were reproduced in the Official Records of the General Assembly (GAOR, Sess.XXVII, Annexes, agenda item 41). The fifth report of the Working Group (A/AC.121/L.16), of 31 October 1972, appeared as an annex to the 1972 report of the Special Committee (Ibid., A/8888), issued on 13 November 1972.

Action in 1973

In 1973, the Special Committee held four meetings between 16 February and 19 November; the Working Group held 13 meetings from March to November. Both bodies considered further replies from Members (A/AC.121/L.20); a communication from the representatives of the United Kingdom (A/9144) and from Denmark, Finland, Norway, and Sweden (A/SPC/165), both reproduced in the Official Records of the General Assembly (GAOR, Sess.XXVIII, Annexes, agenda item 44); a

working document entitled "A comprehensive listing under specific headings of concrete proposals received and a description of progress made
to date" (A/AC.121/L.18), of 23 January 1974,
which had been prepared by the Rapporteur at the
request of the Working Group.

The report of the Special Committee (Ibid.,
A/9236), of 21 November 1973, contained in annexes I and II, the sixth and seventh reports
of the Working Group (A/AC.121/L.19 and L.21,
and Corr.1).

Officers

1965 - The meetings of the Special Committee
were chaired by Alex Quaison-Sackey (Ghana),
the General Assembly President, until his absence during part of May and June. It had been
arranged at the sixth meeting of the Special
Committee that the chairmanship would rotate
alphabetically until the Chairman's return. At
the seventh meeting, on 17 May 1965, Lucio
García del Solar (Argentina) took over. Others
who served were: at the eighth meeting, 25 May,
D. McCarthy (Australia); the ninth meeting, 2
June, Kurt Waldheim (Austria); the tenth meeting,
9 June, José Sette Camara (Brazil); from the
11th to the 14th meetings, 11, 14 and 15 June,
Mr. Quaison-Sackey presided, having returned to
New York.

At four further meetings held from 16 to 31
August 1965, the chairmen were: 15th meeting,
Paul Tremblay (Canada); 16th meeting, Professor
Jiři Hajek (Czech); 17th meeting, Dr. Tesfaye
Gebre-Egzy (Ethiopia); 18th meeting, Alex
Quaison-Sackey (Ghana).

<u>1966</u> - At the opening meeting, on 4 February
1966, the Special Committee, under Acting Chairman U Thant (Burma), elected Dr. Francisco
Cuevas Candino (Mexico) as Chairman; Paul
Tremblay (Canada) and Dr. Milan Klusak (Czech)
as Vice-Chairmen; Ahmed Tawfik Khalil (UAR) as
Rapporteur.

<u>1967</u> - At the opening meeting on 16 February,
the Special Committee elected George Ignatieff
(Canada) to replace Mr. Tremblay (Canada) as
Vice-Chairman, and Shaffie Abdel-Hamid (UAR)
to replace Mr. Khalil (UAR) as Rapporteur.

<u>1969</u> - At its 37th meeting, on 14 February,
the Special Committee elected Yvon Beaulne (Can-
ada) as one of the two Vice-Chairmen to succeed
George Ignatieff (Canada); and Abdel Halim Badawi
(UAR) as Rapporteur to succeed Shaffie Abdel
Hamid (UAR).

<u>1971</u> - At the first meeting of the year, the
49th, held on 1 April, it was announced by the
Secretary-General, in the capacity of Acting
Chairman, that Mr. Cuevas Cancino (Mexico) had
been transferred to another assignment by his
Government, and that the Committee would meet
alternately under the chairmanship of the two
Vice-Chairmen, Mr. Beaulne (Canada), and Mr.
Cernik (Czech). It was also announced that
Mahmoud Kassem (Egypt) would replace Mr. Badawi
(Egypt), who had left New York, as Rapporteur.

The third report of the Working Group (A/AC.121/
L.12) noted that it was continuing to work under
the rotating and effective chairmanship of the
two Vice-Chairmen, but expressed the hope that
it would soon be possible for the Special Committee to elect a chairman.

<u>1972</u> - At its 55th meeting, on 28 June, the Special Committee endorsed the consensus among the members on the following points:

    (a) The representative of Nigeria should be Chairman of the Special Committee, and Dr. E. O. Ogbu took the chair;

    (b) the number of the Vice-Chairmen should be increased from two to four, and those four places should be filled by representatives of Brazil, Canada, Czechoslovakia, and Japan;

    (c) the representative of Egypt, Mahmoud Kassem, should continue as Rapporteur.

The officers should serve a term of one year, it being understood that they should be eligible for reelection.

The Working Group should include, in addition to the six officers, the representatives of Argentina, France, India, Pakistan, USSR, United Kingdom, and United States of America.

Documents under the Special Committee's document series symbol (A/AC.121/-) were issued in mimeographed form, unless otherwise indicated.

<u>Working Group on the Financing of the United
Nations Relief and Works Agency for Palestine
Refugees in the Near East (UNRWA)</u>

Established by Assembly resolution 2656 (XXV),
of 7 December 1970, after considering the UNRWA
report (<u>GAOR</u>, Sess.XXV, <u>Suppl.13</u> (A/8013)),
covering the period from 1 July 1969 to 30 June
1970.

Terms of Reference

The Working Group's terms of reference were established under General Assembly's resolutions
2656 (XXV), 2728 (XXV), 15 December 1970, and
2791 (XXVI), of 6 December 1971.

Under the applicable provisions, the Working
Group was entrusted with:
(a) assisting, as appropriate, the Secretary-General and the Commissioner-General of
the United Nations Relief and Works Agency for
Palestine Refugees in the Near East in reach-
ing solutions to the problems posed by the
Agency's financial crisis;
(b) as appropriate, pursuing urgently with
Governments, both bilaterally and on a regional
basis, with specialized agencies and other organizations and individuals concerned, the implementation of the recommendations approved by
the General Assembly in resolution 2791 (XXVI)
as well as the implementation of other resolutions relating to the mandate of the Working
Group;
(c) after consultation with all concerned,
in particular the Secretary-General and the
Commissioner-General of UNRWA, and taking into
account the views expressed in the course of
the debate during the 25th and 26th sessions of
the General Assembly relevant to the mandate of
the Working Group, -- preparing and submitting

a comprehensive report on all aspects of the financing of the Agency to the General Assembly at its 27th session.

Assembly resolutions 2964 (XXVII), of 13 December 1972, and 3090 (XXVIII), of 28 December 1973, requested the Working Group to continue its efforts, in cooperation with the Secretary-General and the Commissioner-General, for the financing of UNRWA for a further period of one year.

Membership

The establishing resolution called for a membership of nine Member States. At the 1926th plenary meeting, on 11 December 1970, the President of the Assembly, who was authorized by the resolution, in consultation with the Secretary-General, to designate the members, selected the following:

> France, Ghana, Japan, Lebanon, Norway, Trinidad and Tobago, Turkey, United Kingdom, and United States of America.

Their representatives were: Henri Servant (France); H.R. Amonoo, R.M. Akwei, and Joseph G. Cleland (Ghana); Kunio Katakura, Massaki Noguchi (Japan); Edouard Ghorra (Lebanon); Jan Arvesen, P.O. Ravne (Norway); Frank G. Abdulah, Eustace E. Seignoret (Trinidad and Tobago); E. Nuri Eren, Osman Olcay (Turkey); Michael C.S. Weston (UK); Robert B. Oakley, Robert G. Mahon, C. O. Coudert (USA).

Action

At its first meeting, on 9 December 1970, the Working Group elected Nuri Eren (Turkey) as Chairman; H.R. Amonoo (Ghana) as Vice-Chairman; and J. Arnesen (Norway) as Rapporteur.

An interim report (GAOR, Sess.XXV, Annexes, agenda item 35, A/8264), was issued on 14 December 1970. Its recommendations were approved by Assembly resolution 2728 (XXV), of 15 December 1970.

At the next session of the Working Group, R.M. Akwei (Ghana) served as Vice-Chairman, and P.O. Ravne as Rapporteur. The report of the Working Group (GAOR, Sess.XXVI, Annexes, agenda items 38 and 12, A/8476), prepared in compliance with resolutions 2656 (XXV) and 2728 (XXV), was issued on 26 October 1971. It recommended, inter alia, that its mandate should be extended for another year.

In 1972, Joseph O. Cleland (Ghana) was Vice-Chairman, and Jan Arvesen was the Rapporteur. The second report of the Working Group (GAOR, Sess.XXVII, Annexes, agenda item 40 (b),A/8849) was issued on 24 October 1972. Annex III of the report listed the contributions to UNRWA for 1971, and pledges and expected contributions for 1972.

In 1973, Osman Olcay (Turkey) served as Chairman. The third report of the Working Group (A/9231, offset) was issued on 19 October 1973. Annex II reported the contributions to UNRWA for 1972, and pledges and expected contributions for 1974.

C.   Financing of Economic Development

I. Committee of Nine (1953)

Established by ECOSOC resolution 416 A (XIV),
of 23 June 1952.

Terms of Reference

The Committee was asked to prepare a thorough
study of the many and complex aspects of the
detailed plan requested by Assembly resolution
520 A (VI), of 12 January 1952, for establishing, as soon as circumstances permitted, a
special fund for grands-in-aid and for low-
interest, long-term loans to underdeveloped
countries for the purpose of helping them, at
their request, to accelerate their economic
development and to finance non-self-liquidating
projects which are basic to their economic development; the resolution listed five recommendations to be considered and prepared for the
seventh session of the Assembly.

The Committee was to be convened not later than
December 1952 and to complete its report to
ECOSOC not later than 1 March 1953; to be guided by relevant discussions in the General Assembly and the Council and by the proposals,
principles and alternatives set forth in a report of the Secretary-General entitled "Measures of financing economic development", of 27
May 1952 (ESCOR, 14th Sess., Annexes, agenda
item 5 (b), E/2234), issued in compliance with
Assembly resolution 520 A (VI).

In resolution 622 A (VII), of 21 December 1952,
the Assembly noted that the Council had been
unable to submit the detailed plan in time for
the seventh session of the Assembly, and asked

that it be ready for the eighth session.

Membership

The establishing resolution requested the Secretary-General to select the members to serve
on the Committee on the basis of their having
"the experience and high ability required by
the importance and complexity of the task entrusted to them". It also stated that the
Committee should be composed of not more than
nine persons who would serve in their personal
capacities. The following were appointed:

S. Amjad Ali (Pakistan), Ambassador, and
President of the Economic and Social Council
in 1952;

Fernand Baudhuin (Belgium), Professor of
Economics at the Catholic University of Lou-
vain;

C. V. Bramsnaes (Denmark), member of the
Board of Directors and former Governor of the
National Bank of Denmark;

Miguel Guaderno (Philippines), Governor of
the National Bank of the Philippines;

Sir Cyril Jones (UK), Director of the Mer-
cantile Bank of India, Ltd., London, and former
Finance Secretary to the Government of India;

Leo Mates (Yugoslavia), Ambassador and
Permanent Representative to the United Nations;

Hernán Santa Cruz (Chile), President of
ECOSOC during 1950 and 1951, and former Permanent Representative to the United Nations;

Dr. Eduardo Suárez (Mexico), member of the
Board of Directors of the Nacional Financiera
S.A. and the Bank of Mexico, and former Secre-
tary of Finance of Mexico;

Wayne C. Taylor (USA), former President of
the Export-Import Bank and former Under-Secretary of Commerce of the United States Government.

Action

The Committee of Nine met at United Nations
Headquarters in New York from 21 January to 6
March 1953, under the chairmanship of Dr.
Eduardo Suárez (Mexico). Its report (E/2381,
Sales no: 1953.II.B.1) "Report on a Special
United Nations Fund for Economic Development,
submitted by a Committee appointed by the Sec-
retary-General", on 26 April 1953, formed the
technical background of the discussions in the
Assembly and the Council on the proposed United
Nations development fund during 1953, 1954 and
1955.

II.   Committee of Nine (1954)

Established by Assembly resolution 822 (IX),
of 11 December 1954, pursuant to ECOSOC resolution 532 A (XVIII), of 4 August 1954. After
having considered the report (E/2381) prepared
by the 1953 Committee of Nine, the Assembly decided in resolution 724 B (VIII) to appoint the
then President of the Economic and Social
Council, Raymond Scheyven (Belgium), as a Rapporteur, to examine, with the assistance of
the Secretary-General, the comments of Governments received, to collect them, and, if necessary, to clarify them by consulting the Governments concerned, and to report to the Council
and the Assembly at their 1954 sessions.

Mr. Scheyven prepared a brief interim report
(ESCOR, 18th Sess., Annexes, agenda item 3, E/
2599) dated 13 May 1954, and a more comprehensive report for the ninth General Assembly
(GAOR, Sess.IX, Suppl.19 (A/2728)) issued in
October 1954, in which he concluded that "the
essential conditions for the establishment of
a United Nations fund for economic development

in the near future do not at present exist".
Both were prepared in compliance with Assembly
resolution 724 B (VIII).

Terms of Reference

In resolution 822 (IX), the Assembly expressed
the hope that the United Nations development
fund would "be established as soon as practicable", and requested Mr. Scheyven to prepare
a further report which would (1) give a full
and precise picture of the form or forms,
functions and responsibilities which such a
fund might have, and especially the methods by
which its operations might be integrated with
the development plans of the countries receiving assistance from it, and (2) consider the
working relationship the fund should have with
the Technical Assistance Board, the International Bank and other specialized agencies
concerned.

Membership

The resolution specified that the Secretary-
General, in consultation with Mr. Scheyven,
should appoint an ad hoc group of experts to
assist in the preparation of this report. The
following experts were appointed:
      Raymond Scheyven (Belgium), Member of the
Belgian Chamber of Representatives, former
President of ECOSOC (1953), Chairman;
      John Abbink (USA), Foreign Trade Consultant,
USA;
      A. Nazmy Abdel Hamid (Egypt), Sub-Governor
of the Bank of Egypt;
      B.K. Madan (India), Economic adviser to the
Reserve Bank of India, former executive director
of the International Monetary Fund (IMF) and
alternate executive director of the International Bank for Reconstruction and Development(IBRD);

Sir Francis Mudie (UK), former head of the British Economic Mission to Yugoslavia:

Jacques Oudiette (France), Director of the Banque Nationale pour le Commerce et l'Industrie, Paris;

Nenad Popovic (Yugoslavia), Vice-Governor of the National Bank of the Federal People's Republic of Yugoslavia, former executive director of the IMF, and former alternate executive director of the IBRD;

Jorge Schneider (Chile), Director of the New York Office of the Corporación de Fomento de la Producción de Chile; former alternate executive director of the IBRD;

Jan Tinbergen (Netherlands), Professor of Econometrics, Netherlands School of Economics, Director of the Central Planning Bureau, The Hague.

Action

The Committee met in New York from 7 to 25 March 1955. Its report (GAOR, Sess.X, Suppl.17 (A/2906)), and jointly to ECOSOC (E/2757), was issued in June 1955 as the "Report on a Special United Nations Fund for Economic Development (SUNFED) prepared in pursuance of General Assembly resolution 822 (IX)", and referred to as the "Report of the Scheyven Committee". The report did not represent a new departure but rather clarified or amended some of the conclusions reached by the 1953 Committee of Nine. It suggested that the Assembly establish a Special UN Fund for Economic Development for a five year period to reassure States reluctant to commit themselves for an indefinite period.

Ad Hoc Committee on the Question of the Establishment of a Special United Nations Fund for
Economic Development (SUNFED) (A/AC.83/-)

Established by Assembly resolution 923 (X), of
9 December 1955, pursuant to ECOSOC resolution
583 A (XX), of 5 August 1955.

Terms of Reference

The resolution requested the Secretary-General
to invite States Members of the United Nations
and specialized agencies in the economic and
social sphere, to transmit to him not later
than 31 March 1956, their views relating to the
establishment, role, structure and operations
of a Special United Nations Fund for Economic
Development, bearing in mind particularly the
eight points listed in the annex of the resolution, in order that such views and replies might
provide material for the statute of the Fund
when it was decided to establish such a Fund.

At the same time, the resolution established an
ad hoc committee composed of the representatives
of sixteen governments to analyze the replies
and comments of the Governments with a view to
submitting to the Council at its twenty-second
session and to the General Assembly at its
eleventh session such interim report as it
might be in a position to make, and a final report to the twenty-third session of ECOSOC (Assembly resolution 1030 (XI), 26 February 1957,
amended this request to the twenty-fourth session), it being understood that in making such
reports, it would not commit any Member Government.

Membership

At the 553rd plenary meeting, on 9 December

1955, the Assembly President designated the
following 16 Member States as members of the
Ad Hoc Committee:
Canada, Chile, Colombia, Cuba, France,
Egypt, India, Indonesia, Netherlands,
Norway, Pakistan, Poland, USSR, United
Kingdom, United States of America, and
Yugoslavia.

In resolution 1031 (XI), of 26 February 1957,
the Assembly noted that since the establishment
of the Ad Hoc Committee, there had been a sub-
stantial increase in the membership of the
United Nations, the membership of the Ad Hoc
Committee should be increased to nineteen. At
the 661st plenary meeting, Italy, Japan and
Tunisia were added to the Committee membership.

Action

The Ad Hoc Committee met from 7 May to 6 June
1956. Its elected officers were: Ali Yavar
Jung (India) as Chairman; Rudecindo Ortega
(Chile), as Vice-Chairman; Johan Kaufmann
(Netherlands) as Rapporteur. It issued an interim report (A/3134-E/2896 and Corr.1-2, mimeographed) on 8 June 1956.

Further meetings were held on 11 and 12 March
and 19 March to 22 May 1957. Gopala Menon
(India) replaced Mr. Jung as Chairman. A final
report (GAOR, Sess.XII, Annexes, agenda item
28, A/3579 and Add.1) was issued on 26 May
1957. The addendum was circulated to members
of ECOSOC as document E/2961, Corr.1 and Add.1).
The final report was divided into three parts:
I. Summary of comments of Governments on the
establishment, role, structure and operations
of a Special UN Fund for Economic Development;
II. Analysis of comments of Governments; III.
Conclusions.

A supplementary report (Ibid., A/3580-E/2999), issued on 27 May 1957, was also divided into three parts: I. Different forms of legal framework on which a Special UN Fund for Economic Development may be established and statutes drafted; II. Types of project which might be provided for in programs of operations of a United Nations economic development fund; III. Related suggestions of proposals by Governments.

Committee on a United Nations Capital Development Fund (A/AC.102/-)

Established by Assembly resolution 1521 (XV),
of 15 December 1960, recalling its resolutions
1219 (XII), 14 December 1957; 1240 (XIII), 14
October 1958; 1317 (XIII), 12 December 1958;
1424 (XIV), 5 December 1959; and ECOSOC resolutions 662 (XXIV), 30-31 July 1957; and 740
(XXVIII), 31 July 1959.

Terms of Reference

To lay the groundwork for the Capital Development Fund which the General Assembly decided
in principle to establish, and to consider all
concrete preparatory measures, including draft
legislation, necessary to that end.

Assembly resolution 1706 (XVI), of 19 December
1961, extended the Committee's mandate and instructed it to prepare the necessary draft
legislation for a UN Capital Development Fund
(UNCDF) in the light of the general principles
prepared by the Committee and annexed to the
resolution.

Assembly resolution 1826 (XVII), of 18 December
1962 -- recalling Assembly resolutions 520 A
(VI), 12 January 1952; 622 A (VII), 21 December 1952; 724 B (VIII), 7 December 1953; 822
(IX), 11 December 1954; 923 (X), 9 December
1955; 1030 (XI), 26 February 1957; 1219 (XII),
14 December 1957; 1240 (XIII), 14 October 1958;
1317 (XIII), 12 December 1958; 1424 (XIV), 5
December 1959; 1521 (XV), 15 December 1960, and
1706 (XVI), 19 December 1961 -- again extended
the Committee's mandate, requesting it to:
    (a) Study the replies of the Governments
contained in paragraph 2 of the resolution

(requesting the Secretary-General to transmit
the draft legislation (statute) to the Governments of States Members of the United Nations
and members of the specialized agencies so as
to receive their comments and observations by
April 1963);

(b) Continue to study the need for international financing with a view to ensuring the
attainment of the objectives of the United
Nations Development Decade, taking into account
the study prepared by the United Nations Secretariat ("The Capital Development Needs of the
Less Developed Countries" (A/AC.102/5, 8 February 1962, Sales no.:62.II.D.3, May 1962);

(c) Propose practical measures designed
to ensure the beginning of the operation of
the UNCDF, with special emphasis on, inter alia,
the possibility envisaged in section III of resolution 1219 (XII) and in resolution 1240 C
(XIII);

(d) Cooperate with the Secretary-General
in preparing the report provided for in ECOSOC
resolution 921 (XXXIV), of 3 August 1962, and
report to ECOSOC and the General Assembly.

In resolution 1936 (XVIII), of 11 December
1963, the Assembly also extended the Committee's
mandate to enable it to fulfill the tasks entrusted to it in resolution 1826 (XVII), and
to formulate its recommendations for submission
to the 19th session of the Assembly. In resolution 2042 (XX), of 8 December 1965, the Assembly again extended the Committee's mandate
"so as to enable it to carry out the tasks envisaged in General Assembly resolutions 1826
(XVII) and 1936 (XVIII), taking into account
the results of the work of the Governing Council of the UN Development Program, as well as
the results of the Secretary-General's consultations with Member States".

Membership

The establishing resolution decided that the Committee should consist of 25 members to be designated by the President of the General Assembly. At the 968th plenary meeting, on 27 March 1961, the President nominated the following:

Argentina, Brazil, Burma, Canada, Chile, Czechoslovakia, Denmark, France, Ghana, India, Indonesia, Iraq, Italy, Ivory Coast, Japan, Netherlands, Nigeria, Pakistan, Peru, Sudan, USSR, UAR, United Kingdom, United States of America, and Yugoslavia.

The representatives of members were listed in the Introduction of each report of the Committee.

Action

The Committee met on 17 April and from 15 May to 5 June 1961. The report of the first session (ESCOR, 32nd Sess., Annexes, agenda item 5 (2 and 5), E/3514) was issued on 8 June 1961, pursuant to Assembly resolution 1521 (XV), and elaborated twelve General Principles to govern the establishment and operations of the Fund.

The second session of the Committee was held on 14 February and from 25 May to 13 June 1962. Its report, prepared pursuant to Assembly resolution 1706 (XVI) on 14 June 1962 (ESCOR, 34th Sess., Annexes, agenda item 6 (b), E/3654), submitted the text of a Draft Statute for the Fund.

The third session, held from 5 to 13 September 1963, issued its report, prepared pursuant to

Assembly resolution 1826 (XVII) on 24 September
1963 (GAOR, Sess.XVIII, Annexes, agenda item
33 (e), (agenda items 12,33,34,35,36,37,38 and
76), A/5536), which recommended that the General Assembly consider continuing a study of
needs for capital for development and to continue the Committee's mandate. The Secretary-
General prepared a study dated 15 July 1964
(ESCOR, 37th Sess., Annexes, agenda item 10
(c), E/3947), pursuant to Assembly resolution
1936 (XVIII), on the practical steps to trans-
form the Special Fund into a capital development fund in such a way as to include both pre-
investment and investment activities.

A fourth session, held from 19 to 28 October
1964, issued a report on 10 November 1964. The
report (A/5748, mimeographed) noted that there
was a consensus among members that, in view of
the developments at the 1964 UN Conference on
Trade and Development (UNCTAD) in Geneva and at
the 37th session of ECOSOC, the Committee
should postpone the formulation of substantive
recommendations until the General Assembly had
had an opportunity to consider these new developments.

The Committee's fifth session, held at United
Nations Headquarters from 12 to 16 September
1966, issued its report (GAOR, Sess.XXI, Annexes. agenda item 38, A/6418) on 19 September
1966. The report noted that the majority of
the members of the Committee, who had already
approved the draft statute for a Capital Development Fund at its second session, decided it
was necessary to bring the draft up to date,
taking into consideration the latest developments in the activities of the United Nations;
and consequently, a number of delegations submitted amendments to be incorporated into the
draft statute before its adoption by the General

Assembly at its 21st session.

The United Nations Capital Development Fund was voted into being by the General Assembly in resolution 2186 (XXI), of 13 December 1966.

Officers

Officers elected by the Committee at the five sessions were as follows:

1961 - Chairman: U Thant (Burma)
      Vice-Chairmen: Mario Franzi (Italy)
       Dr. Hector Bernardo (Argentina)
      Rapporteur: Branko Karapandza (Yugo-slavia), and in his absence, Ismat Kittani (Iraq).

1962 - Chairman: Dr. Hector Bernardo (Argentina)
      Vice-Chairmen: Mario Franzi (Italy)
       A.B.H. Abdel Ghaffar (UAR)
      Rapporteur: J.B.P. Maramis (Indochina)

1963 - Chairman: J.B.P. Maramis (Indonesia)
      Vice-Chairmen: Dr. Saad Abdel-Fattah Khalil (UAR)
       Bartolomeo Attolica (Italy)
      Rapporteur: Sergio P. Rouanet (Brazil)

1964 - Chairman: J.P.B. Maramis (Indonesia)
      Vice-Chairman: Dr. Saad Abdel-Fattah Khalil (UAR)
      Rapporteur: Eduardo Bradley (Argentina)

1965 - Chairman: Eduardo Bradley (Argentina)
      Vice-Chairman: J.H. Lubbers (Netherlands)
      Rapporteur: Rafee Uddin Ahmed (Pakistan)

Documents issued under the Committee's document series symbol A/AC.102/- were issued in mimeographed form.

United Nations Capital Development Fund (UNCDF)

Established by Assembly resolution 2186 (XXI), of 13 December 1966, as an organ of the General Assembly which would function as an autonomous organization within the United Nations in accordance with the provisions set forth in the resolution.

Terms of Reference

The purpose and functions of the organization were defined in the following articles of resolution 2186 (XXI): I. Purpose; II. Guiding principles; III. General economic provisions; IV. Resources; V. Forms of assistance, operations; VI. Formulation; VII. General responsibilities of recipient Governments; VIII. Organization and management; IX. Managing Director and staff; X. Cooperation and coordination with other organs of the United Nations and other organizations; XI. Financial administration; XII. Future institutional arrangements.

In paragraph 1 of resolution 2321 (XXII), of 15 December 1967, the Assembly decided to adopt on a provisional basis the following measures in implementation of its resolution 2186 (XXI):

(a) the Secretary-General was invited to ask the Administrator of the UNDP to administer the UN Capital Development Fund by performing the functions of the Managing Director, as set forth in article IX of resolution 2186 (XXI);

(b) the Governing Council of the UNDP should perform, as appropriate, the functions of the Executive Board of UNCDP as set forth in article VIII of resolution 2186 (XXI);

(c) the United Nations Pledging Conference on UNCDF would be convened simultaneously with the annual Pledging Conference on the UNDP.

Under the following resolutions, the Assembly decided to preserve the original functions of the Fund for one year, in accordance with the measures set forth in paragraph 1 of resolution 2321 (XXII) cited above: 2410 (XXIII), 17 December 1968; 2525 (XXIV), 5 December 1969; 2690 (XXV), 11 December 1970; 2812 (XXVI), 14 December 1971; 2976 (XXVII), 14 December 1972; 3122 (XXVIII), 13 December 1973.

In resolution 2525 (XXIV), of 5 December 1969, the Assembly requested the Governing Council of UNDP to undertake, within the context of the objectives of UNCDF an exploratory study with a view to broadening the functions of the Fund so as to normalize, stimulate and develop its activities and make it operational and effective, in order to enable all Member States to give it their support; and decided, meanwhile, to preserve the original functions for a year, in accordance with the measures set forth in paragraph 1 of resolution 2321 (XXII).

ECOSOC resolution 1753 (LIV), of 16 May 1973, endorsed by Assembly resolution 3122 (XXVIII), welcomed the decision of 14 December 1972 of the Governing Council of UNDP that the UN Capital Development Fund should be used to serve primarily the hard-core countries (DP/L.263).

United Nations Capital Development Fund: Executive Board

Established by Article VIII of Assembly resolution 2186 (XXI), of 13 December 1966.

Terms of Reference

The immediate intergovernmental control of the policies and operations of the UN Capital Development Fund should be exercised by an Executive Board. It should have final authority for the approval of grants and loans submitted to it by the Managing Director. It should adopt its own rules of procedure.

The Executive Board should review all the activities of the UNCDF and should report annually to the General Assembly through the Economic and Social Council. The Council may transmit to the UNCDF and to the General Assembly such comments on the report as it deemed necessary.

The General Assembly should review the progress and the general policies of the UNCDF as a separate item of its agenda and make any appropriate recommendations.

Paragraph 1 of resolution 2321 (XXII), of 15 December 1967, decided that the UNDP Governing Council should perform, as appropriate, the functions of the Executive Board of the Fund, as set forth in article VIII of resolution 2186 (XXI).

Membership

Paragraph 4 of Article VIII of the establishing resolution stipulated that the Executive Board should consist of representatives of 24 States Members of the United Nations or members of the specialized agencies or of the IAEA.

The members of the Executive Board should be elected by the General Assembly.

There should be equitable representatives on the Executive Board of economically more developed countries, on the one hand, having due regard to their contributions to the UNCDF, and of developing countries, on the other hand, taking into account the need for equitable geographical distribution among the latter members.

The members of the Executive Board should be elected for a term of three years. Retiring members shall be eligible for reelection.

Sessions

The Executive Board should meet at least once a year and as often as considered necessary for the conduct of the Fund's work.

Officers

Under Article IX of resolution 2186 (XXI), 13 December 1966, the chief executive officer of the fund should be the Managing Director, who is to be appointed by the United Nations Secretary-General for a term of four years, the first term to begin on 1 January 1968, and should be subject to confirmation by the General Assembly.

The Managing Director of the Capital Development Fund should participate without vote in the deliberations of the Executive Board.

Paragraph 1 (a) of resolution 2321 (XXII), 15
December 1967, invited the Secretary-General
to ask the Administrator of UNDP to administer
the UN Capital Development Fund by performing
the functions of the Managing Director, as set
forth in article IX of Assembly resolution
2186 (XXI).

Administrators of UNDP and UNCDF

Paul G. Hoffman (USA) served from 1 January
1966 to mid-January 1972. He had been Managing
Director of the United Nations Special Fund
from its creation in 1959 until it was merged
with the UN Expanded Program of Technical Assistance to form the UN Development Program.

Rudolph A. Peterson (USA) succeeded Mr. Hoffman
and served until 11 December 1975. Mr. Peterson was Chairman of the Executive Committee of
the Bank of America in San Francisco, since
1970, and before that had been President of the
Bank of America Corporation.

F. Bradford Morse (USA), who had served as
Under-Secretary-General for Political and
General Assembly Affairs at the United Nations
since May 1972, and was a former United States
Congressman from Massachusetts, was confirmed
by the General Assembly as Administrator of
UNDP on 28 November 1975, and took office in
January 1976.

Action

On 15 May 1968, a report was issued by the
administrator of the UN Development Program
(UNDP) on the UN Capital Development Fund (DP/
L.82), pursuant to resolution 2321 (XXII).

Further program reports on the Fund and contributions pledged were contained in the following documents:

DP/L.139, 14 May 1970; DP/L.161, 17 December 1970; DP/L.216, 6 January 1972; DP/L.222,
14 April 1972; DP/L.258 and Corr.1, 29 November
1972; DP/L.268, 9 January 1973; DP/L.273 and
Add.1-5, 27 April 1973; DP/L.291/Add.7, 21 June
1973.

Documents in the document series symbol DP/
were issued in mimeographed form.

(For a historical resumé of the steps leading
up to the establishment of the Committee for a
capital development fund, see document A/AC.
102/3 of 19 April 1961.)

D. Investment of Funds and Audit of Accounts

Investments Committee

Established by resolution 185 (II), of 15 November 1947, in accordance with the provisions of Section 25 of the provisional regulations for the United Nations Joint Staff Pension Scheme, adopted during the second part of the first session of the General Assembly.

Terms of Reference

The Secretary-General seeks the advice of the Investments Committee in regard to the investment of special and other funds under the control of the United Nations as well as pension funds.

Membership

The three members were appointed by the Secretary-General for a three-year term, after consultation with the Advisory Committee on Administrative and Budgetary Questions (ACABQ), and subject to the approval of the General Assembly. Members are retired by rotation and are eligible for re-appointment.

The Committee was enlarged from three to six members by resolution 1561 (XV), section II, article XXV, of 18 December 1960.

At its 1926th meeting, on 11 December 1970, the Assembly decided, on recommendation of the Secretary-General (GAOR, Sess.XXV, Annexes, vol.2, agenda item 76 (d), A/7934) included as paragraph 1 of A/8114), in order to ensure continuity of policy in the future, the terms of office of the members be so staggered that the terms of the entire Committee do not end in the same year.

At Plenary meeting 115, on 15 November 1947, the following were elected:

To serve to
31 Dec. 1948: Marriner S. Eccles (USA);
31 Dec. 1949: Ivar Rooth (Sweden);
31 Dec. 1950: Jacques Rueff (France).

31 Dec. 1951: Leslie R. Rounds (USA)
(Plenary meeting 151, 16 Oct. 1948).

31 Dec. 1952: Ivar Rooth (Sweden)
(Plenary meeting 255, 24 Nov. 1949).

31 Dec. 1953: Jacques Rueff (France)
(Plenary meeting 324, 14 Dec. 1950).

31 Dec. 1954: Leslie R. Rounds (USA)
(Plenary meeting 356, 20 Dec. 1951).

31 Dec. 1955: Ivar Rooth (Sweden)
(Plenary meeting 409, 20 Dec. 1952).

31 Dec. 1956: Jacques Rueff (France)
(Plenary meeting 471, 9 Dec. 1953).

31 Dec. 1957: Leslie R. Rounds (USA)
(Plenary meeting 496, 29 Oct. 1954).

31 Dec. 1958: Ivar Rooth (Sweden)
(Plenary meeting 549, 29 Nov. 1955).

31 Dec. 1959: Jacques Rueff (France)
(Plenary meeting 632, 31 Dec. 1956).

31 Dec. 1960: Leslie R. Rounds (USA)
(Plenary meeting 723, 26 Nov. 1957).

To serve to
     31 Dec. 1961: Ivar Rooth (Sweden)
     (Plenary meeting 778, 30 Oct. 1958).

     31 Dec. 1962: Jacques Rueff (France)
     (Plenary meeting 838, 17 Nov. 1959).

To serve to 31 Dec. 1964: (Plenary meeting 1086,
     30 Dec. 1961):
     Dr. William Fiske Frazier (USA), R.
McAllister Lloyd (USA), David Rockefeller (USA),
to serve from date of resolution.
     Dr. Roger de Candolle (Switzerland) for a
three-year term beginning on 1 January 1962;
George A. Murphy (USA) (plenary meeting 1276,
11 December 1963) replacing David Rockefeller,
resigned on 31 December 1963. At plenary meeting 1191, 11 December 1962, Eugene Black (USA)
was elected to replace Dr. Frazier, deceased;
amd B.K. Nehru (India) and Jacques Rueff
(France) to bring up the membership to six,
pursuant to resolution 1561 (XV), of 18 December 1960.

To serve to 31 Dec. 1967 (from 1 Jan. 1965):
(Plenary meeting 1328, 10 Feb. 1965)
     Eugene Black (USA), Roger de Candolle
(Switzerland), R. McAllister Lloyd (USA),
George A. Murphy (USA), B.K. Nehru (India),
Jacques Rueff (France).

To serve to 31 Dec. 1970:
(Plenary meeting 1633, 15 Dec. 1967)
Re-appointed the same membership for three
years.

To serve to 31 Dec. 1971:
(Plenary meeting 1926, 11 Dec. 1970)
     Jacques Rueff (France), Eugene Black (USA).

To serve to 31 Dec. 1972:
(Plenary meeting 2030, 21 Dec. 1971)
    Roger de Candolle (Switzerland), R. Mc
    Allister Lloyd (USA), resigned as of 31
    Dec. 1971), succeeded by Jean Guyot (France)
To serve to 31 Dec. 1973:
    B.K. Nehru (India), George A. Murphy (USA);
To serve to 31 Dec. 1974:
    Eugene Black (USA), David Montagu (UK).

To serve to 31 Dec. 1975:
(Plenary meeting 2111, 15 Dec. 1974)
    R. Manning Brown, Jr. (USA), Jean Guyot
    (France).

To serve to 31 Dec. 1976:
(Plenary meeting 2196, 11 Dec. 1975)
    B.K. Nehru (India), George A. Murphy (USA).

The Secretary-General paid tribute 'GAOR, Sess.
XXVII, Annexes, agenda item 76 (d) A/8764),
included as paragraph 1 of A/8884) on 11 December 1972, to R. McAllister Lloyd (USA), "who
had served with great distinction on the Committee for some 20 years, and as its Chairman
for the past eleven years". Mr. Lloyd proposed
to the Secretary-General that he be allowed to
resign as a formal member of the Committee at
the end of 1971, even though his term did not
expire for another twelve months. The Secretary-General reluctantly accepted this suggestion, but, because he considered continuity of
policy and Mr. Lloyd's abilities very important
to an effective Committee, with the express understanding that Mr. Lloyd would continue to
serve on an ad hoc basis as Chairman of the
Committee through 1972. The Secretary-General
felt that similar arrangements should be made
for 1973, and, accordingly, Roger de Candolle
(Switzerland), who had served as a member for
some ten years and whose term expired at the

end of 1972, indicated a willingness to continue on an ad hoc basis through 1973.

In a note of 5 December 1973 (GAOR, Sess.XXVIII,
Annexes, agenda item 85 (d) A/9104), included
as paragraph 1 of A/9184), the Secretary-General advised the Joint Staff Pension Board and
the Advisory Committee (ACABQ) that he planned
to draw on such expertise, as may be required
from time to time, to provide specialized consultation on investment policy. Specifically,
in order to replace Mr. de Candolle, he planned
to co-opt a highly qualified individual from
Switzerland, who would serve on the Investments
Committee in an ad hoc capacity during 1974.

Action

The Investments Committee issues no reports or
documents.

Panel of External Auditors (of the United
Nations and Specialized Agencies)

Established by Assembly resolution 347 (IV),
of 24 November 1949. Paragraph 2 of the resolution approved the principles regarding a joint
Panel of Auditors for the United Nations and
the specialized agencies as set out in annex
B of the resolution. The Panel operates under
a revised set of provisions set forth in resolution 1438 (XIV), of 5 December 1959, which
superseded the original resolution, and which
changed the name of the panel to the Panel of
External Auditors.

The report of the Secretary-General (A/C.5/L.
902, mimeographed), of 17 October 1967, set
forth in some detail the history, nature and
functions of the Panel, and outlined the relationship between the Panel of External Auditors and the Joint Inspection Unit.

Terms of Reference

Annex B of resolution 347 (IV) listed the following terms of reference:
    1. In principle there should be a panel
of external auditors of the United Nations and
the specialized agencies composed of persons
having the rank of Auditor-General (or its
equivalent in the various Member States);
    2. Such a panel should consist of the
auditors appointed by the United Nations and
the specialized agencies, chosen by common consent for a period of three years in such a manner that the members of the panel would not exceed six in number, and bearing in mind the
location of the specialized agencies, the ability of the governmental audit staffs to undertake the total audit load within the appropriate

time-limits, and the desirability of securing continuity of audit;

3. Each organization should select one or more members of the Panel to perform its audit. Payments of salaries, fees or honoraria should be a matter for settlement between the parties directly concerned;

4. Each auditor (or the auditors) performing an audit should sign his (or their) own report or reports;

5. Members of the panel selected to perform the audit should be requested to take appropriate steps, in particular by meeting together annually, to coordinate their audits and to exchange information on methods and findings. The Panel of Auditors should be invited to submit from time to time any observations or recommendations which it might wish to make on the coordination and standardization of the accounts and financial procedures of the United Nations and the specialized agencies;

6. Cost of the annual meetings of active members of the Panel should be borne by the participating organizations.

Based on recommendations of the Secretary-General in a report (A/C.5/795, mimeographed), of 26 October 1959, the General Assembly resolution 1438 (XIV), of 5 December 1959, specified revised terms of reference in an annex as follows:

1. The members of the United Nations Panel of Auditors and the appointed external auditors of the specialized agencies and of the International Atomic Energy Agency (IAEA) shall constitute a Panel of External Auditors, the purpose of which shall be to further the coordination of the audits for which its members are responsible and to exchange information on

methods and findings;

2.   The Panel may submit to the executive heads of the participating organizations any observations or recommendations it may wish to make in relation to the accounts and financial procedures of the organizations concerned;

3.   The executive heads of the participating organizations may, through their auditor (or auditors), submit to the Panel for its opinion or recommendation any matter within its competence;

4.   The Panel shall elect its chairman and adopt its rules of procedure. Meetings shall be held when necessary, but normally not less frequently than once every two years;

5.   Costs of the meetings of the Panel shall be borne by the participating organizations.

Membership

Annex B of resolution 347 (IV) specified that the Panel should be composed of the auditors appointed by the United Nations and the specialized agencies, chosen by common consent for a period of three years in such a manner that the members of the Panel would not exceed six in number.

On 26 October 1959, the Secretary-General (A/C.5/795, mimeographed) reported that at its fifth session, the Panel felt that annual meetings were not warranted and that in view of the current establishment of new agencies, it was considered that the number of the members of the Panel was unduly restricted. The terms of resolution 1438 (XIV) approved these observations, and the Panel consists of the United Nations Board of Auditors, and the appointed external auditors of the specialized agencies and of the IAEA.

Action

The Panel of External Auditors meets in closed
sessions, acts only in an advisory capacity,
and submits no documents or reports.

(For Board of Auditors, see Chapter I)

Chapter XI

ORGANIZATION OF THE SECRETARIAT
AND STAFF QUESTIONS

A. Organization of the Secretariat

1954 Survey Group (1954)

Committee of Experts on the Review of the
Activities and Organization of the Secretariat (1960-1961)

Expert Committee on the Reorganization of
the United Nations Secretariat (1968)

B. Staff Salaries and Benefits

Working Party on Staff Retirement and
Insurance Funds (1946)

Committee of Experts on Salary, Allowances
and Leave Systems (1949)

Committee of Experts on Salary Differentials,
Cost-of-Living Adjustments and Dependency
Allowances (1955)

Committee to Review the Salary, Allowances
and Benefits System of the United Nations
(1956)

Special Committee for the Review of the
United Nations Salary System (1971-1972)

International Civil Service Advisory Board
(1951--)

Expert Committee on Post Adjustments (1959-
1963)

Appendix - Administrative Committee on
Coordination (ACC)

C. Staff Pensions

United Nations Staff Benefit Committee
(1946--)

United Nations Joint Staff Pension Board
(1946--)

United Nations Staff Pension Committee
(1949--)

Expert Group on Pensionable Remuneration
(1958)

Pension Review Group (1959-1960)

D. United Nations Administrative Tribunal

Advisory Committee on a Statute for a
United Nations Tribunal (1946)

United Nations Administrative Tribunal
(1950--)

Special Committee on Review of Administrative Tribunal Judgments (1955)

Committee on Applications for Review of
Administrative Tribunal Judgments (1956--)

E. Staff Recruitment and Other Personnel
Questions

Commission of Jurists (1952)

Advisory Panel (on Secretariat matters)
(1953)

Special Advisory Board (Secretariat)
(1954-1957)

F. Public Information Activities

Advisory Committee on United Nations
Telecommunications   (1947)

Expert Committee on United Nations Public
Information (1958)

Consultative Panel on Public Information
(1960--)

ORGANIZATION OF THE SECRETARIAT
AND STAFF QUESTIONS

A. Organization of the Secretariat

1954 Survey Group (on the reorganization of the Secretariat)

The question of an extensive reorganization of the Secretariat was discussed at the sixth session of the General Assembly; and in the debate on the budget in the Fifth Committee a number of delegations expressed doubt as to the soundness of the present administrative structure of the Secretariat, and requested the Secretary-General to consider the matter of a revision of the structure and to report to the General Assembly. The report of the Fifth Committee to the Assembly (GAOR, Sess. VI, Annexes, agenda item 41, A/2022. paragraph 15), of 31 January 1952, incorporated an Egyptian proposal constituting a recommendation of the Committee which requested the Secretary-General to review the whole structure and functions of the three Departments of the Secretariat -- the Departments of Economic Affairs, of Social Affairs, and the Technical Assistance Administration --, as well as the system of co-ordination between them, and to report to the General Assembly at its seventh session. The Secretary-General's explanatory memorandum (GAOR, Sess. VII, Annexes, vol. 2, agenda item 69, A/2214, part I), was issued on 7 October 1952, pursuant to this request.

Assembly resolution 681 A (VII), of 21 December 1952, taking note of the report, as well as of the report of ACABQ (Ibid., A/2290) on the proposals therein, requested the Secretary-General

to prepare a full report on the problem of reorganization of the Secretariat, including the
relationship between the three departments cited
above, and to circulate it, with the recommendations of ACABQ, to all Members four weeks before
the opening of the eighth session of the General
Assembly.

The Secretary-General's report, pursuant to this
request, (GAOR, Sess. VIII, Annexes, agenda item
48, A/2554), was issued on 12 November 1953.

Assembly resolution 784 (VIII), of 9 December
1953, authorized the Secretary-General to proceed to the extent possible along the lines he
had proposed in his report, and to prepare 1955
budget estimates within the broad framework of
such proposals, taking into account suggestions
of the Advisory Committee (ACABQ) (Ibid., A/
2606), of 5 December 1953, and the views expressed in Fifth Committee meetings 427 and 428
on 8 February 1953.

Terms of Reference

The review was directed to pursue three main
fields of inquiry:
    (a) The character and volume of the sub-
stantive and administrative responsibilities of
the Secretariat staff required to service the
General Assembly, the Councils and other subsidiary organs and to implement the work programs
of those bodies;
    (b) The main structure of the Secretariat
and an appropriate organization for the units
comprising separate departments or offices;
    (c) The number and the levels of staff
required to enable the Secretariat to fulfill
its essential responsibilities.

Membership

To assist him in further elaboration of the re-organization plans, the Secretary-General appointed, early in 1954, a small Survey Group of six senior members of the Secretariat to undertake a thorough review of the Headquarters establishment.

Action

The conclusions of the Survey Group were issued by the Secretary-General in a report (GAOR, Sess. IX, Annexes, agenda item 53, A/2731), of 21 September 1954, which covered departments at Headquarters only. It contained a chart on a proposed organization of the Secretariat at Headquarters. The Assembly, in resolution 886 (IX), of 17 December 1954, after consideration of the report of the Survey Group and comments thereon by ACABQ (Ibid., A/2745), 9 October 1954, approved the measures recommended by the Secretary-General, and requested a further report on the progress of the problem.

Committee of Experts on the Review of the Activities and Organization of the Secretariat

Established by Assembly resolution 1446 (XIV), of 5 December 1959.

Terms of Reference

The resolution requested the Secretary-General to appoint a committee of six experts, with broad and practical experience in the various aspects of administration and chosen with due regard to geographical distribution, to work together with the Secretary-General in reviewing the activities and organization of the Secretariat of the United Nations with a view to effecting or proposing further measures designed to ensure maximum economy and efficiency.

Resolution 1559 (XV), of 18 December 1960, requested the Committee of Experts to study points related to geographical distribution of the staff of the Secretariat.

Membership

On the recommendation of the Secretary-General (GAOR, Sess. XV, Annexes, agenda item 58, A/4536, and Corr.1), of 14 October 1960, the Assembly, in resolution 1557 (XV), of 18 December 1960, increased the number of the Committee from six to eight.

The members were as follows:
Guillaume Georges-Picot (France), former Permanent Representative of France to the United Nations, and formerly Assistant Secretary-General in charge of the Department of Economic Affairs and the Department of Social Affairs, Chairman;

Francisco Urrutia (Colombia), former Permanent Representative of Colombia, Rapporteur;

A. A. Fomin (USSR), Ministry of Foreign Affairs, replaced on 6 February, by A.A. Roshchin (USSR), Alternate Representative of the USSR to the 15th session of the General Assembly;

Omar Loutfi (UAR), Permanent Representative to the United Nations;

Harold Beeley (UK), replaced as of 1 September 1960 by Sir Harold Parker (UK), member of the International Civil Service Advisory Board, and former Permanent Secretary to the Ministry of Defense;

Kenneth K.S. Dadzie (Ghana), attended as Observer on behalf of Alex Quaison-Sackey, Ghana's Permanent Representative to the United Nations;

C.S. Venkatachar (India), former High Commissioner to Canada;

Dr. Herman B. Wells, President of Indiana University, and former member of the US Delegation to the United Nations; replaced on 6 February 1961, by Professor L.M. Goodrich (USA), Professor of International Organization and Administration, Columbia University.

A footnote to paragraph 1 of the introduction in the report of the Committee of Experts (A/4776) listed the experts.

Action

The Expert Committee met from 23 June to 5 July, and from 1 to 9 September 1960. Its interim report (Ibid., A/4536, and Corr.1, annex) was issued on 14 October 1960.

The Committee resumed meeting on 6 February 1961, and set up two sub-committees, one of which continued to meet at Headquarters in New York, the other proceeding to Geneva, where from 14 to 28 March 1961, it met with the Director of the European Office of the United Nations in Geneva, as well as with the Executive Secretaries of ECAFE and ECE.   On 10 April the full Committee met again in New York, and continued meeting until 18 May 1961.   The report of the Committee (GAOR, Sess.XVI, Annexes, vol. 3, agenda item 61, A/4776) was issued on 14 June 1961.

In its report, the Expert Committee stated it conceived its function in terms different from those of the 1954 Survey Group (GAOR, Sess.IX, Annexes, agenda item 53, A/2731), which the Secretary-General had appointed to assist him in the further elaboration of reorganization plans which he had submitted to the General Assembly on 12 November 1953 (GAOR, Sess.VIII, Annexes, agenda item 48, A/2554) on authorization of resolution 784 (VIII), of 9 December 1953.

Other documents on the subject were the following: comments of the Secretary-General (GAOR, Sess. XVI, Annexes, agenda item 61, A/4794) on the report of the Fifth Committee (Ibid., A/5073), 19 December 1961; report of ACABQ (Ibid., A/4901), 29 September 1961.   A separate report (Ibid., agenda item 64, A/5063) was issued by the Fifth Committee on the geographical distribution of the staff of the Secretariat, on 18 October 1961.

Expert Committee on the Reorganization of the United Nations Secretariat

On 14 December 1967, the Secretary-General stated before the Fifth Committee (meeting 1225) that on the question of the reorganization of the top echelon of the Secretariat, it was his intention to appoint a small team of seven members with wide geographical distribution, to enable him to secure the assistance and advice of people of recognized competence from various parts of the world, including two or three members who had experience of both the work of the Permanent Missions to the United Nations and the work of the Secretariat (GAOR, Sess. XXII, Annexes, vol. 3, agenda item 74, A/C.5/1128, paragraph 17), 18 October 1967.

Terms of Reference

The Secretary-General outlined their duties as follows:

They should undertake a review of the most important aspects of the present organization of the Secretariat, including the United Nations Office in Geneva, the secretariats of UNCTAD, UNIDO, and the regional economic commissions, with a view to ensuring the most efficient functioning of the Secretariat with the optimum use of available resources. The Committee might also consider the division of responsibilities, under the authority of the Secretary-General, of the various units and their inter-relationship, in order to improve the functioning of the Secretariat as a whole. He also believed that, with the available time, the Committee might devote some attention to the management procedures of the Secretariat and propose detailed studies, if considered necessary. The Committee was also requested to take a look at the organization of the top echelon of the Secretariat in the light of comments made in the Fifth Committee at the twenty-second session of the General Assembly.

Membership

On 8 April 1968, the following were named as members of the Expert Committee (paragraph 2 of the report (A/7359)):

Louis Ignacio-Pinto (Dahomey), Bernard de Menthon (France), Platon D. Morosov (USSR), Manuel Pérez-Guerrero (Venezuela), Andrew A. Stark (UK), and Wilbur H. Ziehl (USA).

Ismat T. Kittani and Yasushi Akashi of the Executive Office of the Secretary-General, served as Secretary and Assistant Secretary of the Committee, respectively.

Action

At its first meeting, on 16 April 1968, the Expert Committee elected Mr. Pérez-Guerrero (Venezuela) and Mr. Ignacio-Pinto (Dahomey) as Co-Chairmen. Mr. Stark (UK) participated in his private capacity until 1 October 1968 when he took up his duties as Under-Secretary-General for Administration and Management at the United Nations.

The Expert Committee held 108 meetings, first at United Nations Headquarters in New York where it had an extensive exchange of views with all senior officials, and with the executive heads of UNICEF, UNDP, and UNITAR; and in Geneva where it examined Secretariat units stationed there; followed by brief visits to Rome, Vienna, Beirut, Addis Ababa, Bangkok, Santiago de Chile, where other United Nations organs were located. The report of the Expert Committee was issued as an annex to a note of the Secretary-General (GAOR,

Sess. XXIII, <u>Annexes</u>, vol.2, addendum to agenda
item 74, A/7359) on budget estimates for the
financial year 1969. The report contained an
appendix with the text of the separate opinions
of Platon D. Morosov (USSR).

Assembly resolution 2480 (XXIII), 21 December
1968, noted paragraph 73 of the report, in which
the Committee expressed the feeling that there
was a need for greater discipline and stricter
application of the policy of not recruiting
from countries which were over the upper limit
of their desirable range, save in exceptional
cases and with the Secretary-General's special
authorization in each such case. In any event,
it concluded, nothing should be done to compro-
mise the earliest achievement of the desired
equitable geographical distribution.

B.   Staff Salaries and Benefits

Working Party on Staff Retirement and Insurance Funds

Established by the Secretary-General pursuant to General Assembly resolution 13 (I), of 13 February 1946, on the item "Retirement and Compensation".

Terms of Reference

At its 31st plenary meeting, on 13 February 1946, the Assembly decided that "in order to facilitate the engagement, as members of the staff of the United Nations, of persons who have accrued pension rights as officials, either of the central government of Members, or of subordinate governmental or other administrative authorities within the territory of Members, it is desirable that arrangements should be made secure that accrued pension rights are not lost when such persons accept posts on the staff of the United Nations, by way either of transfer or of secondment. Therefore, the General Assembly recommended that, after such discussion with the Secretary-General as may be necessary to settle details, the governments of Members adopt such legislative or administrative measures as may be required to preserve such pension rights (GAOR, Sess. I, Part 2, Sixth Committee, annex 24b, A/114).

Subsequently, in a letter of 31 May 1946, on behalf of the Secretary-General, the Assistant Secretary-General for Administrative and Financial Services suggested as procedure for making the necessary studies and preparing the recommendations for submission to the General Assembly:

(a) A Working Party of consultants should be appointed at an early date which would consist of not more than five members, including persons with a wide range of experience in the social insurance field. It was tentatively suggested that the Working Party might consist of one or more social scientists familiar with social insurance; an individual who has had experience in the administration of social insurance planning; one or more actuaries; and an individual who was familiar with the problems of the finance of staff retirement and accident compensation plans. The Working Party should be served by a secretary designated from the staff of the Secretariat. It was also tentatively suggested that the Working Party might be attached to the Budget and Administrative Planning Office for purposes of administration and staffing.

(b) The Working Party would take account of the proposals put forward by the General Assembly and related information from staff members, and would prepare a draft plan.

(c) The plan prepared by the Working Party would be submitted to the *Advisory Group of Experts, which would review the plan, or alternative plans, and would prepare recommendations which, subject to approval by the Secretary-General, could be transmitted to the General Assembly at the second part of its first session (Ibid., annex 24, A/90, appendix I).

In his letter of 31 May 1946, the Assistant Secretary-General listed the specific questions on which the Working Party would be asked to prepare recommendations for the Secretary-General as follows:

(1) Report on the existing Provident Fund with such changes in this scheme as may be desirable;

(2)   Proposals for a permanent staff retirement scheme to become operative 1 January
1947;
(3)   System for the provision of benefits
to widows and orphans of members of the staff
of the United Nations;
(4)   Proposals for permanent schemes for
injury compensation, compassionate benefits,
and for idemnification of disability resulting
from sickness directly attributable to work in
the service of the Organization;
(5)   Proposed scheme for children's allowances and education grants;
(6)   Pension Fund for the Judges of the
International Court of Justice (in conjunction
with the Registrar of the ICJ);
(7)   Preservation of pension rights for
officials of Member Governments transferred or
seconded for service with the United Nations
(to be considered in conjunction with the Legal
Department).

Subsequently, the Working Party was asked to
include consideration of the possibility of
providing some form of hospitalization and
medical benefit service for members of the United Nations Staff (Ibid., annex 24, A/90, appendix II).

Membership

The Secretary-General arranged for the appoint-
ment of an expert Working Party consisting of:
D. Norman Chester (UK), Chairman; E.
Schoenbaum (Czech); N.E. Sheppard (Canada); and
Rainard B. Robbins, Consulting Actuary to the
Working Party.

Action

On 26 October 1946, a document (Ibid., annex 24, A/90) entitled "Proposed Scheme for Staff Retirement and Insurance Funds and Related Benefits" was issued. It contained a report by the Secretary-General, which was divided into three main parts: Part I: Analysis of the problems involved in a staff benefit scheme for the United Nations and of the ideas under-lying the main proposals; Part II, Draft regu-lations of the Pension Fund and other staff benefits which would come into effect if the report was accepted by the Assembly (the draft-ing of these clauses had been undertaken in conjunction with the Legal Department): Part III: Report of the Consulting Actuary to the Working Party on the cost and financial implications of the pension plan. The appendices to the report included (1) relevant resolutions of the Gen-eral Assembly;(2) terms of reference and re-port of the Working Party; (3) cost of the proposed schemes.

The Secretary-General made use, for guidance, of a memorandum of the Advisory Group of Ex-perts (GAOR, Sess.I, Part 1, Fifth Committee, annex 2, A/C.5/19/Rev.1), of 29 January 1946, concerning "Proposals on Children's Allowances, Education (Expatriation Allowances and Install-ation Allowances)"; and another entitled "Sug-gestions of the Advisory Group of Experts on the Establishment of a Staff Retirement Scheme and Related Questions" (Ibid., Annex 3, A/C. 5/20), of 28 January 1946; and a statement by the delegate of Canada at the meeting of 1 Feb-ruary 1946 of the Fifth Committee (Ibid., annex 3A, A/C.5/28).

On 16 October 1946, a report of the Working Party on Staff Retirement and Insurance Funds

(<u>GAOR</u>, Sess.I, Part 2, <u>Sixth Committee</u>, annex 24b, A/114) was transmitted to the General Assembly by the Secretary-General. It contained proposals on employer's pension arrangements, and on procedure.

*<u>Note</u>:   The "Advisory Group of Experts" referred to in the text of the Working Party refers to the Advisory Group of Experts on Administrative, Personnel and Budgetary Questions (document series ST/SG/AD/-), which was appointed by the Executive Secretary of the Preparatory Commission of the United Nations in November 1945, and which functioned until the standing committee, Advisory Committee on Administrative and Budgetary Questions (ACABQ) was created and its members elected on November 1946 (see Chapter I).

Committee of Experts on Salary, Allowances and Leave Systems

Established by the Secretary-General pursuant to the approval by the General Assembly on 11 December 1948 of the report of the Fifth Committee on the fourth annual budget of the United Nations (GAOR, Sess.III, Part I, Plenary Meetings, Annexes, A/798), of 10 December 1948.

Terms of Reference

The terms of reference were spelled out in the second report of 1948 of the Advisory Committee on Administrative and Budgetary Questions (ACABQ) (GAOR, Sess.III, Suppl.7A (A/598, chapter II, paragraph 24)).

The ACABQ suggested that a comprehensive review of the salary and allowance system be undertaken by the Secretary-General for consideration at the fourth regular session of the General Assembly, and that a working party of three independent experts, appointed by the Secretary-General in agreement with ACABQ, should assist in this review. It also suggested that this general review of the salary and allowance system should include the review of the question of home leave and comparative study of the salary scales and allowance schemes of other international organizations.

Membership

The Committee finally selected was composed of:
    Arthur S. Flemming, President of Ohio Wesleyan University and former member of the United States Civil Service Commission, Chairman;

Roger Grégoire, Directeur de la Fonction Publique, France;

Uno Brunskog (Sweden), member of the United Nations Board of Auditors and Auditor for ILO and WHO; formerly Auditor of the League of Nations.

They received the help of an expert consultant, A. J. D. Winnifrith (UK), throughout the greater part of the Committee's first session.

Action

The Committee held two sessions at Lake Success, the first from 5 July to 4 August 1949, during which it arrived at provisional decisions based on a critical appraisal of existing salary, allowance and leave arrangements, and the second from 28 September to 12 October 1949 when it re-examined certain of these decisions in the course of drafting and appraising its report.

The report (GAOR, Sess. IV, Fifth Committee, Annex, Vol. II, A/C.5/331, and Corr.1 and Add. 1-3) was issued on 31 October 1949. Addendum 1 to the report (A/C.5/331,Add.1 and Corr.1, contained a report by the Secretary-General on the report of the Committee of Experts; addendum 2 (A/C.5/331/Add.2) contained a memorandum from a group of individual members and alternates of the Staff Committee, regarding the report; and addendum 3 (A/C.5/331/Add.3) contained views of the ILO and WHO on the report.

Committee of Experts on Salary Differentials, Cost-of-Living Adjustments and Dependency Allowances

At its ninth session, the General Assembly, in resolution 894 (IX), of 17 December 1954, adopted a revision of the Staff assessment plan. In taking this action, the Assembly noted that it was the intention of the Secretary-General to appoint, in consultation with the executive heads of the specialized agencies, an expert committee to review during 1955 the whole question of salary differentials, cost-of-living adjustments and dependency allowances.

Terms of Reference

With the concurrence of the Directors-General of the specialized agencies, the Secretary-General appointed a committee of experts to study and report on certain aspects of the present system of remuneration of professional staff in the field offices of the United Nations and of the specialized agencies. The studies of the Committee were to pay particular attention to the question of differentials and cost-of-living adjustments applied to the base salaries of staff members at field duty stations, and to the system of dependency allowances as applied by the United Nations and specialized agencies.

The terms of reference of the Committee, as agreed between the United Nations and the specialized agencies through the machinery of the *Administrative Committee on Co-ordination (ACC) (see appendix) were the following:

(a) to review and report on the system applied in the establishment of differentials (initial adjustments) for field offices, and in the establishment of cost-of-living adjustments (subsequent adjustments), as outlined in the report of the Special Committee of the ACC of 17 April 1952;

(b) review and report on the systems of dependency allowances as applied by the United Nations and specialized agencies;

(c) it was not to review the level of basic salary rates for the professional staff, but should feel free to bring to the attention of the ACC any observations which the Committee might wish to offer as a result of its review of the special problems outlined above;

(d) at its discretion, the Committee might receive statements or testimony from the appropriate representative of the staffs of the United Nations and specialized agencies.

It was to submit its report to the ACC.

Membership

The Expert Committee was composed of the following:

Sir A. Ramaswami Mudalier (India), Chairman;

Senator César Charlone (Uruguay);

Dr. Philip J. Idenburg (Netherlands); and

James M. Mitchell (USA).

Action

The Expert Committee met in New York from 16 to 28 May 1955. Its report on salary differentials, cost-of-living adjustments and dependency allowances was contained in an annex to the Secretary-General's report on salary differentials (GAOR, Sess.X,Annexes, agenda item 56,A/C.5/632),

14 October 1955. An appendix to the report contained the report of the Special Committee of ACC of April 1952 on principles and procedures for establishing salary differentials and cost-of-living adjustments. The Secretary-General also issued a note on Headquarters cost-of-living adjustment (Ibid., A/C.5/636), on 18 October 1955.

Committee to Review the Salary, Allowances and Benefits System of the United Nations (A/AC.84/- restricted series)

Known as the "Salary Review Committee," it was established by Assembly resolution 975 (X), of 15 December 1955, after the Assembly had considered the reports of the Secretary-General relating to salary differentials, cost-of-living adjustments and dependency allowances (GAOR, Sess.X, Annexes, agenda item 56, A/C.5/632 and 636), and recommendations thereon of ACABQ (Ibid., A/3036 and A/3039), of 21 November 1955.

Terms of Reference

The resolution decided to establish a Committee of eleven experts nominated by Governments to undertake a comprehensive review of the United Nations salary, allowance and benefits system, and to report its findings and recommendations to the General Assembly at its eleventh session.

Membership

The resolution requested the Governments of Argentina, Denmark, Egypt, France, India, New Zealand, USSR, United Kingdom, and USA, to nominate an expert to serve on the Committee; and requested the Secretary-General, in consultation with the heads of the specialized agencies, to invite the Governments of two States which were members of the specialized agencies but not of the United Nations, to nominate one expert each to serve on the Committee. The Secretary-General subsequently invited the Governments of Switzerland and Japan to nominate members to the Committee.

The representatives of the Committee members were as follows:

F. Friis (Denmark), Chairman

Pascal Frochaux (Switzerland), Vice-Chairman

K. Harada (Japan), replaced by M. Ogiso at second session

J. K. Hunn (New Zealand), Rapporteur

R. S. Mani (India)

A. El-Messiri (Egypt)

James M. Mitchell (USA), replaced at times by Miss Carol Laise and A. F. Bender, Jr.

V. G. Molchanov (USSR)

M. J. Nadal (France)

Dr. R. Quijano (Argentina)

Sir Arthur Rucker (UK)

Action

The Committee met in New York in May; in Geneva from 29 May to 9 June; again in New York from 12 to 29 June and from 11 September to 18 October 1956. Its report (GAOR, Sess.XI, Annexes, agenda item 51, A/3209), issued in November 1956 as a separate document.

Resolution 1095 (XI), of 27 February 1957, expressed appreciation for the valuable work of the Committee, and having considered the comments thereon by the Secretary-General and by executive heads of specialized agencies (Ibid., A/C.5/691), of 18 October 1961, observers of ACABQ (Ibid., A/3505), of 18 January 1957, and the report of the Fifth Committee (Ibid., A/3558), of 25 February 1957, requested the Secretary-General to take certain measures (paragraphs 3 to 6) and amended Staff Regulations as of 1 January 1957 (paragraph 7).

Special Committee for the Review of the United
Nations Salary System (A/AC.150/-)

Established by Assembly resolution 2743 (XXV),
of 17 December 1970, after consideration of the
Secretary-General's report of 25 September 1970
on salary scales for the professional and higher
catagories (GAOR, Sess.XXV, Annexes, agenda item
73, A/C.5/1303 and Add.1), and the related report of the ACABQ (Ibid., Suppl.8A, (A/8008/Add.
3)), and recalling the report of the Salary Review Committee established in 1955 (GAOR, Sess.
XI, Annexes, agenda item 51, A/3209).

Terms of Reference

The Special Committee was requested to undertake a thorough review of the long-term principles and criteria which should govern the
whole United Nations common system of salaries,
allowances, grants, superannuation and other
benefits, and to report its conclusions and recommendations on the following:
     (a) the structure of categories and grades
which would best enable the international civil
service to discharge its functions with efficiency and reasonable economy;
     (b) the base of the system;
     (c) the principles which should govern the
establishment of the salary scales and other
conditions of service for the various categories;
     (d) the level of salaries and allowances,
and the fringe benefits for the various grades;
     (e) such other matters concerning the sys-
tem as it might deem relevant.

The resolution suggested the Special Committee
could establish such panels or subsidiary groups
of experts as would ensure that adequate time
was devoted to the subjects under study; and

requested the Special Committee, _inter alia_,
to transmit its report, together with the comments of the International Civil Service Advisory Board (ICSAB), through the Secretary-
General, in his capacity as Chairman of the
*Administrative Committee on Co-ordination (ACC)
(see appendix), to the General Assembly at its
twenty-sixth session.

Membership

The Special Committee was to consist of government experts from eleven Member States to be
nominated by the President of the General Assembly, with due regard to geographical balance,
it being understood that these States would
nominate individuals of recognized standing and
experience to serve on the Committee.

At the same meeting, on 17 December 1970, the
General Assembly approved the following nomina-
tions by the President:
    Argentina, France, India, Japan, Niger,
    Nigeria, Peru, Poland, USSR, United
    Kingdom, and United States of America.

The eleven Governments designated the following
experts:
    Zakari M. Bello (Nigeria), Permanent Secre-
tary, Ministry of Agriculture and Natural Resources, Kano State;
    Masao Chiba (Japan), Director, Institute of
Public Administration, National Personnel Authority;
    Zbigniew Dembowski (Poland), replaced by Jan
Chowaniec, Ministry of Foreign Affairs, from 5
July 1971;
    Oscar R. Faura (Peru), Minister Counsellor
for Press and Information, Permanent Mission of
Peru to the United Nations;

A.H.M. Hillis (UK), formerly Comptroller-General, National Debt Office;

Dayton W. Hull (USA), formerly Director, Compensation Division, Department of State;

K. A. Meriko (Niger), Counsellor, Embassy of Niger, Brussels;

Guillermo J. McGough (Argentina), Counsellor, Ministry for Foreign Affairs, replaced by Miss Ruth Guevara Achaval, Ministry for Foreign Affairs, from 18 January to 7 April 1972;

P. Robert-Duvilliers (France), replaced by Michel Maler, Deputy to the Chief, Bureau of Statutory Coordination, Secretary of State for the Civil Service, from 15 July to 24 August 1971, and by Jules Milliez, Counsellor, French Embassy, Algeria; as of 18 February 1972;

S. K. Roy (India), Ambassador of India to Mexico, concurrently accredited to Cuba, Nicaragua and Panama;

Aleksei V. Zakharov (USSR), replaced by A. G. Koulazhenkov, Ambassador, Ministry of Foreign Affairs, as of 18 January 1972.

Annexes of both reports listed the members of the Committee.

Action

The first session of the Committee was held at United Nations headquarters in New York from 1 June to 1 July; at the World Health Organization (WHO) headquarters in Geneva from 5 to 29 July; and again in New York from 9 to 24 August 1971. Elected officers were: Chairman: Mr. Roy (India); Vice-Chairman: Mr. Faura (Peru); Rapporteur: Mr. Mariko (Niger). The interim report of the Special Committee (GAOR, Sess.XXVI, Suppl.28 (A/8428, and Corr.1)) was issued in September 1971.

The Special Committee resumed its work in New York from 18 January to 7 April and from 22 May to 1 June 1972. The final part of the session took place at WHO headquarters in Geneva from 5 June to 7 July 1972. The report of the session (GAOR, Sess.XXVII, Suppl.28 (A/8728, and Corr.1)) was issued in three volumes and an addendum, as follows: Vol.I, August 1972, contained a summary of conclusions and recommendations, and annexes I-VI; vol.II, October 1972, contained annexes VII-XI, giving the views of United Nations Members, of executive heads of organizations of the United Nations common system, of the Federation of International Civil Servants' Association (FICSA), and of staff associations; vol.III, October 1972, contained annex XII, a report on "Salaries, Allowances and Benefits in Seven United Nations Headquarters Countries", prepared by an outside consultant, and annex XIII, a "Study of the Post Adjustment System", prepared by Pascal Frochaux (Switzerland). The addendum (Ibid., Suppl.28A (A/8728/Add.1)), October 1972, contained the comments of the International Civil Service Advisory Board (ICSAB).

Resolution 3042 (XXVII), of 19 December 1972 -- noting the report recommended the establishment of a new organ for the regulation and coordination of the conditions of service of the United Nations common system, and that ICSAB and ACABQ (A/8914, offset) recommended the establishment of an international civil service commission, composed of experts who should be independent of executive heads, staff associations and Governments, but accountable as a body to the General Assembly -- decided to establish in principle, as of 1 January 1974, an International Civil Service Commission.

Documents issued by the Committee:

The Development of the United Nations Salary System, 20 April 1971 (A/AC.150/3)

The Existing Conditions of Service in the United Nations Common System, 20 April 1971 (A/AC.150/4)

Criteria and Methods for Determining International Salaries, 20 April 1971 (A/AC.150/5)

The Determination of Salaries for General Service Personnel, 20 April 1971 (A/AC.150/8)

Information on the Organization of the United Nations Common System, 3 June 1971 (A/AC.150/9 and Add.1-11)

Documents under the Committee document series symbol (A/AC.150/-) were issued in mimeographed form.

International Civil Service Advisory Board (ICSAB)

Established by General Assembly resolution 13 (I), III, of 13 February 1946, which instructed the Secretary-General to establish, in consultation with the executive heads of the specialized agencies, an International Civil Service Commission, to advise with regard to methods of recruitment and related matters.

Its last session was held in 1974, after which it was succeeded by the International Civil Service Commission (ICSC).

Terms of Reference

At its fourth session, held in July 1948, the *Administrative Committee on Co-ordination (ACC) (see appendix) agreed on the establishment of an International Civil Service Advisory Board with the following terms of reference:

The purpose of the Board should be to contribute to the improvement of recruitment and related phases of personnel administration in all of the international organizations through:

(a) Advice and interchange of information in methods of recruitment and on the means by which appropriate standards of recruitment in the United Nations Secretariat and the specialized agencies may be ensured;

(b) Consideration, at the request of the Co-ordination Committee (ACC), of related phases of personnel administration, and developing and making recommendations for guiding principles and appropriate policies arising from the consideration of such problems;

(c) At the request of an individual agency, provision of advice or assistance on a personnel problem of the agency.

The Board should be advisory and consultative; it should have no responsibility for, or control of, the operation of recruitment or related phases of personnel administration.

These terms of reference were slightly modified in 1950 by the ACC. Paragraph 2 (b) was revised so that the Board should contribute to the improvement of recruitment and related phases of personnel administration in all the international organizations through:

"consideration, after consultation with the ACC, of related phases of personnel administration and advice on methods of further assimilating and improving major personnel policies in the United Nations and the specialized agencies".

In 1955, the Salary Review Committee, -- a body consisting of eleven experts nominated by Governments and set up by the General Assembly (resolution 975 (X), 15 December 1955) to undertake a comprehensive review of the United Nations salary, allowance and benefits systems -- devoted considerable attention to the inter-agency machinery for dealing with personnel problems and to the role of ICSAB in this field, and made recommendations on additional terms of reference for ICSAB. No action was taken on these recommendations until 1963 when, on the Board's recommendation, the terms of reference were revised by resolution 1981 B (XVIII), of 17 December 1963. Its functions were to be:

I. To advise the Administrative Committee on Co-ordination on:

(a) methods of recruitment and the means by which appropriate standards of recruitment may be ensured in the United Nations and specialized agencies;

(b)   aspects of personnel administration related to the recruitment, training and conduct of staff;

(c)   such other matters of personnel policy as the ACC may refer to it.

II. To foster the development of co-ordination in conditions of service in the organization following the United Nations common system, and in particular, to review and make recommendations through the ACC on:

(a)   the system of classification of posts and its application;

(b)   salaries and allowances of staff in the professional and higher categories;

(c)   the methods of and the criteria for establishing the conditions of service of staff in the General Service category and the manner in which the criteria are applied in the headquarters areas;

(d)   divergencies in the application of the common system, the extent to which they should be eliminated, and the manner in which such elimination might be accomplished;

(e)   any other matter which may be referred to it by the ACC (acting either at the request of an executive head or of a legislative or executive authority of an organization in the common system) including:

(i)   the determination of the specific conditions of service of the General Service category in a particular headquarters area;

(ii)   questions of application and administration of conditions of service in the common system and proposals for changes in the conditions on which the separate organizations concerned have been unable to agree;

(iii)   matters of particular importance to an individual organization, within the general field of personnel administration.

The reports of the Board were transmitted to
the appropriate authorities of each organization through the ACC.

The Board had a Secretary, appointed by the
Secretary-General, with the advice and consent
of ACC, after consultation with the Board, and
was removable only with the agreement of the
Board. In carrying out his duties, he was subject only to the instructions of the Board.

Membership

Originally the Board was composed of a Chairman
and eight other members, appointed by the Secretary-General, with the advice and consent of
the ACC, for a two-year term.

The 1963 revision increased the membership to
ten members besides the Chairman.

The Board is a continuing body, and its members
normally appointed for a three-year term. Their
terms of office expired in rotation, the terms
of three members expiring at the end of the
first year, those of four members each at the
second and third years, and they were eligible
for reappointment.

The members of the Board were appointed in their
personal capacity as individuals who had earned
wide public trust for judgment, and whose high
qualifications ensured respect for the Board's
advice. They were representative of different
regions and cultures and brought to the Board
diverse experience appropriate to its work.
They were not chosen or regarded as representatives of organizations. No Board member would
serve concurrently as a member of the Secretariat of the United Nations or any related agency.

The terms of reference and functions of the International Civil Service Advisory Board were published in a document (ICSAB/INF.1) of 31 May 1966. Annex II of the document listed the members and terms of office of ICSAB from 1949 to 1966; Annex III listed the sessions and reports of ICSAB from the first in March 1949 to the 13th session, in May 1965.

Action

The reports of ICSAB included, *inter alia*, a list of its members, and annex I of each report contained a list of all participants in its sessions. They were as follows:

COORD - CIVIL SERVICE/1, 17 May 1949 (mimeographed). Its members were: Thanassis Aghnides (Greece), Chairman; Leon Baranski (Poland), Charles H. Bland (Canada), Ebbe Groes (Denmark), Luiz Simoes Lopes (Brazil), Jean Morellet (France), Sir A. Ramaswami Mudaliar (India), Dame Mary G. Smieton (UK), John A. Stevenson (USA). The first session was held in New York from 16-22 March 1949, and was devoted to a preliminary discussion of recruitment methods and standards.

COORD/CIVIL SERVICE/2/Rev.1 (Sales no.: 1950.X.4), Report on Recruitment Methods and Standards for the United Nations and the Specialized Agencies. The second session was held in Geneva from 22-28 March 1950. Arthur S. Flemming (USA) served on the Board during this session in place of John A. Stevenson (USA).

COORD/CIVIL SERVICE/3, 11 June 1951 (mimeographed), "Provisional report on In-Service-Training in the United Nations and Specialized Agencies". The third session, held in

New York from 21-25 May 1951, was devoted to the question of in-service training in the international secretariats. Its membership was as follows: Thanassis Aghnides (Greece), Chairman; Dame Mary G. Smieton (UK), Vice-Chairman; Leon Baranski (Poland), Charles H. Bland (Canada), Arthur S. Flemming (USA), Roger Grégoire (France), Ebbe Groes (Denmark), Luiz Simoes Lopes (Brazil); Sir Ramaswami Mudaliar (India).

COORD/CIVIL SERVICE/4 (Sales no.:1952. X.1), Report on In-Service Training in the United Nations and Specialized Agencies, final report. The fourth session was held in Geneva, from 12-16 May 1952.

COORD/CIVIL SERVICE/5, October 1954. Report on Standards of Conduct in the International Civil Service. The fifth session was held in New York from 23-30 March 1954.

COORD/CIVIL SERVICE/6, 10 August 1955 (mimeographed); "Report on Educational Facilities for the Children of International Civil Servants." The ACC at its 18th session requested ICSAB to undertake a "study of the problems concerning the education of children which face international staff members who are expatriated, with the view especially to clarifying the degree and character of responsibility employing agencies should assume". General Assembly resolution 883 (IX), of 14 December 1954, requested ICSAB "to consider appropriate measures for providing children of staff members with special facilities for the study of their mother tongue in cases where they are obliged to attend local schools in which the instruction is given in a language other than the mother tongue". The sixth session was held in Geneva, from 9-13 May 1955.

COORD/CIVIL SERVICE/7, 20 April 1956, (mimeographed), "Report on Age of Retirement in the United Nations and the Specialized Agencies." The seventh session was held in New York from 12-17 April 1956.

COORD/CIVIL SERVICE/8, "Common Grading Standards (Preliminary report)";
COORD/CIVIL SERVICE/9, "Problems in Administering the Post Adjustments System". The eighth session was held in New York in March 1958.

ICSAB/IX/5, "Report on Common Grading Standards". The ninth session was held in Geneva in August 1960.

ICSAB/X/7, 13 May 1951 transmitted by the Secretary-General to the General Assembly (GAOR, Sess.XVI, Annexes, vol.3, agenda item 65, A/4823/Add.1), on 31 July 1961, "Report on the Base Salary Scales of Staff in the Professional and Higher Categories of the International Civil Service." The 10th session was held in Geneva in May 1961. Its members were: Sir Ramaswami Mudaliar (India), Chairman; Mahmoun Beheiry (Sudan), Charles H. Bland (Canada), Dr. César Charlone (Uruguay), Arthur D. Flemming (USA), Guillaume Georges-Picot (France), Dr. Manfred Lach s (Poland), Sir Harold Parker (UK), Adrian Pelt (Netherlands).

ICSAB/XI/3 (annex to document A/C.5/976), a report of the Secretary-General, 23 July 1963 (GAOR, Sess.XVIII, Annexes, agenda item 64 (b)), "Report on Inter-Organizational Machinery for Matters of Pay and Personnel Administration." Annex 2 contained text of the draft terms of reference, which were endorsed by General Assembly resolution 1981 (XVIII), of 17 December 1963.

The 11th session was held in New York from 20-29 May 1963. The Board issued a second report, ICSAB/XI/4, on a "Proposed Study of Career Prospects (Outline of Study)".

ICSAB/XII/5, "Proposed Review of International Base Salary Scales (Outline of Study)"; ICSAB/XII/6, "Career Prospects in the International Civil Service"; ICSAB/XII/7, "Working Arrangements of the Board", were issued by the 12th session of the Board, held in Geneva in July 1964.

ICSAB/XIII/1, "Constitutional Procedures followed for the consideration and implementation of the Board's recommendations"; ICSAB/XIII/2, "Divergencies in the application of the Common System"; ICSAB/XIII/3, "Determination of Revision of Conditions of Service of Staff in the General Services Category"; ICSAB/XIII/4, "Salary Scales of the Professional and Higher Categories of the International Civil Service", were issued at the 13th session, held in Geneva from 17-28 May 1965. A Secretary-General's report on the subject (GAOR, Sess. XX, Annexes, vol.3, agenda item 77, A/5918/Add.1), of 8 September 1965, transmitted the text of ICSAB/XIII/4). Assembly resolution 2050 (XX), 13 December 1965, took action on the report by amending UN Staff Regulations.

The Board in 1966 and thereafter issued only one report for each session, covering all the subjects with which it dealt at that session.

ICSAB/XIV/1, 15 July 1966. The 14th session, held in New York from 30 June to 15 July 1966, reviewed principles underlying the establishment of salaries for International Civil Service, and the questions of education grants, career prospects, and standards of air travel accomodation for International Civil Service. A Secretary-General's report (GAOR, Sess.XXI, Annexes, vol.3, agenda item 81 (b), A/6491), 1 November 1966, published in an annex the text of section III of the Board report concerning education grants.

Members of the Board were as follows: Sir Harold Parker (UK), Acting Chairman; Sir Adetokunbo Ademola (Nigeria), John J. Carson (Canada), Senora Amalia de Castillo Ledon (Mexico), Dr. César Charlone (Uruguay), Guillaume Georges-Picot (France), Dr. Manfred Lache (Poland), John W. Macy Jr. (USA), Sir Ramaswami Mudaliar (India), H.F. Katsuzo Okumura (Japan), Vasilly F. Zaitsev (USSR).

ICSAB/XV/1, 15 July 1967. The 15th session was held at WHO headquarters in Geneva, from 28 June to 12 July 1967, and reviewed the United Nations salary system.

ISCAB/XVI/1, 15 July 1968. A report of the Secretary-General (GAOR, Sess.XXIII, Annexes, vol.2, agenda item 81 (b), A/C.5/1170), 16 October 1968, on education grants, contained excerpts from the ICSAB report on the same subject. Another Secretary-General report on salary scales for the professional and higher categories (Ibid., agenda item 74, A/7236), of 24 September 1966, in annex 1, carried excerpts from the text on the same subject, paragraphs 6-29, of the ICSAB report. Assembly resolution 2485 (XXIII), of 21 December 1968, took action on the report by amending UN Staff Regulations.

The 16th session was held at UNESCO headquarters, Paris, from 26 June to 10 July 1968, and its members were: Dr. Jamshid Amouzegar (Iran), Chairman; Sir Adetokunbo Ademola (Nigeria), Guillaume Georges-Picot (France), Toru Haguiwara (Japan), Alberto Lleras (Colombia), John W. Macy Jr. (USA), Sir Harold Parker (UK), Raúl A. Quijano (Argentina), Dr. Gertruda Sekaninova-Cakrtowá (Czech), Nikolai K. Tarassov (USSR), Sir Frederick H. Wheeler (Australia).

ICSAB / XVII/1, 9 June 1969. The 17th session was held in New York in May-June 1969. A Secretary-General note (GAOR, Sess.XXIV, Annexes, vol.2, agenda item 83 (b), A/C.5/1240), 20 October 1969, in an annex transmitted excerpts from section II of the ICSAB report on principles underlying the international salary system. Assembly resolution 2541 (XXIV) noted the report and requested the Secretary-General to keep the General Assembly informed of ICSAB's progress in examining matters cited in the report.

ICSAB/XVIII/1, July 1970. The 18th session, held at ILO headquarters in Geneva from 1-17 July 1970, reported, inter alia, on salary scales for professional and higher categories, and also made recommendations on the subject of compensation for termination of appointment. A Secretary-General report on the subject of salary scales for the professional and higher categories (GAOR, Sess.XXV, Annexes, agenda item 73, A/1303), of 25 September 1970, transmitted in an annex excerpts from section II of the ICSAB report. Assembly resolution 2743 (XXV), of 17 December 1970, took action on the report by amending UN Staff Regulations.

The membership of the Board was as follows: Dr. Jamshid Amouzegar (Iran), Chairman; Sir Adetokumbo Ademola (Nigeria), Guillaume Georges-Picot

(France), Toru Haguiwara (Japan), Robert E. Hampton (USA), Gustavo Martinez-Cabañas (Mexico), Sir Harold Parker (UK), Raúl Quijano (Argentina), Dr. Gertruda Sekaninova-Cakrtova (Czech), Nikolai K. Tarassov (USSR), Sir Frederick H. Wheeler (Australia).

ICSAB/XIX/1, July 1971. The 19th session was held at IAEA headquarters in Vienna, from 21 June to 1 July 1971. Annex II of the report contained a letter from the Chairman of the Board to the Secretary-General on the question of the establishment of an International Civil Service Commission. Its membership was the same except that Sir Wilfred Horton (UK) replaced Sir Harold Parker (UK).

ICSAB/XX/1, July 1972. The 20th session was held in Geneva from 4-15 September 1972, and was devoted to consideration of the report of the Special Committee for the Review of the UN Salary System (GAOR, Sess.XXVII, Suppl. 28A (A/8728/Add.1)), October 1972, "Comments of the International Civil Service Advisory Board" . Section III of the report contained a proposal for a civil service commission for international organizations. The Board continued with the same membership, except for the following changes: Pascal Frochaux (Switzerland) and Vladimir Velebit (Yugoslavia) were new members, and Dr. Sekaninová-Cakrtowá (Czech) and Sir Frederick H. Wheeler (Argentina) were no longer members.

ICSAB/XXI/1, June 1973. The 21st session was held at Geneva from 21 May to 1 June 1973. Pursuant to General Assembly resolution 3042 (XXVII), of 19 December 1972, the Board devoted the entire session to an examination of the draft statute for the International Civil Service Commission (ICSC) as approved by the ACC. Annex I of a report of the Secretary-General on the draft statute (A/9147, and Corr.1, offset) contained the text of the draft statute of the ICSC, and annex II the report of the first session of ICSAB. The membership remained the same except for the replacement of Mr. Tarassov (USSR) by A.G. Koulazhenkov (USSR).

A/9630 (GAOR, Sess.XXIX, Suppl.30), September 1974, report of the International Civil Service Advisory Board on its 22nd session, which was convened in compliance with a request of the General Assembly of the United Nations that the Board "submit, as a matter of priority, to the Assembly at its twenty-ninth session a report with recommendations concerning the salaries of staff in the professional and higher categories and staff allowances of the United Nations common system, to be effective from 1 January 1975" (A/PV.2206, 18 December 1973).

The 22nd and final session of the Board met at WHO headquarters in Geneva from 1-12 July 1974, with the same membership as that of the 21st session. The contents of the report contained an interpretation of its mandate, base salaries and post adjustment, dependency allowances in the professional and higher categories, assignment allowance, education grant, status of proposals for the International Civil Service Commission. A note by the Secretary-General of 17 October 1974 (A/9709, offset) commented on the report of ICSAB; and Assembly resolution 3358 (XXIX), of 18 December 1974, decided on some amendments to the Staff Regulations of the United Nations with effect from 1 January 1975.

General Assembly resolution 3042 (XXVII), of 19 December 1972, had established in principle, as of 1 January 1974, an International Civil Service Commission, and decided to continue to keep the International Civil Service Advisory Board in being until such time as the International Civil Service Commission was constituted and became operational. Resolution 3357 (XXIX), of 18 December 1974, approved the statute of the International Civil Service Commission, as set out in the annex of the resolution, and requested the Commission to review, as a matter of priority, the United Nations salary system in accordance with the decision in paragraph 5 of resolution 3042 (XXVII), and to submit a report to the 30th session.

Expert Committee on Post Adjustments (ECPA)

During a discussion in the Fifth Committee at the eighth session of the General Assembly (A/C. 5/SR.674, 675), on 4 November 1958, several delegations emphasized the need for an independent review of the application of the post adjustment system, notably in respect of the classification of the main centers of the United Nations activity.

The Secretary-General informed the Fifth Committee that, acting on the recommendation of the International Civil Service Advisory Board (ICSAB), and in agreement with the executive heads of the specialized agencies, he had appointed an independent expert committee composed of persons from outside the United Nations. He indicated that the first major task of this committee would be the conduct of an inquiry into the basic problem of the New York-Geneva relationship.

Terms of Reference

The Expert Committee was to make recommendations "on the general administration of the system of post adjustments, including questions of statistical methodology and the elements of judgment to be applied", and on classification of duty stations within that system.

The Expert Committee reported to the *Administrative Committee on Coordination (ACC) (see appendix), and met once a year.

Membership

The members of the Expert Committee were appointed by the Secretary-General of the United Nations with the advice and consent of ACC.

The membership remained more or less the same during the five sessions held, as follows:

Ewan Clague (USA), F.L. Closon (France), Pascal Frochaux (Switzerland), Dr. Ph.J. Idenburg (Netherlands), Herbert Marshall (Canada), and T.J. Natarajan (India).

At the fourth session, the membership was the same except that Mr. Natarajan (India) did not serve; and at the fifth session, both Mr. Natarajan and Mr. Marshall (Canada) did not serve.

Action

The Expert Committee's first session, held in Geneva from 31 March to 7 April 1959, considered the request of ACC that a comprehensive study be made on the relationship of the cost of living for international officials in New York as compared with Geneva in January 1956. The study was completed and reported at the Expert Committee's second session in New York, from 9-12 May 1960. Mr. Clague (USA) served as Chairman. The report of the first two sessions (ECPA/S.2/8) was transmitted to ACC in annex I to the Secretary-General's report of 12 May 1960 (GAOR, Sess.XV, Annexes, vol.2, agenda item 50, A/C.5/816).

The Expert Committee's third session, held in Geneva, 4-7 April 1961, reported (ECPA/S.3/6) on base salary scales and post adjustments of staff in the professional and higher categories of international civil service. It was transmitted by ACC's report to the Secretary-General, on 31 July 1961 (GAOR, Sess. XVI, Annexes, vol. 3, agenda item 65, A/4823/Add.2).

The fourth session of the Expert Committee was held at the headquarters of the Economic Commission for the Far East (ECAFE) at Bangkok, Thailand, from 11-17 April 1962. The report (ECPA/S.4/11), of 17 April 1962, was transmitted in annex IV of the Secretary-General's report on Personnel Questions (GAOR, Sess. XVII, Annexes, vol.3, agenda item 70, A/C.5/932), of 15 October 1962. A report of the Secretary-General on supplementary estimates (Ibid., Annexes, vol.2, agenda item 62, A/C.5/946), of 14 November 1962, discussed the report.

The fifth session of the Expert Committee was held at the headquarters of the Economic Commission for Latin America (ECLA), at Santiago, Chile, from 17-23 April 1963. Mr. Frochaux (Switzerland) served as Chairman at the third, fourth and fifth sessions. The report (ECPA/S.5/12), of 23 August 1963, was transmitted in annex III of the Secretary-General's report, of 18 September 1963, on Personnel Questions (GAOR, Sess. XVIII, Annexes, vol.3, agenda item 66, A/C.5/979).

Appendix

Administrative Committee on Coordination (ACC)

Established by Economic and Social Council resolution 13 (III), of 21 February 1946, as the "Coordination Committee". It was referred to in Council resolution 128 E (VI), of 10 March 1948, as the "Secretary-General's Committee on Co-ordination"; and in Council resolution 166 (VII), of 29 August 1948, as the "Administrative Committee on Co-ordination".

Terms of Reference

The resolution requested the Secretary-General to establish a coordination committee, which would report to the Economic and Social Council, would take appropriate steps to ensure the fullest and most effective implementation of the agreements entered into between the United Nations and the specialized agencies, and the coordination of activities among the organizations. ECOSOC resolution 992 (XXXVI), of 2 August 1963, requested the Committee to "study possibilities for further enhancing its contribution to the work of the Council, by strengthening its secretariat, including the possibility of secondment of staff by the various organizations of the United Nations working together in the Administrative Committee on Coordination."

While its mandate was never formally revised, the ACC's role has gradually been extended by the General Assembly and the Economic and Social Council. In the early years, the stress was on clarifying responsibilities in areas of interest in several organizations, such as the apparent overlapping or duplication of activi-

ties of the United Nations and specialized
agencies in the economic, social, cultural,
educational, health and related fields. One
of its early functions was in regard to setting
priorities . Over the years, the ACC has been
increasingly drawn into the co-ordination of
activities in key program sectors.

Considering it desirable for the Council and
ACC to maintain a stronger working partnership,
at a meeting held in 1965, the Council arranged
that the ACC would henceforth meet jointly with
the Special Committee for Programme and Co-ordination (an ECOSOC body), and the terms of reference were laid down for these Joint Meetings
by ECOSOC resolution 1090 G (XXXIX), 31 July
1965.

The range and scope of the activities which
the ACC has been called upon by the Council to
perform grew constantly during the 1960's. The
expansion of international activities under the
Development Decade, the emphasis laid by the
Council and the Assembly upon decentralization
and evaluation of development assistance activities, and such major institutional developments as the establishment of UNDP, UNIDO,
UNCTAD, gradually altered the character of co-
ordination and therefore the tasks performed
and the kind of contribution expected of the
ACC.

Membership

The establishing resolution requested the Secretary-General to establish a standing committee of administtative officers consisting of
himself, as Chairman, and the corresponding officers of the specialized agencies brought into relationship with the United Nations, for
the purpose of taking all appropriate steps,

under the leadership of the Secretary-General, to insure the fullest and most effective implementation of the agreements entered into between the United Nations and the specialized agencies.

Since that time, its membership has been increased to include not only the executive heads of specialized agencies, but also of all the organizations and programs in the United Nations system.

Sessions

The ACC meets one or more times a year, at Geneva, at United Nations Headquarters in New York, and some sessions are held at the headquarters of a specialized agency. The sessions are attended by the executive heads of all the organizations and programs of the United Nations system, or their deputies.

Reports

The ACC reports annually to the Economic and Social Council, and also issues from time to time special reports at the request of ECOSOC or of the General Assembly concerning a special problem or field of endeavor. The reports are issued under the E/- document series symbol. No other documents are distributed by the ACC.

Subsidiary Bodies

A great part of the work of the ACC, whose members can meet for only brief periods two or three times a year, is carried out through its subsidiary bodies. Its principal subsidiary body is the Preparatory Committee, established in 1947.

Preparatory Committee is attended by deputy
representatives from the same organizations
and programs that are represented at ACC sessions, and chaired by a Deputy Director-General
or Assistant Director-General. Its functions
have grown more important as the ACC found it
necessary to delegate a growing proportion of
the tasks arising from the increasingly complex
agenda. In 1966, the ACC confirmed the authorization given to the Preparatory Committee to
dispose of all inter-agency business that did
not require specific consideration and decision
by the executive heads themselves.

There are also consultative committees of a
permanent character for administrative and public information questions.

Consultative Committee on Administrative
Questions (CCAQ) - created in 1948, is empower-
ed to deal with personnel, budgetary and financial questions as well as other administrative
questions. It meets annually for ten weeks,
usually in March, and its main task is to ensure as much uniformity as possible in administrative arrangements, and to deal with problems
arising in connection with the common system of
salaries and allowances.

Consultative Committee on Public Information,
established in 1946, meets annually usually
for one week early in the year, to deal with
public information questions and arrangements
of concern to a number of organizations.

Computer Users' Committee, established in 1948,
shares many of the features of the Consultative
Committees. Its main function is to develop
inter-organization cooperation and the pooling
of resources wherever possible in the field of

computers. It also has specific functions regarding coordination of the computer facilities
or organizations based in Geneva.

Finally, there are a number of sub-committees
and working groups for individual program sectors which meet only as necessary and to deal
with specific problems. Their activities cover
program areas in development, population, statistical activities, human resources, education
and training, science and technology, water resources development, and marine science and its
application. There are also informal working
groups in such fields as housing and urbaniza-
tion, rural and community development, outer
space, youth, and the evaluation of technical
assistance programs.

A "Note on the mandate, subsidiary machinery
and staff support of the Administrative Committee on Co-ordination prepared by the Secretariat" (A/AC.51/35/Rev.1-CO-ORDINATION/JM/10/Rev.
1, mimeographed), 17 October 1969, was prepared
at the request of the Committee for Programme
and Co-ordination for its Joint Meetings with
the ACC to be held in Geneva on 10-11 July 1969.

C. Staff Pensions

United Nations Staff Benefit Committee

Established by Assembly resolution 82 (I), of
15 December 1946, having adopted the United
Nations Joint Staff Pension Scheme Provisional
Regulations as set forth in annex I of the re-
solution. It was terminated by resolution 248
(III), of 7 December 1948.

Terms of Reference

The Staff Benefit Committee was charged with
the administration of the Scheme, which was
inaugurated on 27 January 1947.

In accordance with Section E (Transitional Provisions) of the Provisional Regulations of the
Joint Staff Pension Scheme, the Staff Benefit
Committee adopted provisional administrative
rules to apply for such time as Section E was
in force (GAOR, Sess.II, Fifth Committee, Annexes, annex 12, A/397, annex I).

Section E also provided that until such time as
a member organization was admitted to the Joint
Staff Pension Scheme under section 28, the
Staff Benefit Committee was to exercise the
powers and perform the functions of the Joint
Benefit Committee*, and for the time being, the
Secretary of the UN Staff Benefit Committee, appointed on the recommendations of the Committee
by the Secretary-General, was to exercise the
powers and perform the functions of the Secretary of the Joint Benefit Committee.

Resolution 162 (II), of 20 November 1947, decided that the Provisional Joint Staff Pension
Scheme should continue unchanged, and on a provisional basis, for a further period of one

year; and that a permanent pension scheme should be promulgated, if possible, in 1948.

Membership

Section 20 of annex I of resolution 82 (I) provided that the Staff Benefit Committee should consist of three members elected for three years by the General Assembly, three members appointed by the Secretary-General, and three members who must be participants, elected for three years by the participants by secret ballot. The Assembly and the participants were respectively to elect for three years three alternate members. The members of the Staff Benefit Committee and their alternates might be re-elected.

Part B of the resolution listed the members and alternates elected by the General Assembly at the 66th plenary meeting, on 15 December 1946, to serve to 31 December 1949, as follows:

    Members: Roland Lebeau (Belgium); P.M. Chernyshov (USSR); A.J. Altmeyer (USA).

    Alternates: S.K. Kirpalani (India); G. Peissel (France); Diego Mejía (Colombia).

Assembly 156 (II), of 15 November 1947, elected E. de Holte-Castello (Colombia), Edward A. Ghorra (Lebanon), J. Katz-Suchy (Poland), as alternate members to serve for two years, beginning 1 January 1948, replacing the alternate members who had resigned during the second session of the General Assembly.

The full composition of the Staff Benefit Committee was listed in the Introduction of its first and second annual reports.

Action

The Committee held 29 meetings from 4 February
to 15 September 1947, and its first annual re-
port, acting as the Joint Benefit Committee
(Ibid., A/397), was issued on 25 September 1947.
The Committee appointed its Chairman, and the
Secretary-General appointed a Secretary and a
Deputy Secretary on the recommendations of the
Committee. They were: Chairman: Roland Lebeau
(Belgium); Secretary: D. Bannerman Clark;
Deputy Secretary: Miss Mary Eadie. The con-
tents of the report included membership in the
Scheme as of 31 August 1947; administrative
rules; and annex I contained the provisional
administrative rules proposed by the Staff Bene-
fit Committee.

On 2 October 1947, the Staff Benefit Committee,
acting as the Joint Benefit Committee, issued
a review of the provisional regulations (Ibid.,
annex 13, A/398). The Committee, after consultation with the Secretary-General, convened a
commission of internationally representative
actuaries: Dr. Hans Wyss (Switzerland), formerly
the Consulting Actuary of the League of Nations;
Pinto de Moura (Brazil); Dr. Rainard B. Robbins
(USA); and George B. Buck (USA), well-known
actuary practicing in the United States. The
actuaries submitted an agreed set of basic
tables and a general report. The Commission
decided that Mr. Buck should complete the detailed calculations required and submit them to
the Committee.

The Staff Benefit Committee submitted a report
on regulations for a permanent pension scheme
(GAOR, Sess.III, Part 1, Plenary Meetings, Annexes, agenda item 35 (a), A/584), on 22 July
1948.

A second annual report submitted by the Staff
Benefit Committee, acting as the Joint Benefit
Committee (GAOR, Sess.III, Part 1, Plenary
Meetings, Annexes, agenda item 35 (b), A/622
and Add.1), issued on 25 August and 6 October
1948, reported on the operation of the Pension
Scheme, together with such financial statements
as would enable the General Assembly to observe
the position of the Pension Fund as of 31 December 1947 and 30 June 1948 (annexes A and B).
Annex C contained a list of members who had
served on the Staff Benefit Committee during
the period under review.

Resolution 248 (III), of 7 December 1948, established, inter alia, a permanent pension
fund, and a United Nations Staff Pension Committee, which took over the functions of the
Staff Benefit Committee.

*Note: The Joint Benefit Committee was es-
tablished by Section 22 in Annex I of the
"Provisional Scheme for Staff Retirement and
Insurance Funds and Related Benefits" adopted
by General Assembly resolution 82 (I), of 15
December 1946. Its duties were outlined in the
following sections of annex I of the resolution:
31 concerning actuarial valuations of the Pension Fund; 35 concerning the presentation annually to the General Assembly and to member
organizations a report, including a balance
sheet, on the operation of the regulations; 36
instructing it to make administrative rules
necessary for carrying out the regulations. Its
membership, as provided for in Section 22, consisted of three members appointed by the Staff
Benefit Committee, and three members appointed
by each of the Staff Benefit Committees of the

member organizations, provided for in Section 21 of Annex I of the resolution. The Joint Benefit Committee was never constituted, its functions having been exercised by the Staff Benefit Committee, and in 1948 was replaced by the United Nations Joint Staff Pension Board.

United Nations Joint Staff Pension Board

The General Assembly in 1946 (resolution 82 (I)), when planning a pension scheme for the United Nations Secretariat, made provision for the specialized agencies to become member organizations in that Scheme and to share in its administration. By October 1950 three specialized agencies became member organizations in the Fund, thus establishing a Joint Fund, and the first session of the joint administrative body, the Joint Staff Pension Board, was held.

Assembly resolution 248 (III), of 7 December 1948, approved the Regulations for the United Nations Joint Staff Pension Fund, Article 14 of which established the Pension Fund and Article 22 the Joint Staff Pension Board.

The Regulations adopted in 1946 were amended from time to time and approved by the General Assembly in the following resolutions: resolution 248 (III) effective 23 January 1949 and amended by resolution 680 (VII) effective 1 January 1953, resolution 772 (VIII) effective 1 January 1954 and 1 January 1955, resolution 874 (IX) effective 4 December 1954, resolution 955 (X) effective 3 November 1955, resolution 1073 (XI) effective 7 December 1956, resolution 1201 (XII) effective 1 January 1958, resolution 1309 (XIII) dated 10 December 1958, resolution 1561 (XV) and 1614 (XV) effective 1 April 1961, resolution 1799 (XVII) effective 1 January 1963, resolution 2122 (XX) effective 1 March 1965, resolution 2191 (XXI) effective 1 January 1967, and resolution 2524 (XXIV) effective 1 January 1970, resolution 2887 (XXVI) effective 1 January 1972, resolution 2944 (XXVII) effective 1 January 1973, and resolution 3100 (XXVIII) effective 1 January 1974.

The Regulations provide, <u>inter alia</u>, for contributions to the Fund by the participants and the
member organizations, the payment of benefits
of various kinds, and the administration of the
Fund by a Board on which the General Assembly
and the legislative organs of the organization,
the executive heads, and the participants are
equally represented. The Board currently meets
in regular session every two years, and reports
annually to the General Assembly and the member
organizations either directly or through its
Standing Committee.

The Fund started with four member organizations:
the United Nations, WHO, FAO, and ILO. It is
presently made up of eleven organizations as
follows:
      United Nations
      International Labour Organization
      Food and Agriculture Organization of the
United Nations
      United Nations Educational, Scientific
and Cultural Organization
      World Health Organization
      International Civil Aviation Organiza-
tion
      World Meteorological Organization
      Interim Commission for the International
Trade Organization
      International Atomic Energy Agency
      Inter-Governmental Maritime Consultative
Organization
      International Telecommunication Union

<u>Terms of Reference</u>

The Joint Staff Pension Board administers the
Fund separately from the assets of the United
Nations in accordance with the Regulations, and
the Fund is used solely for the purposes provided for in these Regulations.

Article 22 provides that the Joint Staff Pension Board may appoint a Standing Committee, which will act on its behalf when the Board is not in session.

Article 31 requires the Board to have actuarial valuations of the Fund at stated intervals.

Article 35 provides that the Board shall present annually to the General Assembly of the United Nations and to the member organizations a report, including a balance sheet, on the operation of these Regulations. The Secretary-General shall inform each member organization of any action taken by the Assembly upon the report.

Assembly resolution 3100,III.2 (XXVIII), of 11 December 1973, requested the UN Joint Staff Pension Board to carry out an in-depth study on various selective systems designed to compensate for currency changes and inflationary movements in the countries of residence of pensioners and to explain the administrative and financial implications thereof, and to report thereon to the 29th session of the General Assembly.

The Board met annually from 1950 to 1960, after which it met every two years at a time and place decided by the Board or its Standing Committee. It reports annually to the General Assembly, and when it is not in session, the report is submitted by the Standing Committee.

At the opening of each regular session, the Board elects a chairman, two vice-chairmen and a rapporteur.

Summary records of all meetings of the Board and its Standing Committee are prepared under the responsibility of the Secretary and distributed to all members of the Board and Standing Committee as well as the Chairmen and Secretaries of the Staff Pension Committee. Only the annual report of the Board is published in the Official Records of the General Assembly.

Membership

Article 22 of annex I of the establishing resolution provided that the Joint Staff Pension Board should consist of nine members appointed by the United Nations Staff Pension Committee, and three members appointed by each of the staff pension committees of the member organizations. Members of the Board were appointed by each staff pension committee in equal numbers from each of the three groups referred to in article XX (which stated that each member organization should have a staff pension committee, which should include members chosen by the body of the member organization corresponding to the General Assembly of the United Nations, by the chief executive officer, and by the participants).

Effective 1 April 1961, the Board consisted of 18 members:
    (a) Six members appointed by the United Nations Staff Pension Committee; two from the members elected by the General Assembly, two from the members appointed by the Secretary-General, and two from the members elected by the participants, and
    (b) twelve members appointed by the staff pension committees of the other member organizations in accordance with a table fixed by the Administrative Rules of the Fund which provided for equal representation of the three groups referred to in article XX (JSPB/G.H/Rev.3, resolutions 1561 (XV) and 1614 (XV).

Effective 1 January 1963, the Board consisted
of 21 members:

(a) Six members appointed by the United
Nations Staff Pension Committee, two from the
members elected by the General Assembly, two
from the members appointed by the Secretary-
General, and two from the members elected by
the participants, and

(b) Fifteen members appointed by the
staff pension committees of the other member
organizations in accordance with a table fixed
by the Administrative Rules of the Fund which
provide for equal representation of the three
groups referred to in article XX.

Effective 1 January 1971, the United Nations
Joint Staff Pension Board consists of:

(a) Six members appointed by the UN
Staff   Pension Committee, two of whom shall be
from the members and alternate members elected
by the General Assembly, two from those appointed by the Secretary-General and two from
those elected by the participants in service
in the United Nations; and

(b) Fifteen members appointed by the
staff pension committees of the other member
organizations in accordance with a table fixed
by the Administrative Rules, five of whom shall
be from members and alternate members chosen by
the bodies of the member organizations corresponding to the General Assembly, five from those
appointed by the chief administrative officers
of the member organizations, and five from those
chosen by the participants in service.

Alternate members may be appointed by each
staff pension committee.

The Regulations provide that the staff pension
committee of the member organizations, other

than the United Nations, should consist of members and alternate members chosen by the body of the organization corresponding to the General Assembly of the United Nations, its chief administrative officer, and its participants in service, in such a manner that the number representing each is equal and in the case of the participants that the members and alternate members are themselves participants in the service of the organization. Each member organization makes its own rules for the election or appointment of the members and alternate members of the committee.

Standing Committee of the Joint Staff Pension Board

At each regular session the Board appoints a Standing Committee, elected from among the members and alternates of the Board, to exercise on its behalf the powers vested in the Board, with certain exceptions, and to report to each session of the Board.

From 1951-1956, membership comprised all members or their alternates of the Board. Five members constituted a quorum, provided that there were present three members representing the United Nations, and at least one member representing a member organization other than the United Nations, and that among those present there was a representative from each of the following three groups: (a) representatives of the General Assembly and the corresponding body of a member organization; (b) representatives of the competent authorities of member organizations; (c) representatives of the participants (JSPB/G.5/and Rev.2).

In April 1957 (JSPB/G.5/Rev.3), the Standing Committee was composed of 12 members and alternates, elected from among the members and alternates of the Board, according to the representational distribution set forth in Section E.9 of the Administrative Rules of the Board (GAOR, Sess.XII, Suppl. 8 A/3611, annex III)).

From January 1963 to date (JSPB/G.5/Rev.5), Section E, paragraphs 10-17, the Standing Committee was composed of nine members and nine alternates elected from the members and alternates of the Board or of Staff Pension Committees, according to the representational distribution chart.

Action

Reports of the Board contain in general a list of member organizations of the Fund, information on operation of the Fund during the period under review, on the session or sessions of the Board and a list of attending members; or, if the Board did not meet that year, the Standing Committee reports on action it has taken on behalf of the Board during the period under review and lists its own membership. Annexes contain financial statements for the year reviewed, a report of the Board of Auditors on the accounts of the Fund, statistics on the operation of the Fund, a list of its investments, resolutions adopted by the Board at its sessions, recommendations to the General Assembly for amendment of the Regulations of the Joint Staff Pension Fund, and amendments to the Administrative Rules of the Fund by the Board.

A list of the dates, sites, and officers of the sessions held follows the list of reports of the Board.

The following is a list of annual reports issued by the Board or by the Standing Committee and the sessions of the Board covered in the reports:

A/1846 (GAOR, Sess.VI. Suppl.8), August 1951. Report for the year ended 31 December 1950 and Supplementary Report as of 31 May 1951. Covered the first and second sessions of the Board, and referred to the First Actuarial Valuation of the Fund (paragraph 3 (a)).

A/2189 (GAOR, Sess.VII, Suppl.8), October 1952. Report for the year ended 31 December 1951; also reported on the second session of the Board.

A/2190 (Ibid., Suppl.8A), October 1952. Report on the Second Actuarial Valuation on the Fund as of 31 December 1961.

A/2203 (Ibid., Annexes, agenda item 45), 25 September 1952. Report of the Board on amendments to the regulations of the UN Joint Pension Fund.

A/2421 (GAOR, Sess. VIII, Suppl.8), August 1953, for the year ended 31 December 1952; covered third session.

A/2422, 28 July 1953 (Ibid., Annexes, agenda item 47). Report of the Board on amendments to the regulations of the UN Joint Staff Pension Fund.

A/2659 (GAOR, Sess. IX, Suppl.8), July 1954, for the year ended 31 December 1953; covered the fourth and fifth sessions.

A/2914 (GAOR, Sess.X, Suppl.8), August 1955, for year ended 30 September 1954; covered the sixth session. The period under review changed to the twelve months from 1 October to 30 September.

A/2916 (Ibid.,Suppl.8A, August 1955. Report of the Board on the Third Actuarial Valuation of the Fund as of 30 September 1954.

A/3146 (GAOR, Sess. XI, Suppl.8), August 1956, for the year ended 30 September 1955; covered the seventh session.

A/3611 and Corr.1 (GAOR, Sess. XII, Suppl. 8), September 1957, for year ended 30 September 1956; covered eighth session.

A/3642 (Ibid., Suppl. 8A), September 1957. Report of the Board on the Fourth Actuarial Valuation of the Fund as of 30 September 1956 and Second Review of the Basic Tables of the Fund.

A/3938 (GAOR, Sess. XIII, Suppl. 8), October 1958, for year ended 30 September 1957; covered the ninth session.

A/4158 (GAOR, Sess. XIV, Suppl. 8), August 1959, annual report for the year ended 30 September 1958, submitted by the Standing Committee on behalf of the Board, which did not meet in 1959. Contained a summary of the actions of the Standing Committee, and a list of its members.

A/4266 (Ibid., Suppl.8A), December 1959. Report on the Fifth Actuarial Valuation of the Fund.

A/4467, 3 September 1960 (GAOR, Sess.XV, Annexes, vol.2, agenda item 63). Report of the Board at its 10th session on the report of the Expert Group, established under General Assembly 1310 (XIII), to make a comprehensive review of the Pension Fund. (For the work of the Pension Review Group, see Section C of this chapter).

A/4469 and Corr.1 (Ibid., Suppl. 8), September 1960, for the year ended 30 September 1959; covered the tenth session.

A/4807 (GAOR, Sess. XVI, Suppl. 8), August 1961. Report for the year ended 30 September 1960, presented by the Standing Committee, on behalf of the UN Joint Staff Pension Board. Contains a summary report on action taken by

the Standing Committee since the Board's tenth
session (July 1960); lists membership of the
Standing Committee.

A/5208 (GAOR, Sess. XVII, Suppl.8), August 1962, for the year ended 30 September 1961;
covered the 11th session of the Board. Paragraph 40 noted the revised membership of the
Standing Committee at the tenth session to take
effect at the 11th; paragraph 42 listed the
membership.

A/5508 (GAOR, Sess. XVIII, Suppl.8), August 1963, for the year ended 30 September 1962,
submitted by the Standing Committee on behalf
of the Board. Covered action taken by the
Standing Committee since the Board's 11th session (April-May 1962), and listed the Standing
Committee's membership.

A/5808 (GAOR, Sess. XIX, Suppl. 8), November 1964, for the year ended 30 September
1963; covered the 12th session.

A/6008 (GAOR, Sess. XX, Suppl. 8), September 1965, for the year ended 30 September 1964,
submitted by the Standing Committee, on behalf
of the Board. Contained a summary of the action
taken by the Standing Committee since the
Board's last session (July 1964) and a list of
its members.

A/6308 (GAOR, Sess. XXI, Suppl. 8), November 1966, for the year ended 30 September
1965; covered the 13th session.

A/6708 (GAOR, Sess. XXII, Suppl. 8), October 1967, for the year ended 30 September 1966,
submitted by the Standing Committee, on behalf
of the Board. Contained a summary of the action
taken by the Standing Committee since the 13th
session of the Board, and included the membership of the Committee.

A/7208 (GAOR, Sess. XXIII, Suppl. 8),
December 1968, for the year ended 30 September
1967. Covered the 14th session of the Board,
which now meets regularly every two years and

reports annually to the General Assembly directly or through the Standing Committee.

A/7609 (GAOR, Sess. XXIV, Suppl. 9), November 1969, for the year ended 30 September 1968; covered the 15th session, and elected the members and alternate members of the Standing Committee to serve at the 16th session.

A/8009 and Add.1 (GAOR, Sess. XXV, Suppl. 9), November 1970, for the year ended 30 September 1969, submitted by the Standing Committee on behalf on the Board which did not meet in 1970. Annex IV contained the text of Administrative Rules of the Fund which went into effect 1 January 1970, replacing those which came into effect on 1 January 1967.

A/8409 (GAOR, Sess. XXVI, Suppl.9), November 1971, for the year ended 30 September 1970, covered the 16th session, and contained a list of members and alternate s elected by the Board (paragraph 43) to the Standing Committee.

A/8709 and Corr.1 (GAOR, Sess. XXVII, Suppl. 9), September 1972, for year ended 30 September 1971; covered the 17th session. The Board elected the members and alternate members of the Standing Committee, as listed in paragraph 40.

A/9009 and Corr.1-2, Vols. 1 and 2 (GAOR, Sess. XXVIII, Suppl. 9), covered the 18th session held in July 1973. Volume II contained a study by the Committee of Actuaries on "Rates of Contribution under the United Nations Joint Staff Pension Scheme."

Officers and sessions of the Joint Staff Pension Board:

First session, UN Headquarters, New York. 18-25 October 1950.
   Chairman: R.T. Cristobal (General Assembly GA))

Second session, Geneva, April 1951
    Chairman: G.A. Johnston (ILO)

Third session, New York, July 1952
    Chairman: Marc Schreiber (UN participants)
    First Vice-Chairman: C.S. Booth (ICAO
Assembly)
    Second Vice-Chairman: R. Harper-Smith
(UNESCO Director-General (DG))
    Rapporteur: K.G. Brennan (GA)

Fourth session, FAO Headquarters, Rome, April
1953
    Chairman: C.S. Booth (ICAO Assembly)
    1st Vice-Chairman: H.C. Anderson (Secretary-
General (SG))
    2nd Vice-Chairman: P.L. Sherman (FAO parti-
cipants)
    Rapporteur: F.L. Gutteridge (WHO partici-
pants)

Fifth session, New York, April 1954
    Chairman: H.C. Anderson (SG)
    1st Vice-Chairman: Dr. A. Zelenka (ILO par-
ticipants)
    2nd Vice-Chairman: H.J. McCann (FAO Confer-
ence)
    Rapporteur: V.J. Bahr (WMO SG)

Sixth session, UNESCO Headquarters, Paris,
April 1955
    Chairman: Dr. A. Zelenka (ILO participants)
    1st Vice-Chairman: T.W. Cutts (GA)
    2nd Vice-Chairman: R. Harper-Smith (UNESCO
DG)
    Rapporteur: Pierre Obez (UN participants)

Seventh session, New York, March 1956
    Chairman: R. Harper-Smith (UNESCO SG)
    1st Vice-Chairman: A.E. van Braam Houckgeest (GA)
    2nd Vice-Chairman: Carey Seward (UN participants)
    Rapporteur: D. Chakraverti (ICAO Assembly)

Eighth session, Geneva, April 1957
    Chairman: Arthur C. Liveran (GA)
    1st Vice-Chairman: Carey Seward (UN participants)
    2nd Vice-Chairman: J. L. Armstrong (WHO DG)
    Rapporteur: E.S. Abensour (FAO participants)

Ninth session, ICAO, Montreal, September 1958
    Chairman: Arthur C. Liveran (GA)
    1st Vice-Chairman: Carey Seward (UN participants)
    2nd Vice-Chairman: J. L. Armstrong (WHO DG)
    RapporteurL Dr. K.K.P.N. Rao (FAO participants)

Tenth session, ILO, July 1960
    Chairman/Rapporteur: Professor H.S. Kirkaldy (ILO Conference)
    1st Vice-Chairman: Philippe Roux (UNESCO participants)
    2nd Vice-Chairman: Bruce Turner (SG)

11th session, New York, 24 April-4 May 1962
    Chairman: Marc Schreiber (UN participants)
    1st Vice-Chairman: C.R. McCord (ILO Governing Body)
    2nd Vice-Chairman: J. Berrier (ICAO Executive Head)
    Rapporteur: F.X. Byrne (ICAO participants)

12th session, UNESCO, Paris, 13-24 July 1964
    Chairman: J. Berrier (ICAO Executive Head)
    1st Vice-Chairman: Philippe Roux (UNESCO participants)
    2nd Vice-Chairman: James Gibson (GA)
    Rapporteur: Dr. B.D.B. Layton (WHO Governing Body)

13th session, IAEA, Vienna, 18-29 July 1966
    Chairman: James Gibson (GA)
    1st Vice-Chairman: W. Yalden-Thomson (ILO Executive Head)
    2nd Vice-Chairman: H. Bittencourt (IAEA Governing Body)
    Rapporteur: F.X. Byrne (ICAO participants)

14th session, IMCO, London, 15-26 July 1968
    Chairman: J. L.   Armstrong (WHO Executive Head)
    1st Vice-Chairman: A. Landau (UN)
    Rapporteur: J.I.M. Rhodes (GA)

15th session, FAO, Rome, 1-13 August 1969
    Chairman: E.S. Abensour (FAO participants)
    1st Vice-Chairman: W. McCaw (SG)
    2nd Vice-Chairman: H.S. Kirkaldy (ILO Governing Body)
    Rapporteur: F.X. Byrne (ICAO participants)

16th session, WHO, Geneva, July 1971
    Chairman: E. Aujaleu (WHO Governing Body)
    1st Vice-Chairman: Mrs. P.E. Tsien (UN participants)
    2nd Vice-Chairman: R. Piat (FAO Executive Head)
    Rapporteur: N.F. MacCabe (ILO participants)

17th session, UNESCO, Paris, July 1972
    Chairman: R. Prohme (UNESCO Governing Body)
    1st Vice-Chairman/Rapporteur: N.F. MacCabe
(ILO participants)
    2nd Vice-Chairman: M. Landey (IMCO Executive
Head)

18th session, IAEA, Vienna, July 1973
    Chairman: G.J. McGough (GA)
    1st Vice-Chairman: F.X. Byrne (ICAO parti-
cipants)
    2nd Vice-Chairman: P.M.C. Denby (ILO Exec-
utive Head)
    Rapporteur: A.J. Friedgut (UN participants)

Following is a list of pertinent documents concerning the United Nations Joint Staff Pension
Fund and its administrative bodies:
    JSPB/G.4/Rev.7/Amend.1, January 1972, Regu-
lations of the United Nations Joint Staff Pension Fund.
    JSPB/G.5/Rev.6, January 1967. Administrative
Rules, adopted by the Joint Staff Pension Board.
    JSPB/G.7/Rev.3, July 1971. Your Pension Fund:
what it does, how it works, how you benefit.
    JSPB/G.9, April 1963. Report to Participants
for the year ended 30 September 1962. First of
a series of annual reports, the purpose of which
is to keep participants informed of developments
in their Pension Fund. It contains information
on member organizations, administration of the
Fund, operation of the Fund for the period indicated, sessions of the Board held during the
year, and the annexes and list of members of the
Board and the Standing Committee, and assets and
liabilities of the Fund as of the date indicated.
    JSPB/G.10, December 1964. Report to Partici-
pants for the year ended 30 September 1963.

JSPB/G.9/3, December 1966. Report to Participants for the year ended 30 September 1965.
JSPB/G.9/4, January 1970. Report to Participants for the year ended 30 September 1968.

United Nations STaff Pension Committee
(A/CN.6/-)

Established under Article 20 of the Regulations
of the United Nations Joint Staff Pension Fund,
approved by General Assembly resolution 248
(III), of 7 December 1948. The Regulations
were published in an annex to the resolution.

Terms of Reference

Provision D of the "Transitional Provisions, relating to the United Nations, of the Regulations,"
on administration of the Fund, provided that until such time as a member organization was admitted to the United Nations Joint Staff Pension
Fund under article 28, the United Nations Staff
Pension Committee should exercise the powers and
perform the functions of the Joint Staff Pension
Board, and the secretary of the United Nations
Staff Pension Committee, appointed on the recommendation of the Committee by the Secretary-General, should exercise the powers and perform the
functions of the secretary of the Joint Staff
Pension Board.

After 1950 when the Joint Staff Pension Board
was constituted and convened in its first session
in October 1950, the Staff Pension Committee no
longer performed the functions of the Board,
since the latter elected a Standing Committee to
act for it when it was not in session.

The Staff Pension Committee meets several times
a year, and deals chiefly with review and appeal as outlined in Section K of the Administrative Rules of the UN Joint Staff Pension Fund
(JSPB/G.4/Rev.1, annex I), effective 1 January
1971.

Membership

Article 20 of the Regulations in the establishing resolution (and Article 21 in the amendments
to the Regulations) designated the following
membership for the Staff Pension Committee:
three members elected for three years by the
General Assembly, three members appointed by the
Secretary-General, and three members, who must
be participants and on the staff of the United
Nations, elected for three years by such participants by secret ballot. The Assembly and the
participants each elect three alternate members
for three years, and the Secretary-General appoints three alternate members.

The terms of office of elected members of the
United Nations Staff Pension Committee begins on
1 January following the election, and terminates
on 31 December following the election of their
successors. The elected members are eligible
for re-election.

A secretary to the UN Staff Pension Committee is
appointed by the Secretary-General upon the recommendation of the Staff Pension Committee. The
secretary of the Joint Staff Pension Board may
be appointed to this office.

The members appointed by the General Assembly
are found in the resolutions of the Assembly.
Members elected by the participants and appointed
by the Secretary-General may be identified from
the members of the Joint Staff Pension Board
listed in each report of the board.

Following is a list of members and alternates of
the UN Staff Pension Committee (1949-1973)
elected by the General Assembly, on recommendation of the Fifth Committee:

Members	Alternates

Resolution 348 (IV), 24 November 1949 - to serve
from 1 January 1950 to 31 December 1952:

R.T. Cristóbal (Philippines)	Miss Carol C. Laise (USA)
E. de Holte-Castello (Colombia)	Dr. A. Nass (Venezuela) Pierre Ordonneau
N.I. Klimov (USSR)	(France)

Resolution 581 (VI), 20 December 1951, elected
Keith G. Brennan (Australia) and Warren B. Irons
(USA) to replace Dr. Nass and Miss Laise, re-
spectively, resigned.

The full list of members, including those appointed by the Secretary-General and those
elected by the participants, was published in
the report of the Staff Pension Committee (A/
1335,III).

Resolution 671 (VII), 20 December 1952 - to
serve to 31 December 1955:

Keith G. Brennan (Australia)	Arthur H. Clough (UK) Warren B. Irons (USA)
R.T. Cristobal (Philippines)	Fazlollah Nouredin Kia (Iran)
Francisco A. Forteza (Uruguay)	

Resolution 870 (IX), 29 October 1954, elected T.
W. Cutts (Australia) to replace Mr. Brennan, resigned in September 1954.

Resolution 968 (X), 15 December 1955 - to serve
to 31 December 1958:

Arthur H. Clough (UK)	A.E. van Braam Houck-
Rigoberto Torres Astorga (Chile)	geest (Netherlands) F. Nouredin Kia (Iran)
Albert S. Watson (USA)	Arthur C. Liveran (Israel)

Resolution 1080 (XI), 21 December 1956, appointed Johan Kaufmann (Netherlands) to replace Mr. van Braam Houckgeest, resigned; and resolution 1196 (XII), 13 December 1957, appointed A.H.M. Hillis (UK) to replace Mr. Clough, resigned.

Resolution 1293 (XIII), 5 December 1958 - to serve to 31 December 1961:

A.H.M. Hillis (UK)	Bahman Ahaneen (Iran)
Albert S. Watson (USA)	Johan Kaufmann (Netherlands)
R. Torres Astorga (Chile)	Arthur C. Liveran (Israel)

Resolution 1372 (XIV), 17 November 1959, appointed Albert F. Bender (USA) to replace Mr. Watson, resigned.

Resolution 1690 (XVI), 18 December 1961 - to serve to 31 December 1964:

Albert F. Bender (USA)	Arthur C. Liveran (Israel)
C.H.W. Hodges (UK)	Brendan T. Nolan (Ireland)
R. Torres Astorga (Chile)	Nathan Quao (Ghana)

Resolution 1796 (XVII), 11 December 1962, appointed James Gibson (UK) for a period from 1 May 1963 to 31 December 1964, replacing Mr. Hodges, resigned in April 1963. Resolution 1895 (XVIII), 6 November 1963, appointed Shilendra K. Singh (India) to replace Mr. Liveran (Israel), resigned in May 1963.

Resolution 2001 (XIX), 10 February 1965 - to serve to 31 December 1967:

Albert F. Bender(USA)	Shilendra K. Singh (India)
José Espinoza (Chile)	(two vacancies)
James Gibson (UK)	

Resolution 2117 (XX), 21 December 1965, appointed Brian J. Lynch (NZ) and Jean-Claude Renaud
(France) as alternates for a two-year term. Resolution 2141 (XXI), 26 October 1966, appointed
John I.M. Rhodes (UK) and Wilbur H. Ziehl (USA)
to replace Mr. Gibson and Mr. Bender, respectively, resigned in October 1966.

Resolution 2303 (XXII), 13 December 1967 - to
serve to 31 December 1970:

John I.M. Rhodes (UK)   André J. Cahen
Guillermo Valdés   (Belgium)
   (Chile)   John R. Kelso
Wilbur H. Ziehl (USA)   (Australia)
                        Harry L. Morris
                           (Liberia)

Albert F. Bender (USA) was appointed by resolution 2523 (XXIV), 5 December 1969, for a one-
year term, replacing Mr. Ziehl, resigned in
December 1969.

Resolution 2695 (XXV), 11 December 1970 - to
serve to 31 December 1973:

Albert F. Bender (USA) Harry L. Morris
Guillermo J. McGough   (Liberia)
   (Argentina)   Takeshi Naito (Japan)
John I.M. Rhodes (UK) Svenn Refshal (Norway)

Resolution 2756 (XXVI), 11 October 1971, appointed Miss Kathleen Whalley (UK) to replace Mr.
Rhodes, resigned in September 1971. Resolution
2943 (XXVII), 4 December 1972, appointed Richard
V. Hennes (USA) to replace Mr. Bender, resigned
in December 1972.

Resolution 3099 (XXVIII), 31 December 1973 - to
serve to 31 December 1976:

Sol Kuttner (USA)   Harry L. Morris (Liberia)
Guillermo J. McGough Svenn Refshal (Norway)
   (Argentina)   Miss Kathleen Whalley(UK)
Rudolf Schmidt (Germany, (Fed. Rep.)

Action

The Joint Staff Pension Committee held 52 meetings up to 31 August 1949, under the chairmanship of Roland Lebeau (Belgium). The third annual report of the Committee (the first two reports having been issued by the Staff Benefit Committee), acting as the Joint Staff Pension Board (GAOR, Sess.IV, Fifth Committee, Annex, vol.1, agenda item 46, A/987) was issued on 21 September 1949. It contained information on the operation of the Fund, and two annexes: A, statement showing cash receipts and cash disbursements from the inception of the Fund on 27 January 1947 to 31 July 1949, and B, statement on the investments of the Joint Staff Pension Fund as of 31 July 1949. It also contained a complete list of its members, including those elected by the General Assembly, those appointed by the Secretary-General, and those elected by the participants by secret ballot.

The (fourth) annual report of the Committee, acting as the Joint Staff Pension Board (GAOR, Sess. V, Annexes, agenda item 44, A/1335) was issued on 24 August 1950. Its officers were R.T. Cristóbal (Philippines), Chairman; Marc Schreiber (elected by participants), Vice-Chairman. It reported, inter alia, on the financial position of the Fund as of 31 December 1949. At a joint meeting of the new and old Committees, appreciation was expressed for the work performed by the members retiring at that time, special reference being made to the devoted services of Roland Lebeau (Belgium), who had been Chairman of the Committee since it began its work in January 1947.

The Committee decided that an actuarial valuation of the Fund should be carried out as of 31 December 1948 prior to the entry of the specialized agencies into the Fund, and appointed George

B. Buck of New York and Dr. Hans Wyss of Zurich to collaborate in that valuation and to prepare a report, which would be distributed by the Board as directed in Article 31 of the Regulations.

Documents

No documents are issued under the document series symbol (A/CN.6/-) assigned to the UN Staff Pension Committee.

Expert Group on Pensionable Remuneration

Assembly resolution 1095A (XI), of 27 February 1957, followed a recommendation by the Salary Review Committee (GAOR, Sess.XI, Annexes, agenda item 51, A/3209, paragraph 129), that the question of pensionable remuneration be examined by an expert body.

Terms of Reference

The resolution requested the Secretary-General, in conjunction with the executive heads of the specialized agencies concerned and in cooperation with the Joint Staff Pension Board, to review the question of the pensionable remuneration of the staff with a view to making recommendations for action by the General Assembly.

Membership

In accordance with a decision of the Administrative Committee on Coordination (ACC) (ESCOR, 24th Session, Annexes, agenda item 4, E/2993), of 11 May 1957, the Secretary-General appointed a small expert committee with terms of reference limited to a study of pensionable remuneration, consisting of:
>   Dr. Gonzalo Arroba (Ecuador), Chairman;
>   George A. Graham (USA); and Robert Letrou
>   (France).

Action

The Expert Group met in Geneva and in New York, and submitted a report to the Secretary-General on 10 June 1958. The Secretary-General's report (GAOR, Sess.XIII, Annexes, agenda item 53c, A/C. 5/760, 3 November 1958, and Add.1, 20 November 1946) traced developments on the question since the date of the establishing resolution, and also contained the report of the Expert Group and its comments thereon. The addendum (A/C. 5/760/Add.1) transmitted the statement of the United Nations Headquarters Staff Association.

Pension Review Group

Established by Assembly resolution 1310 (XIII),
of 10 December 1958.

Terms of Reference

The first three operative paragraphs of the resolution decided (1) that a comprehensive review
of the system of benefits and their pensionable
remuneration could be revised, and of the financial and technical bases of the United Nations
Joint Staff Pension Fund should be undertaken in
the light of the observations and suggestions
made on this subject in the Fifth Committee;
(2) requested the Secretary-General, in consultation with the UN Joint Staff Pension Board and
the Administrative Committee on Coordination
(ACC) (an ECOSOC body), to appoint such experts
as might be required to accomplish this comprehensive review; (3) requested the Secretary-
General, in conjunction with the executive heads
of the other member organizations and in cooperation with the Joint Staff Pension Board, to submit proposals for action by the General Assembly
at its fifteenth session.

Membership

The Secretary-General appointed the following as
members of the Expert Group:
    George F. Davidson (Canada), Deputy Minister
of Welfare
    Dr. Gonzalo Arroba (Ecuador), former Chairman
of the 1958 Expert Group on Pensionable Remuneration
    Dr. Josef Knap (Czechoslovakia), Director of
Research, Institute of the National Social Security Office in Prague

Arthur Liveran (Israel), former Chairman of the UN Joint Staff Pension Board

Dr. Reinhold Melas (Austria), Director-General of the Central Association of Participants in Austrian Social Insurance

Robert J. Myers (USA), Chief Actuary of the United States Social Security Administration

W. R. Natu (India), former Executive Director of the International Monetary Fund; Chairman, Forward Markets Commission, India

The Baroness Wootton of Abinger (UK), formerly Professor of Social Studies in the University of London.

Action

The Expert Group held three sessions, under the Chairmanship of Mr. Davidson (Canada), in New York from 25 November to 10 December 1959; in Geneva from 28 March to 12 April 1960. Its report (GAOR, Sess. XV, Annexes, agenda item 63, A/4427), a comprehensive review of the United Nations Joint Staff Pension Fund, was issued on 5 August 1960. Annexes included (1) report of the Actuary-Members; (2) origin and development of the Fund and the origin of the present review; (3) note on the salary-scale tables; (4) advice from the UN Investment Committee on certain matters within the scope of the comprehensive review; (5) to (8) contained relevant tables. The report also contained an index.

The UN Joint Staff Pension Board on 3 September 1960 in a report (GAOR, Sess.XV, Annexes, vol.2, agenda item 63, A/4467) made its observations on the report of the Pension Review Group.

Assembly resolution 1614 (XV), of 21 April 1961, recommended several amendments, as of 1 April 1961, in Articles IV (retirement benefits), VIII (child's benefits), and X (withdrawal settlements).

D. United Nations Administrative Tribunal

Advisory Committee on a Statute for a United Nations Tribunal

Established by Assembly resolution 13 (I), of 13 February 1946, concerning the organization of the Secretariat, Part III, paragraph 11.

Terms of Reference

Under Section 3, IV, paragraph 11, of the resolution, the Secretary-General was authorized to appoint a small advisory committee, possibly including representatives of the staff, to draft, for submission to the second part of the first session of the General Assembly, a statute for an administrative tribunal.

Membership

The Advisory Committee comprised the following members appointed by the Secretary-General: Thanassis Aghnides (Greece), Chairman; Manley O. Hudson (USA), Joseph Nisot (Belgium), Ladislav Radimsky (Czech); and the following from the Secretariat: Jean Herbert (Chairman of the Permanent Staff Committee), and Frank Bagley as alternate; Manuel Pérez-Guerrero, with James G. Stewart as alternate; Marc Schreiber, with Egon F. Ranzhofen-Wertheimer as alternate.

Mrs. Isobel Wallace and David M. Levitan, of the Secretariat, served as secretary and technical consultant to the Advisory Committee.

Action

The Advisory Committee met at Lake Success,
New York, from 16 to 26 September 1946. Its
report (<u>GAOR</u>, Sess. I (Part 2), <u>Fifth Committee</u>,
annex 24a, A/91), issued on 16 October 1946, included a draft of a Statute for the Tribunal.

United Nations Administrative Tribunal (AT/-)

Established by Assembly resolution 351 A (IV), of 24 November 1949; came into force on 1 January 1950; and was amended by resolution 782 B (VIII), of 7 December 1953.

Terms of Reference

An International Court of Justice advisory opinion of 1954 described the status of the Administrative Tribunal as not being an advisory organ or a mere subordinate committee of the General Assembly, but an independent and truly judicial body pronouncing final judgments without appeal within the limited field of its functions. The Tribunal is competent to pass judgment upon application alleging non-observance of contracts of employment of staff members of the United Nations Secretariat or of their terms of appointment. Its competence may be extended to specialized agencies in accordance with a special agreement made with each agency by the Secretary-General.

Resolution 678 (VII), of 21 December 1952, recommended that specialized agencies which were members of the UN Joint Staff Pension Fund should accept the jurisdiction of the Administrative Tribunal in matters involving applications alleging non-observance of Pension Fund Regulations. In any dispute as to whether the Tribunal has competence, the matter should be settled by decision of the Tribunal.

The Statute and Rules of the United Nations Administrative Tribunal, Provisions in force with effect from 3 October 1972 (AT/11/Rev.4, Sales No.:E.73.X.1) (earlier editions of the Statute and Rules were issued with the symbols A/CN.5/A, Rev.1 and 2, AT/11, Rev.1 to 3).

Membership

The resolution provided for a membership of
seven, no two of whom may be nationals of the
same State. Only three may sit in any particular case. The members are appointed by the
General Assembly for three years, and may be re-
appointed, provided, however, that of the members initially appointed, the terms of ten members shall expire at the end of two years. A
member appointed to replace a member whose term
of office had not expired should hold office for
the remainder of his predecessor's term.

Following is a list of members of the United
Nations Administrative Tribunal elected annually
by the General Assembly for a three-year term
commencing, at first on 1 December of the year
of their appointment, and later (resolution 670
(VII)), of 20 December 1952, extended to 1 January of the following year.

Plenary meeting 274, 9 December 1949,
to serve one year to 1950:
   Sir Sydney Caine (UK)
   Dr. Vladimir Outrata (Czech)
to serve two years to 1951:
   Roland Andrews Egger (USA)
   Dr. Emilio N. Oribe (Uruguay)
to serve three years to 1952:
   Madame Paul Bastid (France)
   Lt.Gen. His Highness Maharaja Jam Shri
      Digvijayasinhji Sahib (India)
   Omar Loutfi (Egypt), replaced on 14 Dec-
      ember 1950 by Hamed Sultan (Egypt)

Plenary meeting 324, 14 December 1950,
to serve to 30 November 1953, and extended
 to 31 December 1953 (resolution 670 (VII)):
   Lord Crook (UK)
   Dr. Vladimir Outrata (Czech)

Plenary meeting 356, 20 December 1951,
to serve to 31 December 1954:
> Bror Arvid Sture Petrén (Sweden)
> Homero Viteri Lafronte (Ecuador)

Plenary meeting 409. 20 December 1952,
to serve to 31 December 1955:
> Djalal Abdoh (Iran)
> Madame Paul Bastid (France)
> Omar Loutfi (Egypt)

Plenary meeting 471, 29 December 1953,
to serve to 31 December 1956:
> Lord Crook (UK)
> Jacob Mark Lashly (USA)

Plenary meeting 496, 29 October 1954,
to serve to 31 December 1957:
> Víctor Manuel Pérez Perozo (Venezuela)
> Bror Arvid Sture Petrén (Sweden)

Plenary meeting 549, 29 November 1955,
to serve to 31 December 1958:
> Madame Paul Bastid (France)
> Omar Loutfi (Egypt)
> R. Venkataraman (India)

Plenary meeting 632, 21 December 1956,
to serve to 31 December 1959:
> Lord Crook (UK)
> Francisco A. Forteza (Uruguay)
> Jacob Mark Lashly (USA), on 30 October
> 1958 replaced by Harold Riegelman (USA)
> to fill out unexpired term.

Plenary meeting 723, 26 November 1957,
to serve to 31 December 1960:
> Francisco A. Forteza (Uruguay)
> Bror Arvid Sture Petrén (Sweden)

Plenary meeting 778, 30 October 1958,
to serve to 31 December 1961:
  Madame Paul Bastid (France)
  Omar Loutfi (Egypt)
  R. Venkataraman (India)

Plenary meeting 838, 17 November 1959,
to serve to 31 December 1962:
  James J. Casey (USA), appointed to fill
    out unexpired term to 31 December
    1959 of Mr. Riegelman (USA), resigned
    as of 26 October 1959, and to serve
    a three-year term, from 1 January 1960
  Lord Crook (UK)

Plenary meeting 954, 18 December 1960,
to serve to 31 December 1963:
  José A. Corréa (Ecuador), replaced on
    21 April 1961 by Hector Gros Espiell
    (Uruguay) to fill out his unexpired
    term
  Bror Arvid Sturm Petrén (Sweden)

Plenary meeting 1044, 30 October 1961,
to serve to 31 December 1964:
  Madame Paul Bastid (France)
  Omar Loutfi (Egypt), replaced by Louis
    Ignacio-Pinto (Dahomey) on 11 December
    1962 to fill out his unexpired term
  R. Venkataraman (India)

Plenary meeting 1191, 11 December 1962,
to serve to 31 December 1965:
  James W. Barco (USA)
  Lord Crook (UK)

Plenary meeting 1255, 6 November 1963,
to serve to 31 December 1966:
  Héctor Gros Espiell (Uruguay)
  Bror Arvid Sture Petrén (Sweden)

Plenary meeting 1328, 10 February 1965, to serve to 31 December 1967:

Madame Paul Bastid (France)
Louis Ignacio-Pinto (Dahomey)
R. Venkataraman (India)

Plenary meeting 1383, 13 December 1965, to serve to 31 December 1968:

Lord Crook (UK)
Francis T.P. Plimpton (USA)

Plenary meeting 1485, 6 December 1966, to serve to 31 December 1969:

Héctor Gros Espiell (Uruguay)
Zenon Rossides (Cyprus)

Plenary meeting 1598, 16 November 1967, to serve to 31 December 1970:

Madame Paul Bastid (France)
Louis Ignacio-Pinto (Dahomey) resigned as of 31 December 1969, and replaced by Vincent Mutuale (Congo (K)) on 5 December 1969, to fill out his unexpired term
R. Venkataraman (India)

Plenary meeting 1752, 21 December 1968, to serve to 31 December 1971:

Lord Crook (UK)
Francis T.P. Plimpton (USA)

Plenary meeting 1791, 28 October 1969, to serve to 31 December 1972:

Francisco A. Forteza (Uruguay)
Zenon Rossides (Cuprus)

Plenary meeting 1898, 9 November 1970,
to serve to 31 December 1973:
    Madame Paul Bastid (France)
    Vincent Mutuale (Congo (K))
    R. Venkataraman (India)

Plenary meeting 1979, 8 November 1971,
to serve to 31 December 1974:
    Francis T.P. Plimpton (USA)
    Sir Roger Bentham Stevens (UK)

Plenary meeting 2097, 4 December 1972,
to serve to 31 December 1975:
    Francisco A. Forteza (Uruguay)
    Zenon Rossides (Cyprus)

Plenary meeting 2196, 11 December 1973,
to serve to 31 December 1976:
    Madame Paul Bastid (France)
    Mutuale Tshikantshe Mamba (Zaire)
        (listed previously as Vincent Mutuale
        (Congo (K))
    R. Venkataraman (India)

The 1974 membership of the UN Administrative
Tribunal was composed of the following seven
members:
    Madame Paul Bastid (France), Francisco A.
    Forteza (Uruguay), Mutale Tshikantahe Mamba
    (Zaire), Francis T.P. Plimpton (USA), Zenon
    Rossides (Cyprus), Sir Roger Bentham
    Stevens (UK), R. Venkataraman (India).

Action

Plenary sessions of the Administrative Tribunal
are held at United Nations Headquarters in New
York, unless otherwise indicated.

Panel sessions held to hear cases and to render judgments are found in documents bearing the symbol AT/PV (the first ordinary or panel session in June 1950 bore the symbol A/CN.5/PV.1). Through March 1973, 36 panel sessions have been held, most of them at United Nations headquarters in New York, but some were held in Geneva. The November-December 1953 meetings were held in Paris and no documents were issued. Documents for some of the meetings were issued only in the "limited" category of distribution.

Annual reports of the Secretary-General on the work of the Organization also provide useful information on the work of the Administrative Tribunal.

At its third plenary session, held in Paris on 20 December 1951, the Administrative Tribunal decided that at future annual plenary sessions there should be approved for submission to the President of the General Assembly a note on the work of the Tribunal for the year, and that the first such annual note to be presented in December 1952 should cover the period from the appointment of the Tribunal to that date.

The annual notes transmitted by the Secretary-General to the General Assembly, included inter alia, the composition of the Tribunal, election of its officers, composition of the panels for the consideration of cases on the list (in accordance with Article 3 of the Statute only three members shall sit in any particular case; under Article 6 of the Rules, the President designates these three members and may, in addition, designate one or more members to serve as alternates); and the list of judgments delivered during the year.

Following is a list of the annual notes by the United Nations Administrative Tribunal submitted to the President of each session of the General Assembly:

A/INF/52, 15 December 1953, contained information on the first four plenary sessions of the Tribunal, officers elected, composition of the Tribunal for the years 1950 to 1953, the first two held in New York, 1-7 June and 14 December 1950; the third in Paris from 17 to 20 December 1951; the fourth in New York from 10 to 12 December 1951. It also contained the composition of panels for consideration of the cases on the list, and the list of judgments delivered during those years.

A/INF/58, 15 December 1953, fifth plenary session, 3 December 1953.

A/INF/62, 16 December 1954, sixth plenary session, 2-9 December 1954.

A/INF/68, 8 December 1955, seventh plenary session, 29 November to 2 December 1955.

A/INF/74, 27 December 1956, eighth plenary session, 4 December 1956.

A/INF/78, 17 December 1957. The President, having been advised that the holding of the plenary session would involve the voting of a supplementary credit by the Assembly and considering no case was pending before the Tribunal, decided to adjourn the convocation of this session in application of Article 20 of the Rules. In conformity with Article 2 of the Rules, the President and Vice-Presidents would remain in office until their successors were elected.

A/INF/81, 9 December 1958, ninth plenary session, 4 December 1958.

A/INF/85, 7 December 1959, 10th plenary session, 4 December 1959.

A/INF/88, 11 November 1960, 11th plenary session, 7 November 1960.

A/INF/95, 14 December 1961, 12th plenary
session, 29 November 1961.

A/INF/98, 29 September 1952, 13th plenary
session, 28-30 August, 3 and 14 September 1962.

A/INF/103, 14 October 1963, 14th plenary
session, 30 September 1963.

A/INF/107, 10 December 1964, 15th plenary
session met in Geneva, 7 November 1964.

A/INF/111, 7 October 1965, 16th plenary
session, 20 September 1965.

A/INF/116, 11 October 1966, 17th plenary
session, 6 October 1966.

A/INF/123, 27 October 1967, 18th plenary
session, 17 October 1967.

A/INF/130, 7 November 1968, special plenary
session in Geneva on 16 April 1968, and the 19th
plenary session in New York on 24 October 1968.

A/INF/135, 17 October 1969, 20th plenary
session, 9 October 1969.

A/INF/141, 6 November 1970, 21st plenary
session, 16 October 1970.

A/INF/146, 28 October 1971, 22nd plenary
session, 7 October 1971.

A/INF/151, 30 October 1972, 23rd plenary
session, 3 October 1972.

A/INF/157, 30 October 1973, 24th plenary
session, 10 October 1973.

Judgments rendered by the Administrative Tribunal were issued in four volumes to date:

AT/DEC/1-70, 1950-1957 (Sales no.: 58.X.1),
July 1959.

AT/DEC/71-86, 1958-1962 (Sales no.: 63.X.),
March 1964.

AT/DEC/87-113, 1963-1967 (Sales no.:68.X.1),
June 1969.

AT/DEC/114-166, 1968-1972 (Sales no.: 73.X.
2), August 1974.

Further judgments appear in mimeographed documents (AT/DEC/167 from 23 March 1973 to AT/DEC/207, 10 October 1975.

Officers of the Plenary Sessions

Under Article 2 of its Rules, the Administrative Tribunal at its annual plenary session elects a President, a First and Second Vice-President. Following is a list of the officers through 1973:

1950 to 1952
President: His Highness the Maharaja Jam Saheb (India)
First Vice-President: Madame Paul Bastid (France)
Second Vice-President: Sir Sydney Caine (UK) (1950), Rowland A. Egger (USA) (1951), and Lord Crook (UK) (1952)

1953 to 1963
President: Madame Paul Bastid (France)
First Vice-President: Lord Crook (UK)
Second Vice-President: Bror Arvid Sture Petrén (Sweden)

1964 to 1968
President: Madame Paul Bastid (France)
First Vice-President: Lord Crook (UK)
Second Vice-President: R. Venkataraman (India)

1969 to 1971
President: R. Venkataraman (India)
First Vice-President: Lord Crook (UK)
Second Vice-President: Hector Gros Espiell (Uruguay) (1969) and Madame Bastid (1970-1971)

1972 to 1973

President: R. Venkataraman (India)
First Vice-President: Madame Bastid (France)
Second Vice-President: Francis T.P. Plimpton
(USA)

Special Committee on Review of Administrative
Tribunal Judgments (A/AC.78/-)

Established by Assembly resolution 888 B (IX), of
17 December 1954.

Terms of Reference

The resolution accepted in principle judicial
review of judgments of the UN Administrative
Tribunal; requested Member States to communicate to the Secretary-General before 1 July 1955,
their views on the establishment of procedure to
provide for review of the judgments of the Tribunal and invited the Secretary-General to consult on this matter with the specialized agencies
concerned; established a Special Committee to
meet at a time to be fixed in consultation with
the Secretary-General to study the question of
the establishment of such a procedure in all its
aspects and to report to the General Assembly at
its tenth session.

Membership

Paragraph 5 of section B of the resolution de-
signated the following membership:
Argentina, Australia, Belgium, Brazil,
Canada, China, Cuba, El Salvador, France,
India, Iraq, Israel, Norway, Pakistan,
Syria, USSR, United Kingdom, and USA.

Their representatives were listed in paragraph
3 of the report.

Action

The Special Committee convened at the United
Nations headquarters on 4 April 1955, and held
twelve meetings between 4 and 21 April; and

concluded the session with the adoption of the report at the 13th meeting on 31 May 1955. With the exception of the USSR, which did not send a representative, all States Members of the Committee were represented.

The following officers were elected at the first meeting: Chairman: Carlos Blanco (Cuba); Vice-Chairman: Viqar Ahmed Hamdani (Pakistan); Rapporteur: Erik Dons (Norway). The report (GAOR, Sess.X, Annexes, agenda item 49, A/2909), issued on 10 June 1955, contained inter alia: draft amendments to the Statute of the United Nations Administrative Tribunal, and annex I contained proposals and suggestions considered by the Special Committee, memoranda and working papers submitted to the Special Committee by the Secretary-General, and views of the Staff Council of the Secretariat of the United Nations. Another report (Ibid., A/2917, and Add.1-2), of 21 July 1955, contained views of Member States and specialized agencies concerned with the subject.

Assembly resolution 957 (X), of 8 November 1955, on recommendation of the Special Committee, decided to amend the Statute of the United Nations Administrative Tribunal as indicated in the text of the resolution, as of the date of the adoption of the resolution, including the establishment of a committee to review Administrative Judgments.

<u>Committee on Applications for Review of Adminis-</u>
<u>trative Tribunal Judgments (A/AC.86/-. re-</u>
<u>stricted series)</u>

Established by Assembly resolution 957 (X), of
8 November 1955, after consideration of the report of the Special Committee on Review of Administrative Tribunal Judgments (<u>GAOR</u>, Sess. X,
<u>Annexes</u>, agenda item 49, A/2909).

Terms of Reference

The resolution, which amended the Statute of the
United Nations Administrative Tribunal, added a
new Article 11, paragraph 4 of which stated -
"For the purpose of this article, a Committee
is established and authorized under paragraph
2 of Article 96 of the Charter to request advisory opinions of the Court. The Committee
shall be composed of Member States, the representatives of which have served on the General
Committee of the most recent regular session of
the General Assembly. The Committee shall meet
at United Nations Headquarters and shall establish its own rules".

Article 11 further stated that if a Member State,
the Secretary-General or the person in respect
of whom a judgment has been rendered by the Tribunal objects to the judgment, they may within
thirty days from the date of judgment make writ-
ten application to the Committee asking it to
request an advisory opinion of the International
Court of Justice. Within thirty days from the
receipt of such an application, the Committee
shall decide whether or not there is a substan-
tial basis for the application.

The provisional rules of procedure adopted by
the Committee at its first meeting on 16 October

1956 and amended at its second and third meetings on 25 October 1956 and 21 January 1957 were published in a document (A/AC.86/2/Rev.1, and Corr.1, mimeographed), on 4 April 1975. The Committee also decided that its meetings at which applications were discussed should be held in private and that its decisions would be announced at public meetings.

Membership

The Committee is composed of Member States, the representatives of which had served on the General Committee of the most recent regular session of the General Assembly. It has held thirteen sessions from 1956 to 1973. Membership at each session was as follows:

November 1956, 15 Member States: Chile, China, Egypt, Ethiopia, France, Haiti, Luxembourg, Mexico, New Zealand, Norway, Poland, Thailand, USSR, United Kingdom, United States of America.

January 1957, 16 Member States: China, Czechoslovakia, Denmark, Dominican Republic, Egypt, El Salvador, France, India, Italy, Pakistan, Peru, Thailand, Turkey, USSR, United Kingdom, United States of America.

June 1958, 17 Member States: Ceylon, China, Czechoslovakia, France, Guatemala, Iran, Netherlands, New Zealand, Norway, Paraguay, Spain, Thailand, Tunisia, USSR, United Kingdom, United States of America, Venezuela.

January 1959, 21 Member States: Australia, Ceylon, China, Czechoslovakia, Ecuador, El Salvador, France, Greece, Indonesia, Ireland, Japan, Lebanon, Mexico, Nepal, Netherlands, Pakistan, Romania, USSR, United Kingdom, United States of America, Uruguay.

November 1965, 25 Member States: Belgium, Burundi, Central African Republic, Chile, China, France, Guatemala, Haiti, Hungary, Iran, Italy, Kuwait, Laos, Malaysia, Mexico, Morocco, Paraguay, Poland, Sierra Leone, Spain, Tunisia, UAR, USSR, United Kingdom, and United States of America.

December 1968 and July 1969, 25 Member States: Austria, Bulgaria, Byelorussia, Canada, China, France, Ghana, Guatemala, Guinea, Guyana, India, Iran, Italy, Lebanon, Mauritania, Peru, Philippines, Somalia, Sweden, Togo, Trinidad and Tobago, Uganda, USSR, United Kingdom, USA.

December 1970, 25 Member States: Afghanistan, Bolivia, Brazil, Cameroon, Canada, Chad, China, Ecuador, France, Iraq, Jamaica, Kenya, Malta, Mauritius, Nepal, Norway, Philippines, Romania, Senegal, Ukraine, USSR, United Kingdom, USA, Venezuela, Zambia.

November 1971 and June 1972, 25 Member States: Belgium, Bulgaria, Burundi, China, Costa Rica, Cyprus, Finland, France, Greece, Hungary, Indonesia, Ireland, Jamaica, Japan, Nigeria, Peru, Philippines, Sierra Leone, Sudan, USSR, United Kingdom, USA, Venezuela, Yemen (PDR), Zambia.

November 1972 and June 1973, 25 Member States: Belgium, Canada, China, Colombia, Cyprus, Czechoslovakia, Ethiopia, France, Guinea, Haiti, Iceland, Japan, Libya, Mauritania, Mauritius, New Zealand, Paraguay, Philippines, Poland, Rwanda, Syria, USSR, United Kingdom, United States of America, Uruguay.

December 1973, 25 Member States: Cameroon, China, Czechoslovakia, Denmark, Ecuador, Ethiopia, Fiji, France, Ghana, Guyana, Honduras, Hungary, Lebanon, Mexico, Netherlands, Spain,

Sri Lanka, Tanzania, Tunisia, Uganda, USSR, United Arab Emirates, United Kingdom, United States of America, Venezuela.

The list of representatives attending the session was annexed to the Committee reports in the A/AC.86/- document series.

Action

The first seven sessions of the Committee were recorded in summary records (A/AC.86/SR.1-18), 16 October 1956 to 3 July 1969. Information on the Committee meetings and the decisions taken is found in a restricted series of documents (A/AC.86/INF.1 to 14), the first to the 15th sessions, 12 October 1956 to 28 November 1975. Following is a list of sessions and officers:

First session, 16 and 25 October 1956. Officers: Chairman: Sir Leslie Munro (NZ); Vice-Chairman: Miguel Bravo (Chile); Rapporteur: W.V. J. Evans (UK).

Second session, 21, 25, 29 January and 1 February 1957. Officers: Chairman: Mohammad Mir Khan (Pakistan); Vice-Chairman: Ambrosio Álvarez Aybar (Dom. Rep.); Rapporteur: W.V.J. Evans (UK).

Third session, 16 June 1958. Officers: Chairman: Sir Leslie Munro (NZ); Vice-Chairman: Sir Claude Corea (Ceylon); Rapporteur: Dr. Eduardo Plaza (Venezuela).

Fourth session, 20, 27 and 29 January 1959. Officers: Chairman: C.W.A. Schurmann (Netherlands); Vice-Chairman: N.T.D. Kanakaratne (Ceylon); Rapporteur: W.V.J. Evans (UK).

Fifth session, 11, 17 and 18 November 1965. Officers: Dr. Abdullah El-Erian (UAR); Vice-Chairman: Miguel Solano Lopez (Paraguay); Rap-

Porteur: Ian M. Sinclair (UK).

Sixth session, 13-20 December 1968. Officers: Chairman: Krishna Rao (India); Vice-Chairman: Rodolfo Rohrmoser (Guatemala); Rapporteur: H.G. Darwin (UK).

Seventh session, 3-17 July 1969. Officers: Chairman: A.S. Gonsalves (India); Vice-Chairman: Maximiliano Kestler (Guatemala); Rapporteur: Angus W.J. Robertson (Canada).

Eighth session, 10-18 December 1970 and 27 January to 12 February 1971. Officers: Chairman: Paul Bamela Engo (Cameroon); Vice-Chairman: Tulio Alvarado (Venezuela); Rapporteur: John Redvers Freeland (UK).

Ninth session, 5 November 1971. Officers: Chairman: J.P.B. Maramis (Indonesia); Vice-Chairman: Tulio Alvarado (Venezuela); Rapporteur: John Redvers Freeland (UK).

Tenth session, 8, 13, 19, 20 June 1972. Officers: Chairman: Chaidir Anwar Sani (Indonesia); Vice-Chairman: Miss Esther Meneses (Venezuela); Rapporteur: John Redvers Freeland (UK).

Eleventh session, 20 and 27 November and 14 December 1972. Officers: Chairman: Erik Suy (Belgium); Vice-Chairman: Luis González Arias (Paraguay); Rapporteur: John Redvers Freeland (UK).

Twelfth session, 5 June 1973. Officers: Chairman: Carlos Giambruno (Uruguay); Vice-Chairman: Henryk Mikucki (Poland); Rapporteur: John Redvers Freeland (UK).

Thirteenth session, 29 November and 12 December 1973. Officers: Chairman: Sergio González Gálvez (Mexico); Vice-Chairman: C.S.M. Mselle (Tanzania); Rapporteur: Henry Steel (UK).

E. Staff Recruitment and Other
Personnel Questions

Commission of Jurists

Established on 22 October 1952, by the Secretary-General, who decided to appoint an international commission of jurists to advise him
on the action he should take to meet the situation on the problem of alleged subversive
activities of staff members (<u>GAOR</u>, Sess. VII,
<u>Annexes</u>, vol. 2, agenda item 73, A/2364, Part
II).

Terms of Reference

The Secretary-General would request the members
of the Commission to advise him on the five
following questions:

(1) Is it compatible with the conduct
required of a staff member for him to refuse
to answer a question asked by an authorized
organ of his government on the ground of the
constitutional privilege against self-incrim-
ination?

(2) What effect should be given by the
Secretary-General in the refusal of the United
States Government to issue a passport to a
staff member for purposes of official travel?

(3) In view of the Charter requirements
and the Staff Regulations, what action should
the Secretary-General take when he received
information from an official source of the United States Government that a staff member of
United States citizenship was alleged to be
disloyal to his government?

(4) In the course of inquiries by agencies of the United States Government, should
the Secretary-General make available archives
of the Organization or authorize staff members

to respond to questions involving confidential information relating to official acts?

(5) If it appeared that the Secretary-General possessed no present authority to dismiss holders of permanent appointments on evidence of subversive activities against their country or refusal to deny such activities, what new legal steps would be necessary and effective to confer such authority?

Membership

The three jurists appointed by the Secretary-General were:
Sir Edwin S. Herbert (UK); William D. Mitchell (USA); and Paul Veldekens (Belgium).

Action

The Commission met in November and presented its opinion to the Secretary-General on 29 November 1952 (Ibid., A/2364, annex III). The Secretary-General transmitted for the information of delegations a note (A/INF 51 and Corr. 1) of 5 December 1952, which contained a copy of the opinion of the Commission of Jurists, and a statement which the Secretary-General had addressed to the staff of the Secretariat concerning his uses of that opinion. The Secretary-General's report (Ibid., A/2364) on personnel policy was issued on 30 January 1953.

Assembly resolution 708 (VII), of 1 April 1953, requested the Secretary-General to report to the eighth session on the progress made in the conduct and development of personnel policy, together with the comments of ACABQ.

Advisory Panel (on Secretariat Matters)

Established by the Secretary-General on 16
January 1953, on advice of the Commission of
Jurists (GAOR, Sess. VII, Annexes, vol. 2,
agenda item 73, A/2364, paragraphs 104-105).

Terms of Reference

To advise the Secretary-General in cases concerning officers with permanent contracts or
fixed term contracts which had not expired.
When the Panel had completed its consideration
of a particular case, it would make recommendations to the Secretary-General. These would
be of an advisory character, as the responsibility for terminating members of the staff is
imposed upon the Secretary-General by the
Charter and the Staff Regulations.

Membership

The Commission of Jurists suggested a panel
consisting of two "very" senior officers of
the Secretariat staff with an independent
Chairman to be selected by the Secretary-General after consultation with the appropriate
bodies representing the staff.

The Secretary-General announced, on 16 January
1953, the appointment of Leonard W. Brocking-
ton (Canada) as Chairman of the Panel, and an
alternate Chairman to serve in his absence.

Members of the Panel were: Ralph J. Bunche
(USA), Principal Director, Department of Trus-
teeship and Information from Non-Self-Governing Territories; Tor Gjesdal (Norway), Principal Director, Department of Public Information;

Gustavo Martínez-Cabañas (Mexico), Deputy
Director-General, Technical Assistance Admin-
istration; Constantin A. Stavropoulos (Greece),
Principal Director in charge of the Legal
Department (Ibid., A/2364, paragraphs 71-72).

Action

Following the amendment of the Staff Regula-
tions at the eighth session of the General
Assembly, and the establishment of the Special
Advisory Board, it became apparent that the
Advisory Panel would have no function to per-
form and, consequently, it was discontinued
(GAOR, Sess.IX, Annexes, agenda item 54, A/
2777, paragraph 21, 28 October 1954).

Special Advisory Board (Secretariat)

Following the adoption of resolution 782 A (VIII), of 9 December 1953, amending Staff Regulations, the Secretary-General issued staff rule 109.1 (i) establishing the composition of the Special Advisory Board (A/C.5/L. 275, mimeographed), 26 October 1954.

Terms of Reference

The amendment of Staff Regulation 9.1 stated that the Secretary-General may also, giving his reasons therefor, terminate the appointment of a staff member who holds a permanent appointment:

(i) if the conduct of the staff member indicates that the staff member does not meet the highest standards of integrity required by Article 101, paragraph 3, of the Charter;

(ii) if facts entering to the appointment of the staff member and relevant to his suitability come to light which, if they had been known at the time of his appointment, should under the standards established by the Charter have precluded his appointment.

No termination under sub-paragraphs (i) and (ii) shall take place until the matter has been considered and reported by a special advisory board appointed for that purpose by the Secretary-General.

Finally, the Secretary-General may terminate the appointment of a staff member who holds a permanent appointment if such action would be in the interest of the good administration of the Organization, and in accordance with the standards of the Charter, provided that the action is not contested by the staff member concerned.

Membership

Staff Rule 109.1 (a) provided that the Special Advisory Board should be composed of a Chairman appointed by the Secretary-General on the nomination of the President of the International Court of Justice (ICJ) and of four members appointed by the Secretary-General in agreement with the Staff Council.

Pursuant to these provisions, the Secretary-General appointed Dr. Georges Kaeckenbeeck (Belgium) as Chairman of the Special Advisory Board; and appointed, in accordance with the provisions of the same staff rule and in agreement with the Staff Council, four officials of the Secretariat to serve as members and four to serve as alternate members of the Board.

In April 1957, Dr. Kaeckenbeeck resigned as Chairman, and on the nomination of the ICJ President, the Secretary-General appointed Justice O.C. Gundersen (Norway) to succeed him. The Secretary-General also appointed, in accordance with the provisions of the same staff rule and in agreement with the Staff Council, three more officials of the Secretariat to serve as additional alternate members of the Board.

Action

The Special Advisory Board held its first session from 8 June to 21 July 1954. Following consideration by the Board of the procedures which it would follow and consultations by the Secretary-General, with the Board and with representatives of the staff, the Secretary-General, in a letter of 1 July 1954 to the Chairman of the Staff Committee, explained

the interpretation which he gave to the
functions of the Special Advisory Board (GAOR,
Sess. IX, Annexes, agenda item 54, A/2777,
paragraphs 15-20, 28 October 1954).

The Special Advisory Board also held sessions
in 1955, 1956, and 1957. Three of the four
sessions were held at United Nations headquarters in New York and one at the European
Office in Geneva. Dr. Kaeckenbeeck presided
at the first three sessions, and Justice
Gundersen at the latest session held from 15
August to 6 September 1957. The Secretary-
General reported on these sessions on 25 October 1957 (GAOR, Sess. XII, Annexes, agenda
item 51 (d), A/C.5/726), and recommended no
change in Staff Regulations at this time.

F. Public Information Activities

Advisory Committee on United Nations Telecommunications

Established at the first session of the General Assembly in London, resolution 13 (I), annex I, on 13 February 1946, when the Assembly approved the recommendations of the Technical Advisory Committee on Information of the Preparatory Commission to the United Nations that the United Nations should have its own radio broadcasting station or stations at headquarters.

The Committee was formerly known as the Panel of Radio Experts, and was summoned by the Department of Public Information to assist in its task.

Terms of Reference

The Advisory Committee was assigned three distinct but related functions:

(a) To prepare a plan for efficient world-wide broadcasting coverage under United Nations auspices of General Assembly proceedings beginning on 23 October 1946;

(b) To investigate and make recommendations concerning United Nations broadcasting and telecommunications arrangements during the period between the close of the General Assembly and the establishment of permanent United Nations telecommunications facilities;

(c) To investigate the technical problems arising in connection with the proposal to give the United Nations independent radio communication, and to submit a plan supported by the necessary technical data by 10 November

1946, on which date it was suggested that five
communications experts designated by China,
Egypt, Uruguay, United Kingdom, and the USSR,
be asked to meet with the Advisory Committee
and examine the plan in order to permit greater participation in its preparation. The recommendations could then, at the discretion of
the Secretary-General, be submitted to the
General Assembly.

The Advisory Committee was also requested to
give careful consideration to all technical
and financial aspects of the problems involved.

Membership

The original committee consisted of the fol-
lowing members:
    Brigadier-General Frank E. Stoner (USA),
Chairman, Assistant Chief Signal Officer, US
Army, former wartime Chief of US Army Communi-
cations Service;
    S. Kagan (France), Former Chief Signal
Officer, HQ, Free French Forces; formerly
Chief, French Mission of Telecommunications;
    G. F. Van Dissel (Netherlands), Chief of
Communications Dept., Netherlands Purchasing
Commission; former Member of Transit and Com-
munications Section, League of Nations (in
charge of League of Nations wireless section).

The augmented committee consisted of the members named above, plus the following nominees
of the Governments named:
    Wen Yuan Pan (China), formerly Technical
Adviser, China Defense Supplies, Inc., Washington, D.C., and Universal Trading Corp., New
York City; Communications Expert to International Civil Aviation Conference, 1944;

Colonel Hassan Bey Ragab (Egypt), Military Attaché, Egyptian Embassy, Washington, D. C., formerly Commanding Officer, Egyptian Army Telecommunications Maintenance System;

Sergei P. Gavrilitsa (USSR), radio engineer in charge of communications, Soviet Delegation to the United Nations; formerly broadcast engineer, Moscow Radio;

Brigadier John Gordon Deedes (UK), Telecommunications Attaché, British Embassy, Washington, D.C., formerly Deputy Director of Signals (Telecommunications), War Office, London;

Roberto Fontaina (Uruguay), President of SADREP, Commercial Broadcasting Network of Uruguay, Alternate Delegate of Uruguay to the Assembly.

Action

The report of the Advisory Committee (GAOR, Sess.II, Suppl.9 (A/335)), was issued on 13 November 1947. Annex C of the report contained the membership of the Committee.

In resolution 158 (II), of 20 November 1947, the Assembly directed the Secretary-General to proceed with negotiations to obtain whatever was necessary for the operation of a United Nations telecommunications system, and to report to the third session.

Resolution 240 (III), of 18 November 1948, approved in principle the establishment of a United Nations Telecommunications system, and requested the Secretary-General to present to the Assembly in 1950 such recommendations as he deemed necessary to establish such a system.

The Secretary-General's report (GAOR, Sess. V, Annexes, vol.2, agenda item 47, A/1454) was issued on 25 October 1950; and in a note of 14 November 1950 to the Fifth Committee (Ibid., A/C.5/401), the Secretary-General reported that the International Telecommunication Union (ITU) had accepted all proposals presented to it, and had accepted the United Nations as an operating broadcasting agency and a non-voting member of the ITU.

Resolution 460 (V), of 12 December 1950, instructed the Secretary-General to proceed with the implementation of the proposals outlined in his report, provided that the capital expenditure involved did not constitute a net addition to the budget of the United Nations. It also authorized him to accept for this purpose such voluntary contributions and/or donations as would be appropriate and necessary to carry out the proposals in whole or in part.

Resolution 588 (VI), of 12 January 1952, took note of the report of the Secretary-General (GAOR, Sess.VI, Annexes, agenda item 47, A/1919) dated 16 October 1951, in which he reported on developments in the use of the United Nations Telecommunications System.

Expert Committee on United Nations Public Information

Established by Assembly resolution 1177 (XII), of 26 November 1957.

Terms of Reference

The resolution requested the Secretary-General to appoint an expert committee of six individuals with practical, administrative and financial experience in the various fields of information, to be nominated by the Governments of the UAR, India, USSR, United Kingdom, United States of America, and Uruguay, with instructions to undertake, in the light of the opinions expressed by delegations during the twelfth session of the General Assembly, a review and appraisal of the work, the methods used and the effectiveness of the results achieved by the public information services of the United Nations (including the information centers). Its specific task was to recommend possible modifications to ensure a maximum of effectiveness of the lowest possible cost, and to report before the opening of the thirteenth session of the Assembly.

Membership

On 10 March 1958, the following experts, having been nominated by their Governments, were appointed by the Secretary-General to constitute the Committee:

R. A. Bevan (UK), A.M. El-Messiri (UAR), P.N. Haksar (India), Louis P. Lochner (USA), E. Rodriguez Fabregat (Uruguay), A. F. Sokirkin (USSR).

Action

The Committee met at United Nations Headquarters
in New York, from 20 March to 16 April 1958.
It had spent the period from 17 April to 24 June
visiting the information centers in various
countries. Its report (GAOR, Sess. XIII, Annexes, agenda item 55, A/3928) was issued on 20
September 1958; and the Secretary-General's
comments on the report (Ibid., A/3945) appeared
on 16 October 1958.

Resolution 1335 (XIII), of 13 December 1958,
requested the Secretary-General to give effect
in 1959 in so far as practicable to the recommendations made by the Expert Committee. In a
statement to the 682nd meeting of the Fifth
Committee (GAOR, Sess. XIII, Fifth Committee,
682nd meeting, A/C.5/764, paragraphs 1-9), on
13 November 1958, the Secretary-General stated
his intention to act upon the many excellent
recommendations included in paragraph 227 of
the Expert Committee's report, in the light of
basic principles as interpreted in his statement referred to above, and to resolutions 13
(I), of 13 February 1946, and 595 (VI), of 4
February 1957, setting forth the basic policy
and principles of the United Nations Information program.

Implementing the recommendations of resolution
1335 (XIII), the Secretary-General on 18 December 1958 appointed a Committee consisting of
Andrew W. Cordier (USA), Executive Assistant to
the Secretary-General; Anatoly Dobrynin (USSR),
Under-Secretary for Political and Security Council Affairs; and Philippe de Seynes (France),
Under-Secretary for Economic and Social Affairs,
with Alfred G. Katzin (South Africa) (temporar-
ily designated as Acting Head of the Office of

Public Infromation) as Executive Secretary of
the Committee.

The Committee was instructed to report recommendations to the Secretary-General in implementation of the Assembly's resolution, taking into
account, inter alia, the recommendations of the
Office of Public Information made in the light
of operational experience.

As a result of their work, the Secretary-General
issued a report (GAOR, Sess.XIV, Annexes, agenda
item 52, A/4122) on 16 June 1959. At the 727th
meeting of the Fifth Committee, on 22 October
1959 (Ibid., A/C.5/792), the Secretary-General
discussed the implementation of the report.

Resolution 1405 (XIV), of 1 December 1959, noted
the report with appreciation; requested the Secretary-General, inter alia, to include in his
report on the Office of Public Information to
the General Assembly at every session outlines
of the policy and programs planned to be executed
by the Office during the coming year, with comments thereon; and also requested him to appoint,
in consultation with the Governments of Member
States, a panel of qualified persons representative of the various geographical areas and main
cultures of the world, and to consult with members of that panel from time to time on United
Nations information policies and programs in order to ensure maximum effectiveness at minimum
cost.

Consultative Panel for Public Information

General Assembly resolution 1405 (XIV), of 1 December 1959, requested the Secretary-General, in consultation with Member States, to appoint a panel of qualified persons representative of the various geographic areas and main cultures of the world, and to consult with members of that panel from time to time on United Nations information policies and programs designed to assure maximum effectiveness at minimum cost.

Terms of Reference

At the first meeting on 9 June 1960, it was decided that the Panel's functions were purely advisory to the Secretary-General, that no voting procedure followed or views expressed would commit the respective Delegations, and that no summary records would be made of the proceedings or Panel discussions.

Resolution 1558 (XXV), of 18 December 1960, requested the Secretary-General, in consultation with the Consultative Panel on Public Information and the Advisory Committee on Administrative and Budgetary Questions (ACABQ), as appropriate:

(a) to give high priority to the opening of information centers or arranging for adequate information facilities in the less-developed areas, particularly in the newly independent countries and Trust territories and Non-Self-Governing Territories, by effecting economies in other directions;

(b) to intensify his efforts to achieve a more effective regional representation at the policy-making level of the Office of Public Information;

(c) to report to the General Assembly at its 16th session on the progress made in implementing the present resolution.

ECOSOC resolution 1176 (XLI), of 5 August 1966, invited the Secretary-General to undertake, with such assistance as deemed necessary, the study of information activities of the United Nations with respect to its economic, social and human rights work, and inform the Council at its 43rd session on measures to be taken to improve information services in these fields of United Nations activity. The Secretary-General issued two reports in response to the request in this resolution, the first on 18 April 1967 (ESCOR, 43rd Sess., Annexes, agenda item 20, E/4341), and the second on 9 June 1967 (Ibid., E/4394).

Assembly resolution 2897 (XXVI), of 22 December 1971, reaffirmed "the importance of United Nations information centers as appropriate instruments for informing the peoples of the world about its objectives and activities", and requested the Secretary-General "to appoint to the United Nations information centers highly qualified professional staff in the fields of information and the building of public support for United Nations activities..."

Membership

The Secretary-General advised in a letter to Delegations dated 16 May 1960 that the most practical approach would be to invite the assistance of a panel composed of the Permanent Heads of Delegations to the United Nations of ten Member States, and announced at the same time that he would approach the Permanent Representatives of nine as follows: France,

India, Japan, Peru, Sudan, USSR, United Kingdom, United States of America, and Venezuela.

The Panel decided at its first meeting on 9 June 1960, that participants were present in their personal capacities, and that representatives could appoint a nominee to represent them.

At a meeting of the Panel on 16 June 1960, it was suggested that the Panel be increased by two and that the Representatives of Czechoslovakia and Italy be invited to participate.

At the meeting of the Panel held on 24 June 1960, the following representatives were present:
  Dr. Zdenek Černík (Czech), representing Karel Kurka (Czech);
  Armand Berard (France);
  C. S. Jha (India);
  Egidio Ortona (Italy);
  Dr. Koto Matsudaire (Japan);
  Carlos Mackehenie (Peru);
  O.A.H. Adeel (Sudan);
  A.A. Sobolev (USSR);
  Sir Pierson Dixon (UK);
  Wallace Irwin (USA), representing Henry Cabot Lodge (USA);
  Dr. Ignacio Silva Sucre (Venezuela), representing Dr. Carlos Sosa-Rodríguez (Venezuela).

By letter of 3 July 1962, the Secretary-General reported that the Ivory Coast would participate as a French-speaking African country, Liberia having already participated as an English-speaking African country, thus bringing up the total membership to 13.

At the 10th meeting held on 15 March 1967, the
following representatives were present:

      Jan Muzik (Czech);

      Claude Chayet (France);

      Ambassador Copalaswani Parthasarathi
(India);

      Carlo Rossi Arnaud (Italy);

      Tokishiro Uemeto (Japan);

      Ambassador Nathan Barnes (Liberia);

      Ambassador Carlos Mackehenie (Peru);

      Ali Sahleul (Sudan);

      Ambassador Nikolai T. Fedorenko (USSR);

      C. Peter Hope (UK);

      Ambassador Seymour M. Finger (USA);

      Ambassador Dr. Pedro Zuloaga (Venezuela).

Resolution 2897 (XXVI), of 22 December 1971,
recommended that the Secretary-General, in accordance with the provisions of resolution 1405
(XIV), should review the composition of the
Consultative Panel on Public Information to ensure that it reflected the present situation in
the United Nations, and requested the Secretary-
General to convene the Panel before the twenty-
seventh session of the Assembly to advise him
on the information policies and activities of
the United Nations.

In 1972, the membership of the Panel had been
increased by the Secretary-General to 26 members as follows:

      Canada, China, Colombia, Czechoslovakia,
      France, India, Italy, Ivory Coast, Japan,
      Jordan, Liberia, Netherlands, Peru,
      Poland, Roumania, Sudan, Sweden, Trinidad
      and Tobago, Tunisia, USSR, United King-
      dom, United States of America, Venezuela,
      Yemen (People's Democratic Rep.), Yugo-
      slavia, and Zaire.

Action

The Panel met in early summer of 1960 and in December 1961 to consider draft reports on public information activities of the United Nations to the fifteenth and sixteenth sessions of the General Assembly. On 25 August 1960, the Secretary-General issued a report (GAOR, Sess. XV, Annexes, vol.2, agenda item 59, A/4429); and a second report, on 19 October 1961 (GAOR, Sess. XVI, Annexes, vol.3, agenda item 63, A/4927, and Corr.1).

It was agreed at the seventh meeting held on 3 March 1964 that the Panel should meet more than once in two years. Meetings were held in July 1962, in March 1964, and in January and March 1967.

The Secretary-General submitted to the twenty-fifth Assembly a report, entitled "Review and Reappraisal of the United Nations Information Policies and Activities"; on 30 October 1970 (A/C.5/1320, and Corr.1); on 15 June 1971, he submitted a revised version of the report (A/C.5/1320/Rev.1); an addendum on 14 October 1971 (A/C.5/1320/Rev.1/Add.1); and a further report on the same subject on 17 October 1972 (A/C.5/1452), all in final offset.

After a lapse of five years, the Panel met from 11 to 13 September 1972. At this session, the Secretary-General submitted a paper on "General Policy Considerations relating to the OPI (Office of Public Information) Work Program for 1973", which had been circulated to the members of the Panel by letter of 18 August 1972.

The second meeting of the reconstituted Panel met on 17-18 April 1973. For this session, by letter of 6 April 1973, the Assistant Secretary-General for the Office of Public Information (OPI) transmitted to the members of the Panel:

(a) a note of the Secretary-General on United Nations Information Centers;

(b) report of the Secretary-General on the Center for Economic and Social Information (CESI);

(c) note of the Secretary-General on the acquisition and replacement of audiovisual equipment.

In the report of the Secretary-General of 12 November 1973 (A/C.5/1547, final offset), he felt it appropriate to mention that the satisfactory results achieved due to the advice extended to him by the reactivated and enlarged Panel, relating to the implementation of the information policies determined by the General Assembly, might lead one to envisage a still broader function for the Panel. Noting that resolutions of a number of United Nations organs call upon Member States to engage in information activities on a variety of specific topics, he believed it would be worth while for the Consultative Panel on Public Information to monitor the role played by the Member States in this regard.

Chapter XII

TRANSFER OF ASSETS OF THE LEAGUE OF
NATIONS; UNITED NATIONS HEADQUARTERS
AND OFFICES; HOST COUNTRY RELATIONS

A. Transfer of Assets of the League of Nations

League of Nations Committee (1946)

Committee on Negotiations with the League
of Nations (1946)

B. United Nations Headquarters and Offices

Interim Committee for Selection of a
Definite Site for the Permanent Headquarters
of the United Nations (1946)

Negotiations Committee on Negotiations
with the Authorities of the United States
of America concerning the arrangements required as a result of the Establishment of
the Seat of the United Nations in the United States of America (1946)

Permanent Headquarters Committee (1946)

Headquarters Commission (1946)

Headquarters Advisory Committee (1947,
1948-1952)

Ad Hoc Committee on Headquarters (1947)

Ad Hoc Committee on Building (Geneva)
(1971-1973)

C. Host Country Relations

USUN-NYC (United States Mission to the United Nations-New York City) Host Country Advisory Committee (1967-1971)

Informal Joint Committee on Host Country Relations (1966-1971)

Committee on Relations with the Host Country (1971--)

TRANSFER OF ASSETS OF THE LEAGUE OF NATIONS;
UNITED NATIONS HEADQUARTERS AND OFFICES;
HOST COUNTRY RELATIONS

A. Transfer of Assets of the League of Nations

League of Nations Committee (A/LN/-)

Established by Assembly resolution 26 (a) (I),
of 28 January 1946, as one of two ad hoc committees of the Whole.

The Preparatory Commission of the United Nations had appointed a Committee on League of
Nations Assets at its third plenary meeting on
18 December 1945, to negotiate with the Supervisory Commission of the League of Nations. It
was composed of representatives of Chile, China,
France, Poland, Union of South Africa, USSR,
United Kingdom, and United States of America.
The Committee was to enter, on behalf of the
Preparatory Commission, into discussions with
the League Supervisory Commission, for the purpose of establishing a common plan for the
transfer of the assets of the League to the United Nations on such terms as were considered
just and convenient. The duly authorized representatives of the International Labor Organization (ILO) were to be consulted on questions
connected with the transfer which affected the
ILO.

The report of the Committee on League of Nations
Assets on a "Common Plan for the Transfer of the
Assets of the League of Nations established by
the United Nations Committee and the Supervisory Commission of the League of Nations" (GAOR,

Sess.I, Part I, <u>League of Nations Committee</u>,
<u>Summary record of meetings</u>, 30 January - 1 February 1946, Annexes 1, 2 and 3, A/18, and Add.
1-3) was issued, as a separate document, on 28 January 1946.

Terms of Reference

The League of Nations Committee was to consider the possible transfer of certain functions, activities and assets of the League of Nations.

Membership

The Committee was established as a Committee of the Whole, that is, each Member having the right to be represented. A list of participants was contained in the Committee's report.

Action

The League of Nations Committee held two meetings in London on 30 January and 1 February 1946. At its first meeting, the Committee elected Erik Andreas Colban (Norway) as Chairman, Sheikh Rafic Nahba (Saudi Arabia) as Vice-Chairman, and H. T. Andrews (Union of South Africa) as Rapporteur.

At its second meeting, it considered the "Common Plan for the Transfer of the Assets of the League of Nations". The report of the Committee (<u>Ibid.</u>, <u>Plenary Meetings</u>, annex 16, A/28), issued on 4 February 1946, proposed the adoption of various resolutions relating to the transfer of certain functions, activities and assets of the League of Nations, which were incorporated in resolution 24 (I), adopted by the General Assembly on 12 February 1946. One of the proposals established a committee on negotiations with the League of Nations to assist the Secretary-

General in negotiating further agreements.

A checklist of documents of the League of
Nations Committee, the Committee on League of
Nations Assets, and the Negotiating Committee
of League of Nations Assets, was issued on 26
April 1946 (A/LN/4, mimeographed).

Committee on Negotiations with the League of Nations (A/NC/-)

Established by the General Assembly at its 29th plenary meeting, under section IV of resolution 24 (I), of 12 February 1946, on recommendation of the League of Nations Committee.

Terms of Reference

The Assembly approved the creation of a small negotiating committee to assist the Secretary-General in negotiating further agreements in connection with the transfer of certain assets in Geneva, and in connection with the premises of the Permanent Court of International Justice in the Peace Palace at The Hague.

Membership

The resolution stated that the committee should consist of one representative designated by the delegations, if they so desired, of each of the same eight Members as previously constituted the Committee on League of Nations Assets created by the Preparatory Commission.

The Member States and their representatives were the following:

Chile	Alvaros Muñoz
China	Y. Dao
France	George Peissel
Poland	W. Moderow, Chairman
South Africa	D. B. Sole
USSR	
United Kingdom	Sir William Matthews, H. McKinnon Wood, Legal Advisor
USA	H. Elting, Jr.

M. P. Ruegger, Swiss Minister in London, represented Switzerland, and Adrian Pelt, an Assistant Secretary-General, represented the Secretary-General.

Action

On 5 March 1946, the Negotiating Committee had completed its work of negotiating a preliminary agreement with the Directors of the Carnegie Foundation for the use of the premises in the Peace Palace at The Hague, and issued its report jointly with the Secretary-General on 17 October 1946 (GAOR, Sess.I, Part 2, Sixth Committee, annex 21, A/109).

In accordance with resolution 21 (I), adopted by the General Assembly at its 28th plenary meeting, on 10 February 1946, the conditions set out in this agreement were to be embodied in an agreement subject to the approval of the General Assembly. The Committee also met with representatives of the Swiss Federal Council at Berne, Switzerland, on 4 April 1946, concerning interim arrangements on the privileges and immunities of the United Nations in Switzerland, and then proceeded to Geneva where final texts of the Agreement on the Ariana site (headquarters of the League of Nations) and on the Interim Arrangement on privileges and immunities of the United Nations in Switzerland were approved by the Committee and by the Swiss Delegation; both were temporary, and permanent arrangements were to be made at a later date. The report on these arrangements (Ibid., annex 17, A/175) was issued on 4 November 1946. Annex III of the report contained the final act, and annex IV the minutes of the five meetings held on 4,5,6 and 19 April 1946. The Interim Arrangement was approved by General Assembly resolution 98 (I), at the 65th plenary meeting, on 14 December 1946.

B. United Nations Headquarters and Offices

<u>Interim Committee for the Selection of a Definite Site for the Permanent Headquarters of the United Nations (A/ICH)</u>

Established by the Preparatory Commission of the United Nations on 20 December 1945.

Terms of Reference

The Interim Committee should:

(a) establish the qualifications and standards for the choice of the site for the permanent headquarters of the United Nations in the light of the criteria set forth in Section 2 of Chapter I of the Report of the Executive Committee (PC/EX/113/Rev.1) and of the decision to locate the permanent headquarters in the east of the United States;

(b) examine the material which had so far been received, in the light of the qualifications and standards mentioned above;

(c) eliminate from consideration those cities and localities which did not satisfy the established qualifications and standards;

(d) receive new offers and, whenever it felt it desirable, invite deputations or suggest additional cities and localities on its own initiative;

(e) inspect, at its discretion, any cities or areas before making its final selection;

(f) report on a list of not more than six cities or areas, as early as possible during the first part of the first session of the General Assembly.

Membership

The Interim Committee was composed of the following members:

Paul Hasluck (Australia); Shuhsi Hsu (China); Dr. Ernesto Dihigo (Cuba); François Brière (France); Sayid Awni Khalidy (Iraq); Adrian Pelt (Netherlands); E. Sobolewski (Poland); Professor Vsevolod N. Durdenevsky (USSR); Sir Charles Webster (UK); Roberto E. MacEachen (Uruguay), Chairman; Julio A. Lacarte Muró (Uruguay); and Dr. Stoyan Gavrilović (Yugoslavia), Rapporteur.

The report of the Permanent Headquarters Committee, published on 24 January 1947, included a list of the members.

Action

The terms of reference and the activities of the Interim Committee were reported on 14 February 1946 (GAOR, Sess.I, Part 1, Plenary Meetings, annex 29, A/58/Rev.1).

The summary records of the Interim Committee meetings were included in the same volume as those of the Permanent Headquarters Committee (GAOR, Sess.1, Part 1, I. Permanent Headquarters Committee, Summary Record of Meetings: 2-14 February 1946; II. Interim Committee for the Selection of a Site for the Permanent Headquarters of the United Nations, Summary Record of Meetings, 22 December 1945--5 February 1946), published on 24 January 1947.

The Interim Committee set up an Inspection Group on 27 December 1945 to inspect and report on proposed sites in the United States. The report of the Inspection Group included its

composition and terms of reference (Ibid., annexes 1, 2, 3, A/Site/2 and Add.1, 2, 3).

Assembly resolution 25 (I), of 14 February
1946, approved the recommendations of the Interim Committee as reported by the Permanent
Headquarters Committee.

<u>Negotiating Committee on Negotiations with the
Authorities of the United States of America
concerning the Arrangements required as a result of the Establishment of the Seat of the
United Nations in the United States of America</u>

Established by Assembly resolution 22 B (I), of
13 February 1946.

Terms of Reference

Paragraph 1 of the resolution authorized the
Secretary-General to negotiate (with the assistance of a committee), with the competent
authorities of the United States of America,
the arrangements required as a result of the
establishment of the seat of the United Nations
in the United States of America.

The resolution suggested that the Secretary-
General use as a basis in these negotiations
the draft convention annexed to the resolution.

It also stated that any agreement apart from
purely temporary agreements with the competent
authorities of the United States resulting from
these negotiations should be subject to approval by the General Assembly before being signed
on behalf of the United Nations.

Membership

The resolution designated the following States
and requested their governments to appoint a
representative:
    Australia, Belgium, Bolivia, China,
    Cuba, Egypt, France, Poland, United
    Kingdom, and USSR.

Their representatives were: K. H. Bailey (Australia), Joseph Nisot (Belgium), G. Salamanca (Bolivia), Shuhsi Hsu (China), G. Belt (Cuba), Mahmoud Bey Fawzi (Egypt), J. Cahen-Salvador (France), A. Rudzinski (Poland), V. F. Tepliakov (USSR), H. McKinnon Wood (UK).

Action

At its first meeting on 15 May 1946, the Negotiating Committee elected Mr. Bailey (Australia) as Chairman. On his being obliged to return to Australia, A. H. Body acted as the Australian member, and H. McKinnon Wood (UK) was elected Chairman. The Secretary-General was represented throughout the negotiations by Ivan Kerno, Assistant Secretary-General in charge of Legal Affairs, assisted by A. Feller, General Counsel and Director of the Legal Department, and Marc Schreiber, Legal Adviser, who acted as secretary to the United Nations delegation.

The joint report of the Secretary-General and the Negotiating Committee (GAOR, Sess. I, part 2, Sixth Committee, annex 25, A/67, and Add.1), was issued on 1 September (Add. 1 on 4 September) 1946. Appendix I of the report contained the text of the working draft of the Convention/Agreement between the United Nations and the United States of America. Add. 1 contained appendix III to the report: the opinion of 20 August 1946 of the Acting Attorney-General of the United States regarding the effectiveness of the proposed Headquarters Agreement.

Assembly resolution 99 (I), of 14 December 1946, having decided that the permanent headquarters of the United Nations should be located in the City of New York (A/67 and Add.1), and recognizing that any agreement with the USA relating to the permanent headquarters would need to be adapted to the circumstances of this site, authorized the Secretary-General to negotiate and conclude with the appropriate authorities of the USA an agreement concerning the arrangements required as a result; and further, that in negotiating this agreement the Secretary-General should be guided by the provisions of the draft agreement set forth in document A/67.

Permanent Headquarters Committee (A/SITE/-)

The question of the site of the permanent headquarters of the United Nations was considered
by the Executive Committee of the Preparatory
Commission of the United Nations, the full Preparatory Commission, the Interim Committee for
the Selection of a Definite Site for the Permanent Headquarters of the United Nations, and
its Inspection Group, and finally by the General Assembly of the United Nations, at the
first part of the first session, held in London
from 10 January to 14 February 1946. In the
course of these discussions, the location of
the site was narrowed down to the region of
Westchester and Fairfield counties in the states
of New York and Connecticut, respectively, in
the United States of America, and it was left
to the Headquarters Commission to recommend
five different sized sites within these counties.

Upon the recommendation of the General Committee, the General Assembly at its 18th plenary
meeting, on 26 January 1946, established, in
resolution 26 (I), a Permanent Headquarters
Committee.

Terms of Reference

The Committee would "consider the question of
the site of the permanent headquarters of the
United Nations", pursuant to chapter X of the
report of the Preparatory Commission (PC/20).
Upon recommendation of the General Committee
(GAOR, Sess.I, Part I, Plenary Meetings, annex
28, A/57), the Assembly, at its 33rd plenary
meeting on 14 February 1946, changed the terms
of reference to read "to consider the site of
the permanent and temporary headquarters of the

United Nations and other matters directly connected therewith".

Membership

The Committee was created as a Committee of the
Whole, all Member States having the right to be
represented. A list of participants was included in the reports of the Committee published on 24 January 1947, and 26 November 1947.

Action

The Committee elected the following officers:
Chairman: Dr. Eduardo Zuleta Ángel (Colombia);
Vice-Chairman: L.D. Wilgress (Canada); Rappor-
teur: Nasrollah Entezam (Iran).

On the basis of the recommendations of the Preparatory Commission and its Interim Committee,
the Permanent Headquarters Committee recommended, and the General Assembly, at its 33rd plenary meeting on 14 February 1946, adopted resolution 25 (I) establishing a Headquarters Commission to deal with the problem.

The report of the Permanent Headquarters Committee (Ibid., Plenary Meetings, annex 29, A/
58/Rev.1), issued on 14 February 1946, reported
on the activities of the Interim Committee. Assembly resolution 25 (I), of 14 February 1946,
approved the recommendations of the Interim Committee as presented by the Permanent Headquarters Committee.

The summary records of the Permanent Headquarters Committee meetings for the first session were included in the same volume, published on 24 January 1947, as those of the Interim
Committee (GAOR, Sess.I, Part I, I: Permanent

Headquarters Committee, Summary Record of Meetings, 2-14 February 1946; II: Interim Committee for the Selection of a Site for the Permanent Headquarters of the United Nations, Summary Record of Meetings, 22 December 1945 - 5 February 1946), which also contained the report and recommendations of the Inspection Group established by the Interim Committee (annexes 1, 2, 3, A/SITE/2 and Add.1, 2, 3).

The Permanent Headquarters Committee met again at Lake Success, New York, from 7 November to 13 December 1946 (GAOR, Sess.I, Part 2, Permanent Headquarters Committee, Summary Record of Meetings, 7 November - 13 December 1946), published on 26 November 1947. At its meeting on 14 November, the Committee appointed a Sub-Committee consisting of the Chairman, Vice-Chairman and Rapporteur of the Permanent Headquarters Committee, and representatives of Australia, Belgium, Bolivia, China, Cuba, Egypt, France, Iraq, Netherlands, Poland, USSR, United Kingdom, United States of America, Uruguay, and Yugoslavia. Its functions were (1) to consider the relative merits of alternative sites for permanent headquarters in the New York area (including the Westchester-Fairfield areas), the San Francisco Bay area, the Boston area, and the Philadelphia area, which might be available without cost or at reasonable cost; (2) to report to the Permanent Headquarters Committee the results of its deliberations, together with its specific recommendation as to the site or sites it considered most appropriate, in ample time for debate by the Permanent Headquarters Committee and its report to the General Assembly; (3) to take such steps as might be necessary for the effective discharge of the foregoing functions, including the study and inspection of sites under consideration. The report of Sub-Committee 1 (Ibid., annex 7, A/SITE/Sub.1/3) was issued on 13 December 1946.

At the meeting of 11 December, the Committee set up a small sub-committee (Sub-Committee 2) to study the offer of John D. Rockefeller, Jr., concerning the purchase of a site in Manhattan (Ibid., annex 9, A/SITE/50) to inspect the site, and to report the following day. Sub-Committee 2 consisted of the members of the Permanent Headquarters Committee and the representative of the United States of America. Its report (Ibid., annex 10, A/SITE/Sub.2/1) appeared on 12 December 1946.

The report on the activities of the Permanent Headquarters Committee (GAOR, Sess.II, Plenary Meetings, annex 79, A/277) was issued on 13 December 1946.

A check list of documents of the Permanent Headquarters Committee, its sub-committees and the Interim Committee (A/SITE/53, mimeographed) was issued on 27 June 1947.

Headquarters Commission (A/HQC/-)

Established by Assembly resolution 25 (I), of
14 February 1946, on the recommendation of the
Permanent Headquarters Committee.

Part I of the resolution was repealed by paragraph 6 of resolution 100 (I), of 14 December
1946.

Terms of Reference

The Headquarters Commission was to carry out
the tasks entrusted to it under Part I of the
resolution, that is, to proceed to the regions
mentioned in the first paragraph, to make an
exhaustive study and to make recommendations
to the General Assembly at the second part of
the first session regarding the exact location
to be selected. The Commission was also to
ascertain what measures the federal, state and
county authorities of the United States of
America were prepared to take in order to control development in the territory adjacent to
the zone selected. Part II of the resolution
stated that the interim headquarters of the
United Nations should be located in New York
City.

Membership

Part III (a) of the resolution designated the
following members, listed herewith with their
representatives:

Australia	Paul Hasluck, J.C. Moore
China	Kien-Wen Yu
France	Charles Le Corbusier
Iraq	Awni Khalidy
Netherlands	Jonkheer Jan de Ranitz

USSR	Nikolai D. Bassov
United Kingdom	Sir Angus Fletcher
Uruguay	Juan Felipe Yriart
Yugoslavia	Dr. Stoyan Gavrilović, Alexander Franić

Chapter I of the report contained a list of members and representatives.

Action

The Headquarters Commission held 38 plenary meetings from 7 May 1946. Sir Angus Fletcher (UK) was elected as Chairman; and Dr. Stoyan Gavrilović (Yugoslavia) as Vice-Chairman. To facilitate its work, the Commission establish-ed five sub-committees: (a) Committee on Re-quirements, (b) Sites and General Questions Committee, (c) Contacts and Legal Committee, (d) Film Committee, and (e) Drafting Committee. The membership of these committees was given in annex 2 of the report.

The Report of the Headquarters Commission (GAOR, Sess. I, part 2, A/69) issued in October 1946, as a separate document. It contained chapters on criteria for selection of sites, method of in-vestigation of sites, information on five sites, special legal, financial and administrative problems arising from the acquisition of any site, considerations of policy which might as-sist the General Assembly in determining the size of the headquarters site. There were 25 annexes containing a variety of pertinent information, a photographic section and a map section.

Headquarters Advisory Committee (A/AC.7/-
and 22/-, restricted series)

Established by Assembly resolution 100 II (I),
of 14 December 1946, which also repealed Part
I of resolution 25 (I), of 14 February 1946,
and reconstituted by resolution 182 (II), of
20 November 1947.

Terms of Reference

Part I of the resolution accepted the offer,
subject to stated terms and conditions, of John
D. Rockefeller, Jr., of a sum of money making
it possible to acquire a tract of land in New
York City in the area bounded by First Avenue,
East 48th Street, the East River and East 42nd
Street. Part II requested the Secretary-General to prepare recommendations with respect to
the matters set forth below pertaining to the
establishment of the permanent headquarters.
He was further requested to prepare a report
on these matters to be distributed to the Members of the United Nations on or before 1 July
1947 for consideration at the next regular session of the General Assembly on:
     (a) general plans and requirements for
official buildings and other necessary facilities;
     (b) arrangements for accomodations, hous-
ing developments and related facilities, on or
off the site, for personnel of the Secretariat,
specialized agencies and national delegations
and their staffs, and for the families of
such personnel;
     (c) approximate costs of construction
and development;
     (d) financial and other arrangements;
     (e) any other matters pertaining to the
development of the site which the Secretary-
General felt the General Assembly should con-

sider at its next regular session.

Reconstituted by paragraph 5 of resolution
182 (II), in which, desiring to proceed as
rapidly as possible with the construction of
the permanent headquarters in accordance with
Assembly resolution 100 (I), of 14 December
1946, noting with satisfaction the letter of
29 October 1947 from the USA to the Secretary-
General (GAOR, Sess.II, Ad Hoc Committee on
Headquarters,(Summary Records of Meetings, annex
2, A/AC.15/7), stating that the Government of
the United States was prepared to enter into
negotiations with the Secretary-General to conclude a loan agreement for the purpose of financing the cost of construction of the United
Nations Headquarters. The Assembly approved
the general plan and design set forth in the
report of the Secretary-General (GAOR, Sess.II,
Suppl. 8, A/311; Sales no.:1947.1.10), and
authorized the Secretary-General to negotiate
and conclude, on behalf of the United Nations,
a loan agreement; to receive and expend, or
direct the expenditure of, the sum borrowed;
to proceed with the construction and furnish-
ing of the General Assembly building, conference area and Secretariat building; to enter
into appropriate arrangements with the United
States Government, the State and City of New
York, with regard to easements, public services,
sub-surface facilities, the approaches to the
site, the vehicular traffic, water front and
pier rights, and similar matters. In carrying
out his responsibilities, the Secretary-General
would be assisted by an Advisory Committee; and
report to the third regular session of the
General Assembly.

Membership

The resolution named the following countries as members of the Advisory Committee:

Australia, Belgium, Brazil, Canada, China, Colombia, France, Greece, India, Norway, Poland, Syria, USSR, United Kingdom, United States of America, and Yugoslavia.

Their representatives and alternates were as follows:

C.V. Kellway (Australia), Roland Lebeau (Belgium), Henrique de Souza-Gómez (Brazil), C.D. Howe and Hugh D. Scully (Canada), Dr. C.L. Hsia and K.W. Yu (China), Dr. Edmundo de Holte-Castello and Dr. Eduardo Zuleta Ángel (Colombia), Guy de la Tournelle (France), Vassili Dendramis (Greece), M.J. Vesugar (India), Finn Moe (Norway), Juliusz Katz-Suchy (Poland), Toufik Humeidi and Rafik Asha (Syria), N.D. Bassov (USSR), V.G. Lawford and P.S. Falla (UK), Warren R. Austin and John C. Ross (USA), and Dr. Stoyan Gavrilović (Yugoslavia).

The resolution also provided for consultants and experts who, at the request of the Secretary-General, should be designated by the Government of the United States of America, or by Governments of other Member States, or local authorities.

Paragraph 5 of resolution 182 (II) designated the following as members of the reconstituted Advisory Committee:

Australia, Belgium, Brazil, Canada, China, Colombia, France, Greece, India, Norway, Poland, Syria, USSR, United Kingdom, USA, and Yugoslavia.

The representatives and alternates of the members were the following:

C.V. Kellway, J.D.L. Hood, H.G. Marshall (Australia); Roland Lebeau, Luc Steyaert, Andre Wendelsen, Robert Fenaux (Belgium); Henrique de Souza-Gómez, Henrique Rodríguez Valle, Carlos Frederico Duarte, Luiz Bastian-Pinto (Brazil); C.D. Howe, Hugh D. Scully (Canada); Dr. C.L. Hsia, Dr. Cheng Poanan, H.C. Kiang (China); Dr. Edmundo de Holte-Castello, Hernando Semper Gomez, Eduardo Carrizosa (Colombia); Guy de la Tournelle, Yves Pierre-Benoist (France); Alexis Kyrou, Byron Theodoropoulos, Stavros G. Roussos (Greece); Dr. P.P. Pillai, S. Sen, S. Dharman, Dr. B. Rajan (India); Finn Moe, Arne Sunde, Finn Seyersted, Erik Nord (Norway); Juliusz Katz-Suchy, Aleksander Rudzinski, Dr. Stefan Baratynski (Poland); Rafik Asha, Rashid Kabbani (Syria); V.I. Kobushko, Nicolai F. Paisov, A.S. Poliansky (USSR); H.A. Cooper, R.T. Callender, S.G. Yorston (UK); Warren B. Austin (USA); Misa Levi, Andjelko Blaževič, Ratko Pleič (Yugoslavia).

Lists of members and representatives were published in the printed reports referred to below under "Action".

The following resolutions reaffirmed the existence and membership of the Headquarters Advisory Committee: 242 (III), 18 November 1948; 350 (IV) 24 November 1949; 461 (V), 12 December 1950; 589 (VI), 2 February 1952. The Advisory Committee did not meet after the year 1952.

Action

At the first meeting on 6 January 1947, of the Advisory Committee, Warren B. Austin (USA), was

elected as Chairman. At various times in the
organization and progress of the work, the
members of the Advisory Committee were called
upon for advice on matters of policy and administration.

A report of the Secretary-General (GAOR, Sess.
II, Suppl.8 (A/311)) was published in July
1947. It contained a report on the activities
of the Advisory Committee in 1947 and a list
of its members and their representatives; as
well as lists of New York City authorities, of
Board of Design consultants, of associate
architects and engineers, of special consultants, consulting engineers, the staff of the
Headquarters Planning Office. It contained
information on the fulfillment of all conditions necessary for the final acquisition of
the site, and on the organization of the planning work on a basis that would assure construction in the shortest possible time. Annexes included a letter and memorandum from
John D. Rockefeller, Jr., to the Permanent
Headquarters Committee (A/SITE/50); resolution
adopted by the Board of Estimate of the City of
New York, 13 December 1946; letter from the
Secretary-General to the Mayor of the City of
New York, 22 March 1947; and letter from the
Mayor of the City of New York to the Secretary-
General, 17 June 1947.

A report on comparative cost estimates of revised plans (A/311/Add.1/Rev.1, mimeographed),
of 6 November 1947; a report on the perspective
design studies of the Permanent Headquarters of
the United Nations (A/311/Add.2), and plans of
revised scheme (A/311/Add.3), were issued as
separate documents.

The reconstituted Advisory Committee held 15
meetings from 6 January 1948 to 1 October 1952.

On 16 February 1948, the Advisory Committee issued a report (A/AC.22/1) entitled "Planning the Permanent Headquarters of the United Nations: A Short Summary 1948" which contained a list of members and representatives of the reconstituted Advisory Committee, repeated the lists of those involved in the planning and construction of the permanent headquarters; and a historical summary from 1945 to 1948.

A report issued on 8 September 1948 (GAOR, Sess. III, Part I, Plenary Meetings, Annexes, agenda item 13, A/627) contained, as an annex, the text of the loan agreement between the United States Government and the United Nations.

The progress reports of the Secretary-General were the following:
    A/1009 (GAOR, Sess. IV, Fifth Committee, Annexes, vol.1, agenda item 36) of 7 October 1948. The Advisory Committee held four meetings during 1949;
    A/1392/Rev.1 (GAOR, Sess.V, Annexes, agenda item 56), 26 September 1950. The Advisory Committee held one formal meeting;
    A/1895, Corr.1 and Add.1 (GAOR, Sess.VI, Annexes, agenda item 46), 5 October 1951. The Advisory Committee held three formal meetings in 1951 and one on 7 January 1952, when it considered the Secretary-General's report and endorsed his draft resolution.

Further reports were requested of the Secretary-General in resolutions: 663 (VII), 25 November 1952; 780 (VIII), 9 December 1953; and 877 (IX), 12 December 1954. Pursuant to these requests, the following reports were issued:
    A/2209 (GAOR, Sess.VII, Annexes, agenda item 47), 2 October 1952;
    A/2544 (GAOR, Sess. VIII, Annexes, agenda

item 41), 5 November 1953;

A/2778 (GAOR, Sess.IX, Annexes, agenda item 40), 29 October 1954);

A/2948 (GAOR, Sess.X, Annexes, agenda item 41), 30 August 1955.

Resolution 969 (X), of 15 December 1955, took note of the report and the comments thereon of the ACABQ (Ibid., A/2997), of 17 October 1955; and requested the Secretary-General to make no further commitments against the Permanent Headquarters Construction Account after 31 August 1953.

Ad Hoc Committee on Headquarters (A/AC.15/-)

Established by the General Assembly at plenary
meeting 90, on 23 September 1947, to consider
item 13 of the agenda for the second session --
the report of the Secretary-General on the headquarters of the United Nations (GAOR, Sess.II,
Suppl.8 (A/311)), and A/311/Add.1 and Add.2 -3,
issued separately)-- on the recommendation of
the General Committee (Ibid., Plenary Meetings,
vol.2, annex 1, A/392, paragraph 2 (a)), of 22
September 1947.

Terms of Reference

The ad hoc committee was to report to the General Assembly on questions of general design,
plans and requirements for official buildings
and other necessary facilities, while questions
of cost and financial arrangements should be
referred by the ad hoc committee to the Fifth
Committee for report to the General Assembly.

Membership

The General Committee recommended that the ad
hoc committee should consist of members of the
Advisory Committee on Headquarters set up under
the terms of resolution 100 (I), of 14 December
1946, as follows:
Australia, Belgium, Brazil, Canada,
China, Colombia, France, Greece, India,
Norway, Poland, Syria, USSR, United
Kingdom, United States of America, and
Yugoslavia.

The representatives of Member States were as
follows: H.V. Evatt (Australia), Roland Lebeau
(Belgium), Henrique de Souza-Gómez (Brazil),
Norman P. Lambert (Canada), Dr. C.L. Hsia

(China), Dr. Julio César Turbay (Colombia),
Guy de la Tournelle (France), Alexis Kyrou
(Greece), Dr. P.P. Pillai (India), Finn Moe
(Norway), Juliusz Katz-Suchy (Poland), Rafik
Asha (Syria), Alexei A. Roschin (USSR), H.A.
Cooper (UK), Warren B. Austin (USA), Misa
Levi (Yugoslavia).

The officers of the Ad Hoc Committee, elected
at the first meeting, were: Warren B. Austin
(USA) as Chairman; Finn Moe (Norway) as Vice-
Chairman; and Alexis Kyrou (Greece) as Rapporteur.

Action

The summary records of the five meetings held
by the Ad Hoc Committee from 24 September to 13
November 1947 were published in January 1949
(GAOR, Sess.II, Ad Hoc Committee on Headquarters), as a separate document, which contained a list of members and their representatives, and texts of pertinent documents of the
Ad Hoc Committee (A/AC.15/2,3,4,7, and 8) as
annexes.

At the same meeting, the Committee heard a
statement by Robert Moses, Coordinator of Construction for the City of New York, and a detailed report from Wallace K. Harrison, Director of Planning, on the architectural and
engineering plan s. The Committee report (GAOR,
Sess.II, Plenary Meetings, vol.2.annex 9, A/
485) was issued on 18 November 1947. Its recommendations to the General Assembly were adopted
in resolution 182 (II), of 20 November 1947.

The report of the Fifth Committee on costs and financing (Ibid., annex 9a, A/486) was issued on 18 November 1947.; and the report of the Sixth Committee on the agreement between the United Nations and the United States of America regarding the headquarters of the United Nations (Ibid., annex 9b, A/427) was issued on 29 October 1947.

Ad Hoc Committee on Building (Geneva)

Established by Assembly resolution 2891 (XXVI), of 22 December 1971, on recommendation of ACABQ (GAOR, Sess. XXVI, Suppl.8A (A/8408/Add.10, paragraph 23)) in order that the Secretary-General might have the advantage of more regular and more frequent guidance during the remaining stages of the program to modernize the Palais des Nations in Geneva.

The modernization of the Palais des Nations had been an ongoing project since 1956, when the Secretary-General in a report (GAOR, Sess.XI, Annexes, agenda item 43, A/C.5/659, and Add.1), of 9 July 1956 and 1 February 1957, submitted a plan for the improvement of the installations in the Palais necessary to meet present requirements and those of the foreseeable future. The possibility of financing the program through a loan from a source external to the Organization was suggested by an ACABQ report (Ibid., A/3379 and Add.1) of 2 November 1956 and 12 February 1957. The General Assembly, in resolution 1101 (XI), of 27 February 1957, approved the program of modernization, and authorized the Secretary-General to accept the offer of a loan from the Swiss Federal Government, and to proceed with the execution of the program.

Progress reports of the Secretary-General and comments thereon by ACABQ, and General Assembly resolutions which noted the reports and in general accepted their recommendations were as follows:
A/C.5/775, 22 June 1959 (GAOR, Sess. XIV, Annexes, agenda item 44); ACABQ report, 22 July 1959 (Ibid., A/4157); Assembly resolution 1447 (XIV), 5 December 1959, approved revisions in

the program for modernization of the Palais des
Nations, and authorized the Secretary-General
to proceed with execution of the program, and
to keep the ACABQ informed of developments in
the progress of the modernization program.

A/C.5/877, 14 September 1961 (GAOR, Sess.
XVI, Annexes, vol.2, agenda item 54); ACABQ report, 10 December 1961 (Ibid., A/4918); resolution 1737 (XVI), 20 December 1961.

A/C.5/982, 26 September 1963 (GAOR, Sess.
XVIII, Annexes, vol.2, agenda item 58); ACABQ
report (Ibid., A/5600), 6 November 1963.

A/C.5/1009, 23 October 1964 (GAOR, Sess.XX,
Annexes, vol.2, agenda item 76); ACABQ report
on an inquiry into the conference facilities
and major maintenance of the Palais des Nations
(Ibid., A/5799), 27 November 1964.

A/C.5/1040, 11 November 1965 (Ibid.) report
on developments concerning conference facilities in the Palais for 1963 and 1964; ACABQ report (Ibid., A/6137), 4 December 1965.

A/C.5/1054, 26 July 1966 (GAOR, Sess.XXI,
Annexes, vol.3, agenda item 74); ACABQ report
(Ibid., A/6385), 5 August 1966; resolution 2246
(XXI), 20 December 1966, expressed gratitude to
the Swiss Government for its cooperation, as-
sistance, and offer of a gift of 4 million
Swiss francs toward the cost of the project.

A/C.5/1076, 28 October 1966 (Ibid.); ACABQ
report (Ibid., A/6524/, 22 November 1966; resolution 2246 (XXI), 20 December 1966, established a special account in which all funds
made available for the project of the extension
of the Palais would be deposited.

A/C.5/1179, 21 October 1968 (GAOR, Sess.
XXIII, Annexes, agenda item 74) on extension
of the Palais; ACABQ report (Ibid., A/7337), 18
November 1968. A/C.5/1189, 14 November 1968
(Ibid.) on maintenance; ACABQ report (Ibid.,
A/7367). Resolution 2488 (XXIII), 21 December
1968.

A/C.5/1245 and 1248, 30 October 1969
(GAOR, Sess. XXIV, Annexes, vol.2, agenda item
74) on maintenance, improvements and extension
of the Palais; ACABQ reports (Ibid., A/7767),
14 November 1969.

A/C.5/1331 and 1332, 16 November 1970
(GAOR, Sess. XXV, Annexes, vol.2, agenda item
73); ACABQ report (Ibid., Suppl.8A (A/8008/
Add.8 and Corr.1, paragraph 30)), 30 November
1970. At its 20th session, in 1964, the Assembly had approved a program of major maintenance of and improvements to the Palais to be
undertaken during the period 1966 to 1974 (GAOR,
Sess.XX, Annexes, vol.2, agenda item 76, A/6223),
21 December 1965. In 1970, the General Assembly approved some additions to the program, and
requested the Secretary-General to submit annual progress reports on implementation of the
program (Ibid., Sess.XXV, Annexes, vol.2, agenda
item 73, A/8099, paragraph 114), 7 December
1970 ; resolution 2744 (XXV), 17 December 1970.

The reports of the Secretary-General, of
29 October 1971, on the extension of the Palais
des Nations and on the program of major maintenance and improvements there, respectively,
were reproduced in Budget Estimates for the
Financial Year 1972 - Revised Estimates (GAOR,
Sess. XXVI, Suppl. 6B (A/8406/Add.2)), pp. 76-
91, 92-101. These reports and the report of
the ACABQ (Ibid., Suppl.8A (A/8408/Add.1-30)),
document A/8408/Add.10, of 23 November 1971,
were the basis for Assembly resolution 2892
(XXVI), of 22 December 1971.

At the twenty-seventh session of the General Assembly, the Secretary-General reported
(A/C.5/1445, paragraph 3, of 3 October 1972,
offset) that an ad hoc Committee on Buildings
had been set up in Geneva.

Membership

The ad hoc Committee was comprised of the representatives of Belgium, France, Ghana, Japan, Mexico, USSR, United Kingdom, and United States of America.

Terms of Reference

The Committee would give the Secretary-General more frequent and more regular guidance during the remaining stages of the Palais des Nations project. Such a committee might meet on an informal basis to review the progress of work and to advise the Secretary-General on any special problems, particularly those which might have a bearing on the cost estimates currently before the Assembly.

Action

The ad hoc Committee held its first meeting on 14 April 1972, and met regularly every month since, advising on all matters within its terms of reference.

A progress report by the Secretary-General (A/C. 5/1512, offset) was issued under agenda item 79 on 6 August 1973. A further report (A/C.5/1518, offset) was issued under agenda item 79 on 13 August 1973, indicating the status, as of 30 June 1973, of the construction and financing of the extension of the Palais des Nations as authorized by resolutions 2480 (XXIII), 21 December 1968; 2744 (XXV), 17 December 1970; and 2891 (XXVI), 22 December 1971.

The Secretary-General transmitted to the General Assembly by note of 24 September 1973 the report on office accomodation for the United Nations staff at Geneva submitted by the Joint Inspection Unit (JIU) (JIU/REP/73/2). The ACABQ's comments on the report were contained in a note of 8 October 1973 (A/9164, Add.1, offset).

The Assembly, at its 220th meeting on 18 December 1973, took note of the reports of the Secretary-General concerning the program of modernization of the Palais, and approved the recommendations of the ACABQ report to the twenty-eighth session of the General Assembly (GAOR, Sess. XXVIII, Suppl.8A (A/9008/Add.1-34), document A/9008/Add. 2, of 19 October 1973) which considered the reports of the Secretary-General on United Nations accomodation at New York, Geneva and other locations (A/C.5/1510, A/C.5/1511 and Add.1), and the reports on major maintenance and extension of the Palais des Nations A/C.5/1512, A/C.5/1518, and Corr. 1-2), and the JIU report cited above.

C. Host Country Relations

USUN-NYC Host Country Advisory Committee

Initiated by the United States Mission to the
United Nations (USUN) and announced as of 8
February 1967, to assist the United States Mission, the City of New York, and cooperating
non-governmental organizations, in carrying
out their responsibilities as host to the United Nations.

Terms of Reference

In announcing the Committee's formation in
February, 1967, Ambassador Goldberg of the United States Mission described its purposes as
follows:

"Having just completed an intensive study
("Problems facing United Nations' Diplomats in
New York City Today", by Louis Harris, April
1966) of the structure and functions of the
principal agencies rendering these services
(active host country responsibilities), I am
concerned with the risk of breakdowns in the
performance of our hostship functions because
of the lack of coordination and communication
among the agencies in the field. There are
areas where I think more effective action can
be taken. An objective and continuing review
of the entire program is needed to assure maximum effectiveness in carrying out these responsibilities. To this end, we have decided, in
consultation with Mayor Lindsay, to establish
a USUN-NYC Host Country Advisory Committee".

It was intended that the Advisory Committee
would explore questions of broad policy, assist

in mapping out action programs, and serve as a consultant and coordinator with respect to agencies functioning at the operational level. Selected problem areas to be considered by the Advisory Committee were housing, education, public relations, as some of the problems encountered by the diplomatic community.

Membership

In addition to the Mayor, representing the City, and Ambassador Goldberg, and later Ambassador Charles Yost, representing the US Mission, the Committee included: Constantin A. Stavropoulos, UN Under-Secretary and Legal Counsel, as the representative of the Secretary-General, and five distinguished citizens of the New York community who would serve as public members of the board. They were: Harding F. Bancroft, Executive Vice-President of The New York Times, and a member of the United States Delegation to the 21st session of the General Assembly; Dr. Kenneth B. Clark, a psychologist, who was President of the Metropolitan Applied Research Center; David L. Guyer, Vice-President, Institute of International Education, and a former member of the United Nations Secretariat and of the US Mission to the United Nations; Christopher H. Phillips, President, US Council of the International Chamber of Commerce, and former US Representative to the United Nations Economic and Social Council, and Deputy Assistant Secretary of State; and Lawrence A. Wien, an attorney and real estate investor and senior partner in the law firm of Wien, Lane, Klein and Malkin.

Dr. Clark resigned from the Committee on 8 May 1967, due to his inability to fulfill his responsibilities as a member, and was replaced on 5 June by James R. Dumpson, Dean of the School of Social Service at Fordham University, New York.

Former Ambassador Arthur J. Goldberg (USA) joined the Committee as a public member in January 1970.

Christopher H. Phillips (USA) resigned in February 1970, upon assumption of his duties as Deputy Permanent Representative in the United Nations Mission to the United Nations.

Dean Dumpson (USA) resigned on 10 March 1970, having undertaken several special projects for the Mayor of New York City.

Mrs. Jean Picker, United States Representative on the United Nations Commission for Social Development, joined the Committee as of 26 May 1970.

Action

The first meeting of the Advisory Committee was held at the US Mission to the United Nations on 27 February 1967. Ambassador Arthur J. Goldberg, Permanent Representative to the United Nations, and Mayor John V. Lindsay, Mayor of the City of New York, served as Co-Chairmen.

The second and third meetings of the Advisory Committee were held at Gracie Mansion, official residence of the Mayor, on 14 April and 28 September 1967. A fourth meeting, held on 27 November 1967 at the headquarters of the New York City Commission, discussed present and projected programs in the area of consumer and life-style education.

In 1968, meetings were held on 11 March at Gracie Mansion, and on 24 July at the US Mission.

Further meetings were held on 2 February 1970 at the New York City Hall; on 11 March 1971 at Gracie Mansion, and on 3 May 1971 at the US Mission.

A reception for the New York business, civic and media leaders was held at the US Mission to meet the new US Ambassador to the United Nations, George Bush, and Mayor John D. Lindsay, on 20 April 1971.

Ernest M. Howell (USA) was appointed Executive Director of the Advisory Committee, and served through 30 June 1967. Upon his resignation, he was succeeded by Miss Sarah H. Goddard (USA), who was appointed as of 1 September 1969.

The Advisory Committee had functioned in three major ways since its inception:
     1.   as a forum to discuss problems and develop solutions, the implementation of which was then assumed by the appropriate agency;
     2.   as a coordinative body, tripartite in structure, able to facilitate coordination among hostship agencies;
     3.   as a conduit of financial assistance in agencies involved in an operational capacity.

Top priority was assigned to the critical area of housing. The Foundation for the Improvement of Housing for Foreign Diplomatic Personnel, Inc., was created as an inducement to the real estate community to make rentals available to the United Nations community. Housing services within the United Nations Secretariat were consolidated into one office.

The Executive Director of the Advisory Committee chaired Bi-Weekly Working Group meetings for senior staff of agencies concerned with operational host responsibilities. Through meetings

of this group and representatives of the Training Service of the Secretariat, it became clear
that there existed inadequate English language
instruction for wives of United Nations diplomatic personnel. The Advisory Committee, therefore, proposed that an English language assistance program for United Nations and Consular
Corps' wives be organized independent of any
existing program. The program, entitled H.E.L.
P. (Hospitality Extension Language Program)
commenced in the fall of 1970 and was adminis-
tered by a consultant in conjunction with the
Hospitality Committee.

In conjunction with the Bi-Weekly Working
Group, the Advisory Committee also put out a
monthly calendar listing the activities being
planned by hostship agencies.

No documents were issued by the Advisory Committee.

Informal Joint Committee on Host Country Relations (A/AC.146/-)

The Informal Joint Committee had been originally established by the United Nations in 1966, largely at the behest of the United States Mission to the United Nations, and following consultations with the Chairmen of the regional groups at the United Nations.

The Committee was reconstituted by paragraph 7 of Assembly resolution 2618 (XXIV), of 17 December 1969. It was superseded by the Committee on Relations with the Host Country, established by resolution 2819 (XXVI), of 15 December 1971.

Terms of Reference

The terms of reference of the original Committee approved by the Committee at its first meeting on 6 April 1966 were:

The Committee would serve as an informal deliberation body or organ of consultation, to help avoid or resolve problems relating to the status of representatives of Members of the United Nations through the exchange of views and the use of good offices. It would deal both with questions by members of Missions relating to their privileges and immunities and with questions relating to obligations of members of Missions, whether contractual or otherwise. While any problem within the broad context of Host Country relations may be brought before the Committee, it was not intended that the Committee would replace the present channels of direct contact between the Permanent Missions and the United States Mission in the handling of day-to-day problems. Wherever feasible, particular cases would continue to be dealt with directly between the Host Country and the Permanent Mission concerned.

The work of the Committee would be in the context of the applicable Articles of the United Nations Charter, the Headquarters Agreement between the United Nations and the United States of America, general principles of international law and comity as well as relevant provisions of national law.

The establishing resolution (resolution 2618 (XXIV)) requested the Secretary-General to reconstitute and convene on a regular basis the Informal Joint Committee on Host Country Relations, so that there would be a continuous interchange of views and exploration of problems between the diplomatic community, the Secretariat and the host Government on matters of mutual interest, and to report the results thereof to the General Assembly at its twenty-fifth session and annually thereafter.

Resolution 2747 (XXV), of 17 December 1970, recommended that the Informal Joint Committee undertake a systematic consideration of the implementation of the Convention on the Privileges and Immunities of the United Nations and the Agreement between the United Nations and the United States of America regarding the Headquarters of the United Nations (resolution 169 (II)), of 31 October 1947, as well as conditions of life and obligations of members of Permanent Missions to the United Nations. It also requested the Secretary-General, in consultation with the Informal Joint Committee, to report in a comprehensive manner to the General Assembly at its twenty-sixth session on the status of the work of the Committee with particular reference to the extent to which existing problems had been solved.

Membership

At the first meeting on 6 April 1966 of the original committee, it was agreed that the Informal Joint Committee should have a tripartite character, being composed of representatives of the Permanent Missions, of the Host Country and of the Secretariat. It was further agreed that for reasons of convenience, the geographic distribution of members of the Permanent Missions would follow that of the Security Council. Thus, in addition to the United States as host country, the Committee would be composed of the other four permanent members of the Security Council, five African and Asian States, one Eastern European State, two Latin-American States, and two Western European and Other States (Secretary-General's third person note, LE 312/1, 13 April 1970).

Pursuant to a request of the Secretary-General for assistance in reconstituting the Informal Joint Committee, the Chairman of the regional groups consulted their respective groups and informed the Secretary-General of the names of the Permanent Missions which would represent their respective groups for the current year. Accordingly, in addition to the United States as Host Country, and the other permanent members of the Security Council (China, France, United Kingdom, USSR), the membership in 1970 was as follows: African States: Cameroon, Liberia, Libya; Asian States: Cyprus, India; Eastern European States: Bulgaria; Latin-American States: Bolivia, Guyana; Western Europe and Other States: Canada, Spain.

In 1971, the membership remained the same except that Iraq took the place of India in the Asian group.

In addition to the Secretary-General as Chairman, the Secretariat was represented by the Chef de Cabinet, the Legal Counsel, and the Chief of Protocol.

It was envisaged that the representatives designated by the regional groups would report to their respective groups and inform them of matters dealt with by the Informal Joint Committee. In turn, they would also inform the Informal Joint Committee of the reactions of their respective groups concerning these matters and of any suggested items which the groups desired to have taken up by the Committee.

Meetings

The General Assembly, in resolution 2747 (XXV), 17 December 1970, requested the Secretary-General to convene the Informal Joint Committee in January 1971 and thereafter as frequently as appropriate in order that it might be in a position to examine carefully the matters specified in the terms of reference, and seek solutions to problems which fell within the broad context of relations with the Government of the host country.

The resolution authorized the Committee to maintain and circulate summary records of its proceedings.

Action

During 1966 and 1967, the Committee held seven meetings from 6 April 1966 to 20 April 1967. During this period, meetings were of an informal nature and only brief minutes of the proceedings were kept. No meetings were held in 1968 and 1969.

The Secretary-General convened the initial meeting of the newly constituted Committee on 17 April 1970; and further meetings were held on 23 April, 22 May, 2 June, 21 September and 15 October 1970. The Secretary-General's report (GAOR, Sess.XXV, Annexes, vol.2, agenda item 73, A/C.5/1319) was issued on 21 October 1970.

During the course of its meetings, the Committee had begun a preliminary examination of the following subjects: housing for diplomatic personnel and for Secretariat staff, parking of diplomatic vehicles, public relations in the host city, privileges and immunities generally and related topics, protection of permanent missions and their staff, education and health, insurance.

On 15 October 1970, the Committee was convened on the basis of a letter from the Permanent Mission of Libya, on behalf of the permanent missions of the Arab States, requesting an urgent meeting of the Committee "to consider the question of the recent threats of bombings to permanent missions of Arab States, and the protection of these missions and their staff". The representative of the host country reviewed for the Committee the various steps which were being taken by the appropriate authorities in respect of protection in general and of recent incidents in particular.

The Committee decided at its meeting on 23 February 1971 that the Chairman should establish a working group on organization of the Committee's work after consultations regarding the composition of such a group. On 10 March 1971, the Working Group, consisting of the representatives of Guyana, Iraq, Liberia, Spain, United Kingdom, USSR, and the USA, met with the Legal

Counsel. The Group noted that the aim of the Committee, as expressed in operative paragraph 2 of resolution 2747 (XXV), was to seek solutions to problems which fell within the broad context of relations with the host country. It was therefore agreed that the Committee should organize its work in such a way as not only to give expression to the problems facing the United Nations community and the host country, but also to achieve progress toward the practical solution of those problems. The Working Group further recommended that the Committee set up one or more small but representative working groups to study and report back to the Committee on parking facilities for diplomatic vehicles and on housing facilities for the personnel of permanent missions and of the Secretariat. In view of the importance of the question of protection of permanent missions and their staff, the Working Group agreed it should remain under continuous consideration by the Committee as a whole and should be a standing item on the agenda.

At the meeting on 31 March 1971, the Committee adopted the suggestion to appoint a working group to study questions of parking and housing facilities, and decided its composition would be of the same members who had attended the Working Group on the organization of work.

During 1971, the Committee held eight meetings; the Working Group on organization of work held one meeting; the Working Group on parking and housing facilities held two meetings and submitted two interim reports, dated 14 May and 23 June, to the Committee.

The Secretary-General's report on the work of the Committee in 1971 (A/8474, offset) under agenda item 86, was issued on 10 October 1971. It contained chapters on protection of permanent missions and their staff, transportation, housing, studies on privileges and immunities, public relations of the United Nations community in the host city; and an annex which contained the membership, terms of reference and procedure of the Committee. In his general remarks, the Secretary-General considered the Committee, with its informal tripartite character, had provided a useful forum for discussion of the different problems faced by the United Nations community in New York City. He stated that the problems confronting the Committee were not amenable to easy resolution, but, nevertheless, with the continued examination by the Committee of these problems and of other issues which the Committee had not yet studied in depth, that improvements might be expected.

Committee on Relations with the Host Country
(A/AC.154/-)

Established by paragraph 5 of resolution 2819
(XXVI), of 15 December 1971.

Terms of Reference

The Committee was to deal with the question of
the security of missions and the safety of their
personnel, as well as all the categories of issues previously considered by the Informal Joint
Committee on Host Country Relations. The Committee was authorized to study the Convention on
the Privileges and Immunities of the United
Nations and to consider, and advise the host
country on, issues arising in connection with
the implementation of the Agreement between the
United Nations and the United States of America
regarding the Headquarters of the United Nations.

The Committee was authorized to have summary records of its meetings, and to convene on a periodic basis and whenever it was convoked by its
Chairman at the request of any State Member of
the United Nations or of the Secretary-General.

The Committee was requested to submit a report
to the twenty-seventh session of the General Assembly on the progress of the work and to make,
if it deemed necessary, appropriate recommendations. Resolution 3033 (XXVII), of 18 December
1972, requested the Committee to report to the
twenty-eighth session of the General Assembly on
the progress of its work.

Resolution 3107 (XXVIII), of 12 December 1973,
decided to continue the work of the Committee
in 1974, in conformity with resolution 2819
(XXVI), with the purpose of examining on a more

regular basis all matters falling within its terms of reference; and requested a report to the twenty-ninth session of the Assembly.

Membership

The Committee was composed of the host country and 14 Member States to be chosen by the President of the General Assembly, in consultation with regional groups and taking into consideration equitable geographic representation thereon.

On 21 December 1971, at the 2029th plenary meeting, the President announced the appointment of 14 States which, together with the United States of America, would comprise the Committee, as follows:

Argentina, Bulgaria, Canada, China, Cyprus, France, Guyana, Iraq, Ivory Coast, Mali, Spain, Tanzania, USSR, United Kingdom.

Argentina (A/9436, offset) and Guyana (A/9437, offset) resigned from the Committee as of 1 January 1974. At the 2201st plenary meeting, on 14 December 1973, the President announced that, after consultation, he had decided to appoint Costa Rica and Honduras to fill the vacancies.

Action

At the first meeting of the Committee, on 28 December 1971, Zenon Rossides (Cyprus) was elected as Chairman; and at its third meeting, on 7 February 1972, Simeon Ake (Ivory Coast), Mrs. Elena Gavrilova (Bulgaria), and A.J. Matheson (Canada) were elected as Vice-Chairmen; and D.E. Pollard (Guyana) as Rapporteur. The Committee report (GAOR, Sess. XXVII, Suppl. 26, (A/8726)), issued in September 1972, was divided into four parts: I dealt with the membership, terms of reference and organization of work of the Committee; II dealt with particular aspects of the Committee's work; III covered general aspects of the Committee's work; IV contained the Committee's recommendations. During the period, 28 December 1971 to 9 August 1972, the Committee held a total of 15 meetings.

The Chairman, on 20 June 1972, submitted a working paper proposing that two working groups be established: Working Group I to examine, from a general standpoint, the question of the security of missions and the safety of their personnel; and II to deal with various specific topics listed in item 2 of the Committee's list of subjects, set out in paragraph 1 of the document "Organization of work" (A/AC.154/L.8, mimeographed). At its 11th meeting, on 23 June 1972, the Committee decided that questions relating to the security of missions and safety of their personnel should continue to be dealt with by the Committee as a whole, and that a Working Group should be set up to consider the various specific items contained in item 2 of the Committee's list of subjects.

The Committee's officers in 1973 were: Chairman: Zenon Rossides (Cyprus); Vice-Chairmen: Guero Grozev (Bulgaria), A.J. Matheson (Canada), and Simeon Ake (Ivory Coast); and Rapporteur: Lionel Samuels (Guyana), and later, Joseph A. Sanders (Guyana). During the period under review the Committee held eight meetings. Its report (GAOR, Sess. XXVIII, Suppl.26 (A/9026, and Corr.1)) was issued in November 1973, and included the two reports of the Working Group as annexes.

I. Working Group

At its 11th meeting, on 23 June 1972, the Committee established a Working Group.

Terms of Reference

The Working Group was requested to examine the 11 topics listed in paragraph 1, item 2 of the document entitled "Organization of work" of the Committee as follows:

(a) Comparative study of privileges and immunities;

(b) obligations of permanent missions and individuals protected by diplomatic immunity;

(c) exemption from taxes levied by states other than New York;

(d) possibility of establishing at United Nations Headquarters a commissary to assist diplomatic personnel as well as staff;

(e) housing for diplomatic personnel and for Secretariat staff;

(f) transportation;

(g) insurance;

(h) the public relations of the United Nations community in the host city; question of encouraging the mass media to publicize the functions and status of permanent missions;

(i) education and health;

(j) question of provision of an identity document for members of the family of diplomatic personnel (also to include the question of provision of an identity document for non-diplomatic staff of missions);

(k) acceleration of customs procedures.

At the 13th meeting of the Committee, on 28 July 1972, a proposal was adopted to add an additional item entitled "entry visas issued by the host country".

Membership

The Committee decided that the Working Group should consist of representatives of the following countries:
  Bulgaria, Guyana, Mali, Spain, Tanzania, United Kingdom, and the United States of America.

Action

At the second meeting, on 27 July 1972, the Working Group elected Ambassador Jaime Alba (Spain) as Chairman, and Lionel Samuels (Guyana) as Vice-Chairman.

The first report of the Working Group (A/AC. 154/L.45) was issued on 26 April 1973. The Group had met on 6 and 27 July, 3 August 1972, and on 16 March, 13 and 24 April 1973. The annex contained a "Program of information measures directed to the local community".

The Working Group continued its work in 1973 with the same membership and the same officers. It held five meetings and submitted its report on the progress of its work (A/AC.154/L.53) on 28 August,1973. Both reports were reproduced as annex I and II in the report of the Committee (A/9026, and Corr.1).

Chapter XIII

INTERNATIONAL LAW AND OTHER LEGAL
PROBLEMS

A. Development, Codification and Promotion of
International Law

Committee on the Progressive Development of
International Law and its Codification
(1947)

International Law Commission (1949--)

Special Committee on Technical Assistance
to Promote the Teaching, Study, Dissemination and Wider Appreciation of International
Law (1964-1965)

Advisory Committee on the United Nations
Programme of Assistance to the Teaching,
Study, Dissemination and Wider Appreciation
of International Law (1966--)

United Nations Commission on International
Trade Law (1957--)

B. Question of Defining Aggression

Special Committee on the Question of Defining Aggression (1954)

1956 Special Committee on the Question of
Defining Aggression (1956-1957)

Special Committees on the Question of Defining Aggression (1958-1974)

C. <u>Special Legal Problems</u>

Committees on International Criminal Jurisdiction (1951 and 1953)

Preparatory Group of Experts to advise the Secretary-General on Preparation of a Conference on the Law of the Sea (1957)

Special Committee on Principles of International Law concerning Friendly Relations and Cooperation among States (1964-1970)

Register of Experts on Methods of Fact-Finding (1968-1970)

Ad Hoc Committee on International Terrorism (1973--)

INTERNATIONAL LAW AND OTHER
LEGAL PROBLEMS

A. Development, Codification and
Promotion of International Law

Committee on the Progressive Development of International Law and its Codification (A/AC.10/-)

Established by Assembly resolution 94 (I), of
11 December 1946, which recognized the obliga-
tion laid upon the General Assembly by Article
13, paragraph 1 (a), of the Charter, to initiate
studies and to make recommendations for the purpose of encouraging the progressive development
of international law and its codification.

Terms of Reference

The resolution directed the Committee to study:
(a) the methods by which the General Assembly
should encourage the progressive development of
international law and its eventual codification;
(b) methods of securing the cooperation of the
several organs of the United Nations to this
end; (c) methods of enlisting the assistance of
such national or international bodies as might
aid in the attainment of this objective; and to
report to the General Assembly at its next regular session.

Membership

The resolution established a Committee of 17
members to be appointed by the General Assembly
on the recommendation of the President, each of
these members to have one representative on the

Committee; and at the same plenary meeting, the 55th, on 11 December, the Assembly appointed the following States to serve on the Committee: Argentina, Australia, Brazil, China, Colombia, Egypt, France, India, Netherlands, Panama, Poland, Sweden, USSR, United Kingdom, United States of America, Venezuela, Yugoslavia.

The following representatives attended the meetings of the Committee: Dr. Enrique Ferrer Vieyra, Dr. Rodolfo Muñoz (Argentina); Dr. W.A. Wynes, A.H. Body (Australia); Gilberto Amado (Brazil); Dr. Shushi Hsu (China); Dr. Antonio Rocha, Dr. Jorge Ortiz Rodríguez, Dr. Alberto Gonzáles Fernández, Professor Jesús M. Yepes (Colombia); Osman Ebeid (Egypt); Professor Henri Donnedieu de Vabres, Michel Leroy-Beaulieu (France); Sir Dalip Singh (India); Dr. J.G. de Beus (Netherlands); Roberto de la Guardia (Panama); Dr. Alexander Rudzinski, Dr. Alexander Bramson (Poland); Erik Szoborg (Sweden); Professor Vladimir Koretsky (USSR); Professor J.L. Brierly (UK); Professor Philip C. Jessup (USA); Dr. Carlo Eduardo Stolk, Dr. Victor M. Pérez-Perozo (Venezuela); Professor Milan Bartoš (Yugoslavia).

Action

The Committee met from 12 May to 17 June 1947. At the first meeting, the officers elected were: Chairman: Sir Dalip Singh (India); Vice-Chairmen: Dr. Antonio Rocha (Colombia), and Professor Vladimir Koretsky (USSR); Rapporteur: Professor J.L. Brierly (UK).

The report of the Committee (GAOR, Sess.II, Sixth Committee Meetings, Annex 1, A/331 and Corr.1) was issued on 18 July 1947. Resolution 174 (II), of 21 November 1947, on the recommendation of the Committee established an International Law Commission.

International Law Commission (ILC) (A/CN.4/-)

Established by General Assembly resolution 174 (II), of 17 November 1947, and generally referred to herein as ILC or "the Commission".

The International Law Commission was established as a permanent body with its own Statute. This characteristic has been at the root of the selection made by the Commission in 1949 of a list of topics for codification, as well as the decisions taken by the Commission from time to time concerning its program and the planning of its future work. It is, however, a subsidiary organ of the General Assembly, and the constitutional and, in the final analysis, operational dependency of the Commission results from the fact that, being embodied in a resolution of the General Assembly, the Commission's Statute can be amended or revoked only by the General Assembly. Also, the General Assembly considers annually the Commission's report and adopts recommendations and instructions regarding the Commission's work. (Working paper prepared by the Secretariat on the review of the Commission's program and methods of work, annex to the ILC report (GAOR, Sess.XXIII, Suppl.9, A/7209/Rev.1, Yearbook of the International Law Commission 1968, vol.II, pp. 226-243).

In preparation for its first session in 1949, a number of studies were published by the United Nations Secretariat, and submitted by the Secretary-General:
Survey of International Law in relation to the Work of Codification of the International Law Commission. Preparatory work within the purview of article 18, paragraph 1, of the Statute of the ILC (A/CN.4/1/Rev.1, 10 February 1949, Sales no.:1948.V.I (1)).

Preparatory Study concerning a Draft Declaration on the Rights and Duties of States (A/CN. 4/2, 15 December 1948, Sales no.: 1949.V.4).

The Charter and Judgment of the Nürnberg Tribunal-History and Analysis (A/CN.4/5, 3 March 1949, Sales no.:1949.V.7).

Ways and Means of Making the Evidence of Customary International Law More Readily Available. Preparatory work within the purview of article 24 of the Statute of the ILC (A/CN.4/6, 7 March 1949, Sales no.:1949.V.6).

Historical Survey of the Question of International Criminal Jurisdiction (A/CN.4/7/Rev.1, September 1949, Sales no.:1949.V.8).

Terms of Reference

The Commission has for its object the promotion of the progressive development of international law and its codification. It is primarily concerned with public international law, but is not precluded from entering the field of private international law. The Commission reports to the General Assembly.

The statute of the International Law Commission was attached to the establishing resolution, and published in February 1962 in a document (A/CN.4/4/Rev.1, Sales no.:62.V.2) which gave the amendments to the original text, and symbols and dates of General Assembly resolutions containing those amendments.

Subsequent resolutions of the General Assembly enlarged the task of the ILC, as follows:
Resolution 177 (II), 21 November 1947, decided to entrust the formulation of international law recognized in the charter of the Nürnberg Tribunal and in the judgment of the Tribunal to the ILC, to (a) formulate the principles of

international law recognized in the Charter of
the Nürnberg Tribunal and in the judgment of
the Tribunal, and (b) prepare a draft code of
offences against the peace and security of mankind, indicating clearly the place to be ac-
corded to the principles cited above.

Resolution 178 (II), 21 November 1947, instructed the ILC to prepare a draft declaration
on the rights and duties of States, taking as a
basis of discussion the draft declaration on
the rights and duties of States presented by
Panama (A/285 and Corr.1, published in A/CN.4/
2, Sales no.:1949.V.4, part III) of 15 January
1947, and taking into consideration other documents and drafts on the subject.

Resolution 260 B (III), 9 December 1948, requested the ILC to study the desirability of
establishing an international judicial organ
for the trial of persons charged with genocide,
and to the possibility of establishing a Criminal Chamber of the International Court of
Justice.

Resolution 374 (IV), 6 December 1949, noted the
ILC decision (GAOR, Sess.IV, Suppl.10 (A/2163)),
to give priority to the following three topics:
law of treaties, arbitral procedure, regime of
the high seas, and recommended that it include
the topic of the regime of territorial waters
in its list of priorities.

Resolution 375 (IV), of 6 December 1947, annexed to the resolution the text of the draft declaration on rights and duties of States prepared by the ILC (Ibid., paragraph 46). Resolution 596 (VI), of 7 December 1951, decided to
postpone consideration of the draft declaration
until a sufficient number of States had transmitted their comments and suggestions.

Resolution 478 (V), of 16 November 1950, invited the ILC to study the question of reservations to multilateral conventions both from the point of view of codification and from that of the progressive development of international law.

Resolution 685 (VII), 5 December 1952, requested the ILC to undertake the codification of the topic "Diplomatic intercourse and immunities", as a priority topic.

Resolution 799 (VIII), 7 December 1953, requested the ILC to undertake the codification of the principles of international law governing State responsibility.

Resolution 899 (IX), of 14 December 1954, noting that the ILC report (GAOR, Sess.VIII, Suppl. 9 (A/2456)) had submitted draft articles on the continental shelf, requested the ILC to complete its work on the study of the régime of the high seas, the régime of territorial waters and all related problems, and to submit its final report to the General Assembly at its eleventh session.

Resolution 1289 (XIII), 5 December 1958, taking note of paragraphs 51 and 52 of the ILC report on the work of its 10th session (GAOR, Sess. XIII, Suppl.9 (A/3859, and Corr.1)), invited the ILC to give further consideration to the question of relations between States and inter-governmental international organizations, after study of diplomatic intercourse and immunities, consular intercourse and immunities and ad hoc diplomacy had been completed by the United Nations.

Resolution 1400 (XIV), 21 November 1959, recalling that the ILC at its first session had in-

cluded the right of asylum in the provisional
list of topics of international law selected
for codification, requested the ILC to undertake the codification of the principles and
rules of international law relating to the
right of asylum. Resolution 2312 (XXII), 14
December 1967, adopted text of the "Declaration
on Territorial Asylum", as annexed to the resolution.

Resolution 1453 (XIV), 7 December 1959-- recalling that, by a resolution adopted on 27 April
1958, the United Nations Conference on the Law
of the Sea (GAOR, vol.II: Plenary Meetings, annexes, A/CONF.13/L.36, resolution VII, Sales no.
58.V.4, Vol.II), requested the General Assembly
to arrange for the study of the juridical régime
of historic waters, including historic bays --
requested the ILC to undertake such a study, and
to make such recommendations regarding the matter as the Commission deemed appropriate.

Resolution 1687 (XVI), of 18 December 1961 --
noting the resolution on special missions
adopted by the UN Conference on Diplomatic Intercourse and Immunities at its fourth plenary
meeting, held on 10 April 1961, recommended
that the subject be referred again to the ILC
(GAOR, Sess. XVI, Annexes, agenda item 71, A/
4773, paragraph 1) requested ILC to study further the subject of special missions and to report thereon to the General Assembly.

Resolution 1903 (XVIII), 18 November 1963, recalling resolution 1766 (XVII), 20 November 1962
and having considered the question of extended
participation in general multilateral treaties
concluded under the auspices of the League of
Nations and the ILC report thereon (GAOR, Sess.
XVIII, Suppl. 9 (A/5509, chapter III)), decided

that the General Assembly was the appropriate
organ of the United Nations to exercise the
power conferred by multilateral treaties of a
technical and non-political character on the
Council of the League of Nations to invite
States to accede to those treaties.

Resolution 2166 (XXI), of 5 December 1966, having considered chapter II of the ILC report on
its 18th session (GAOR, Sess.XXI, Suppl.9 (A/
6309/Rev.1)), which contained final draft
articles and commentaries on the law of treaties, decided to convene an international conference of plenipotentiaries. The first session of the UN Conference on the Law of Treaties
was held at the Neue Hofburg, Vienna, from 26
March to 24 May 1968; the second session from
9 April to 22 May 1969. The report of the Conference was issued in three volumes: First session, Official Records, Summary records (A/CONF.
39/11, Sales no.:68.V.7); Second session, Official Records, Summary records (A/CONF.39/11/Add.
1, Sales no.:70.V.6); First and second sessions,
Official Records, Documents of the Conference
(A/CONF.39/11/Add.2, Sales no.:70.V.5). The
last volume contained inter alia the Final Act
of the Conference (with an annex containing the
declarations and resolutions adopted by the
Conference), and the text of the Vienna Convention on the Law of Treaties.

Resolution 2501 (XXIV), 12 November 1969, recommended the ILC should study, in consultation
with the principal international organizations,
the question of treaties concluded between
States and international organizations or between two or more international organizations,
as an important question.

Resolution 2530 (XXIV), 8 December 1969, having
considered the final draft articles on special

missions in chapter II of the ILC report of its
19th session (GAOR, Sess.XXII, Suppl.9 (A/6709/
Rev.1 and Corr.1)), adopted and opened for sig-
nature and ratification two instruments, the
texts of which were annexed to the resolution:
Convention on Special Missions, and Optional
Protocol concerning the Compulsory Settlement
of Disputes.

Resolution 2669 (XXV), 8 December 1970, recalling resolution 1401 (XIV), of 21 November 1959,
on the desirability of initiating preliminary
studies on the legal problems relating to the
utilization and use of international rivers,
and as a result of which useful legal material
was collected in the report submitted by the
Secretary-General on 15 April 1963 (A/5409,
vols. 1-3, published in ILC Yearbook 1974, vol.
II, part two, Sales no.:E.75.V.7 (Part II))re-
commended that the ILC should, as a first step,
take up the study of the law of the non-naviga-
tional uses of international watercourses with
a view to its progressive development and codification.

Resolution 2780 (XXVI), 3 December 1971, in
part III, requested the ILC to study the question of the protection and inviolability of
diplomatic agents and other persons entitled
to special protection under international law,
with a view to preparing a set of draft articles
dealing with such offences.

Resolution 2966 (XXVII), 14 December 1972, recalling resolution 2780 (XXVI) in which the Assembly noted that the ILC had adopted a final
set of draft articles as the basis of a convention on the representation of States in their
relations with international organizations, decided that an international conference of plenipotentiaries should be convened to consider the

draft articles. Assembly resolution 3072 (XXVIII), 30 November 1973, authorized the decision. The United Nations Conference on the Representation of States in Their Relations with International Organizations met at the Neue Hofburg in Vienna, Austria, from 4 February to 14 March 1975. Its Final Act, together with the resolutions adopted by the Conference and annexed to it, (ACONF.67/15) was issued on 14 March 1975; and the text of the "Vienna Convention on the Representation of States in Their Relations with International Organizations of a Universal Character" (A/CONF.67/16) was published on 14 March 1975.

Resolution 3166 (XXVIII), 14 December 1973, recalling resolution 2780 (XXVI), of 3 December 1971, and having considered the draft articles of the ILC on the protection and inviolability of diplomatic agents and other persons entitled to special protection under international law (GAOR, Sess.XXVII, Suppl.10 (A/8610/Rev.1, chapter III, section B)), adopted the Convention on the Prevention and Punishment of Crimes against Internationally Protected Persons, including Diplomatic Agents, text of which was annexed to the resolution.

Seat
    Article 12 of the ILC Statute designated the European Office of the United Nations at Geneva as the official seat of the Commission, which, however, would have the right to hold meetings at other places after consultation with the Secretary-General.

Meetings held at other sites are indicated in the list of sessions below.

Membership

Articles 2 to 11 of the ILC Statute deal with
the membership of the Commission. The members
of the Commission are elected by the General
Assembly from a list of candidates nominated by
the Governments of States Members of the United
Nations. No two members of the Commission may
be nationals of the same State. In the case of
a casual vacancy, the ILC fills the vacancy,
having due regard to the provisions of articles
2 and 8 of the Statute which deal with nationality and qualifications of the members elected.

Originally there were 15 members elected for a
three-year term. Assembly resolution 486 (V),
of 12 December 1950, extended the term of office
for the members elected in 1948 from three to
five years. Resolution 985 (X), of 3 December
1955, lengthened the term of office from three
to five years. Resolution 1103 (XI), of 18 December 1956, enlarged the Commission from 15 to
21 members; and resolution 1647 (XVI), of 6
November 1961, further increased its membership
to 25 members, at which it has remained since
that time. Members are eligible for reelection.

Following is a list of members from 1948 to
1973, giving the date of election and length
of service:

Plenary meetings 154-155, 3 November 1948
to serve to 31 December 1951 - extended to
31 December 1953
_____

    Ricardo J. Alfaro (Panama)
    Gilberto Amado (Brazil)
    James L. Brierly (UK)
    Roberto Córdova (Mexico)
    J.P.A. François (Netherlands)

Shuhsi Hsu (China)
Manley O. Hudson (USA)
Faris Bey el-Khoury (Syria)
Vladimir M. Koretsky (USSR)
Sir Benegal N. Rau (India)
A.E.F. Sandström (Sweden)
Georges Scelle (France)
Jean Spiropoulos (Greece)
Jesús M. Yepes (Colombia)
Jaroslav Zourek (Czech)

At its fourth session in 1952, the Commission elected F.I. Kozhevnikov (USSR), H. Lauterpacht (UK), and Radhabinod Pal (India) to fill the vacancies caused by the resignations of James L. Brierly (UK), Vladimir M. Koretsky (USSR) and Sir Benegal N. Rau (India).

Plenary meetings 453-454, 23 October 1953
to serve to 31 December 1956

Gilberto Amado (Brazil)
Roberto Córdova (Mexico)
Douglas L. Edmonds (USA)
J.P.A. François (Netherlands)
F.V. García-Amador (Cuba)
Shuhsi Hsu (China)
Faris Bey el-Khoury (Syria)
S.B. Krylov (USSR)
H. Lauterpacht (UK)
Radhabinod Pal (India)
Carlos Salamanca (Bolivia)
A.E.F. Sandström (Sweden)
Georges Scelle (France)
Jean Spiropoulos (Greece)
Jaroslav Zourek (Czech)

Mr. Edmonds (USA) was elected on 28 June 1954 by the ILC to fill the vacancy caused by the resignation of John J. Parker (USA) who had been elected by the General Assembly.

Sir Gerald Fitzmaurice (UK) and Luis Padilla
Nervo (Mexico) were elected members by the Commission on 9 and 16 May 1955, respectively, to
fill the vacancies caused by the resignations
of H. Lauterpacht (UK) and R. Cordova (Mexico).

Plenary meeting 623, 18 December 1956
to serve to 31 December 1961 (21 members)

Roberto Ago (Italy)
Gilberto Amado (Brazil)
Milan Bartos (Yugoslavia)
Douglas L. Edmonds (USA)
Abdullah El-Erian (Egypt)
Sir Gerald Fitzmaurice (UK)
J.P.A. François (Netherlands)
F.V. García-Amador (Cuba)
Shuhsi Hsu (China)
Thanat Khoman (Thailand)
Faris Bey el-Khoury (Syria)
Ahmed Matine-Daftary (Iran)
Luis Padilla Nervo (Mexico)
Radhabinod Pal (India)
A.E.F. Sandström (Sweden)
Georges Scelle (France)
Jean Spiropoulos (Greece)
Grigory I. Tunkin (USSR)
Alfred Verdross (Austria)
Kisaburo Yokota (Japan)
Jaroslav Zourek (Czech)

On 30 April 1958, the Commission elected Ricardo
J. Alfaro (Panama) to fill the casual vacancy
caused by the resignation of Jean Spiropoulos
(Greece). On 2 June 1958, Abdullah El-Erian
(UAR) resigned, stating that, having regard to
the provision in article 2, paragraph 2, of the
ILC Statute no two members shall be nationals of
the same State (Faris Bey el-Khoury now represented the UAR).

On 1 May 1959, the Commission elected Nihat Erim (Turkey) to fill the casual vacancy caused by the resignation of Mr. El-Erian during the previous session.

On 16 May 1960, the Commission elected Eduardo Jiménez de Aréchaga (Uruguay) to fill the casual vacancy caused by the election of Ricardo J. Alfaro (Panama) to the International Court of Justice; and also elected Mustafa Kamil Yasseen (Iraq) to fill the casual vacancy caused by the resignation of Thanat Khoman (Thailand).

On 2 May 1961, the Commission elected André Gros (France), Senjin Tsuruoka (Japan), and Sir Humphrey Waldock (UK), to fill the vacancies caused by the death of Georges Scelle (France), the resignation of Kisaburo Yokota (Japan), and the election of Sir Gerald Fitzmaurice to the International Court of Justice.

Plenary meeting 1067, 28 November 1961
to serve to 31 December 1966 (25 members)

    Roberto Ago (Italy)
    Gilberto Amado (Brazil)
    Milan Bartoš (Yugoslavia)
    Herbert W. Briggs (USA)
    Marcel Cadieux (Canada)
    Erik Castrén (Finland)
    Abdullah El-Erian (UAR)
    Taslim O. Elias (Nigeria)
    André Gros (France)
    Eduardo Jiménez de Aréchaga (Uruguay)
    Victor Kanga (Cameroon)
    Manfred Lachs (Poland)
    Liu Chieh (China)
    Antonio de Luna (Spain)
    Luis Padilla Nervo (Mexico)
    Radhabinod Pal (India)
    Angel M. Paredes (Ecuador)

Obed Pessou (Dahomey)
Shabtai Rosenne (Israel)
Abdul Hakim Tabibi (Afghanistan)
Senjin Tsuruoka (Japan)
Grigory I. Tunkin (USSR)
Alfred Verdross (Austria)
Sir Humphrey Waldock (UK)
Mustafa Kamil Yasseen (Iraq)

On 12 May 1964, the Commission elected Paul
Reuter (France) and José María Ruda (Argentina)
to fill the vacancies which had arisen in conse-
quence of the election of André Gros (France)
and Luis Padilla Nervo (Mexico) as judges of
the International Court of Justice.

On 18 May 1965, the Commission elected Mohammed
Bedjaoui (Algeria) to fill the vacancy due to
the resignation of Victor Kanga (Cameroon).

Plenary meeting 1460, 10 November 1966
to serve to 31 December 1971
Roberto Ago (Italy)
Fernando Albónico (Chile)
Gilberto Amado (Brazil)
Milan Bartoš (Yugoslavia)
Mohammed Bedjaoui (Alberia)
Jorge Castañeda (Mexico)
Erik Castrén (Finland)
Abdullah El-Erian (UAR)
Taslim O. Elias (Nigeria)
Constantin Th. Eustathiades (Greece)
Louis Ignacio-Pinto (Dahomey)
Eduardo Jiménez de Aréchaga (Uruguay)
Richard D. Kearney (USA)
Magendra Singh (India)
Alfred Ramangasoavina (Madagascar)
Paul Reuter (France)
Shabtsi Rosenne (Israel)
José María Ruda (Argentina)

Abdul Hakim Tabibi (Afghanistan)
Arnold J.P. Tammes (Netherlands)
Senjin Tauruoka (Japan)
Nikolai Ushakov (USSR)
Endre Ustor (Hungary)
Sir Humphrey Waldock (UK)
Mustafa Kamil Yasseen (Iraq)

On 21 May 1970, the Commission elected José Sette Câmara (Brazil), Gonzalo Alcívar (Ecuador), and Doudou Thiam (Senegal) to fill the vacancies caused by the death of Gilberto Amado (Brazil), and by the resignations of Eduardo Jiménez de Aréchaga (Uruguay) and Louis Ignacio-Pinto (Dahomey) on their election to the International Court of Justice.

Plenary meeting 1986, 17 November 1971 to serve to 31 December 1976

Roberto Ago (Italy)
Gonzalo Alcívar (Ecuador)
Milan Bartoš (Yugoslavia)
Mohammed Bedjaoui (Algeria)
Suat Bilge (Turkey)
Jorge Castañeda (Mexico)
Abdullah El-Erian (Egypt)
Taslim O. Elias (Nigeria)
Edvard Hambro (Norway)
Richard D. Kearney (USA)
Nagendra Singh (India)
Robert Quentin-Baxter (NZ)
Alfred Ramangasoavina (Madagascar)
Paul Reuter (France)
Zenon Rossides (Cyprus)
José María Ruda (Argentina)
José Sette Câmara (Brazil)
Abdul Hakim Tabibi (Afghanistan)
Arnold J.P. Tammes (Netherlands)
Doudou Thiam (Senegal)
Senjin Tsuruoka (Japan)

Nikolai Ushakov (USSR)
Endre Ustor (Hungary)
Sir Humphrey Waldock (UK)
Mustafa K. Yasseen (Iraq)

On 15 May 1973, the Commission elected Juan
José Calle y Calle (Peru), Alfredo Martínez
Moreno (El Salvador), C.W. Pinto (Sri Lanka),
and Sir Francis Vallat (UK) to fill the vacan-
cies caused by the death of Gonzalo Alcívar
(Ecuador), and by the resignations of Nagendra
Singh (India), José María Ruda (Argentina), and
Sir Humphrey Waldock (UK) on their election to
the International Court of Justice.

Action

At its first session, in 1949, the Commission
reviewed, on the basis of a Secretariat memorandum of 10 February 1969 entitled <u>Survey of
International Law in relation to the Work of
Codification of the International Law Commission</u>
(A/CN.4/1/Rev.1, Sales no.:48.V.I (1)), 25 topics for possible inclusion in a list of topics
for study. The Commission drew up a list of 14
topics selected for codification, which was
provisional and subject to change in compliance
with the wishes of the General Assembly. At its
23rd session, in 1971, the Commission had before
it a working paper, entitled <u>Survey of International Law</u>, prepared by the Secretary-General
(A/CN.4/245, ILC <u>Yearbook 1971</u>, vol.II (part
two), Sales no.:E.72.V.6 (Part II)). At its
25th session, the Commission, in chapter VI of
its report (<u>GAOR</u>, Sess.XXVIII, <u>Suppl.10</u> (A/9010/
Rev.1)), <u>Yearbook 1973</u>. vol.II, Sales no.:E.74.
V.5) reviewed its long-term program of work in
the light of the Secretary-General's working

paper cited above, and the work of the Commission during the first 25 sessions; and concluded that, in accordance with previous decisions of the Commission, endorsed by the General Assembly, the Commission would, for some years, have ample work to do to complete consideration of the five topics upon which it was then actively engaged, namely:

1. Succession of States in respect of treaties;
2. State responsibility;
3. Succession of States in respect of matters other than treaties;
4. The most-favored-nation clause;
5. The question of treaties concluded between States and international organizations or between two or more international organizations.

Methods of Work

The Commission appoints (from its membership), as necessary, special rapporteurs for individual topics, provided they remain members of the Commission. Each special rapporteur prepares substantive reports on the topic entrusted to him, containing draft articles where appropriate, and submits them to the Commission for consideration. In addition to that major responsibility the special rapporteur drafts other working documents of both the Commission and its Drafting Committee, as required by the Commission's progress of work on the topic. The Commission submits final drafts of the special rapporteur's work to the General Assembly with its recommendations as to the action desired.

Since its first session, the Commission has made use of a Drafting Committee, which, in recent years, has been composed in principle of eleven members, presided over by the First Vice-Chairman. The general Rapporteur also takes

part in the Drafting Committee's work, and the
special rapporteurs participate when their
topics are being considered.

In addition, the Commission has made use of
relatively small working groups or sub-committees, on particular topics. For instance, during the years 1962-1963, two sub-committees were
set up for the purpose of considering what plan
the Commission should follow in dealing with
the topics of state responsibility and succession of States and Governments. During 1970-
1971, a sub-committee on treaties concluded between States and international organizations or
between two or more international organizations
was entrusted with the task of considering preliminary problems involved in the study of this
topic. On 25 May 1971, the Commission established a Working Group on relations between
States and international organizations; and on
3 May 1972, the Commission set up a Working
Group on the question of the protection and inviolability of diplomatic agents and other persons entitled to special protection under international law. At its 26th session, in pursuance
of paragraph 4 of Assembly resolution 3071
(XXVIII), 30 November 1973, the Commission established a Sub-Committee on the law of the non-
navigational uses of international watercourses.

The reports of the special rapporteurs, sub-
committees and working groups are published in
the Yearbooks of the ILC.

A United Nations publication which provides a
general introduction to the work of the International Law Commission, with sufficient references to facilitate further research, is The
Work of the International Law Commission, first
issued in 1967 and in a revised edition in
September 1972 (Sales no.:E.72.I.17). Part I

contains a brief historical outline of the various attempts at the development and codification of international law up to the inception of the Commission's work; Part II, an account of the organization, program and methods of work of the Commission, with particular reference to the Statute under which the Commission functions; Part III briefly describes the various topics of international law which have been dealt with by the Commission, the actions decided upon by the General Assembly following the consideration of the topics by the Commission, and the results achieved by diplomatic conferences convened by the General Assembly to consider drafts prepared by the Commission. The table of contents, in Part III, lists (A) topics on which the Commission has submitted final reports; and (B) topics currently under consideration by the Commission. Annexes contain the texts of the Commission's Statute, a list of present and former members of the Commission, and the full texts of selected final drafts prepared by the Commission and of multilateral conventions which were adopted by diplomatic conferences convened under the auspices of the United Nations or the General Assembly itself, following the consideration of the topics by the Commission.

Following is a list of the ILC sessions and the symbols of its reports, which are republished in the ILC Yearbook for the year in which the session took place:

> First session, Lake Success, New York
> 12 April - 9 June 1949
> (GAOR, Sess.IV, Suppl.10 (A/925))
>
> Second session, Geneva
> 5 June - 29 July 1950
> (GAOR, Sess.V, Suppl.12 (A/1316))

Third session, Geneva
16 May - 27 July 1951
(GAOR, Sess.VI, Suppl.9 (A/ 1858))

Fourth session, Geneva
4 June - 8 August 1952
(GAOR, Sess.VII, Suppl.9 (A/2163))

Fifth session, Geneva
1 June - 14 August 1953
(GAOR, Sess.VIII, Suppl.9 (A/2456))

Sixth session, UNESCO House, Paris, France
3 June - 28 June 1954
(GAOR, Sess.IX, Suppl.9 (A/2693))

Seventh session, Geneva
2 May - 8 July 1955
(GAOR, Sess.X, Suppl.9 (A/2934)

Eighth session, Geneva
23 April - 4 July 1956
(GAOR, Sess.XI, Suppl.9 (A/3159))

Ninth session, Geneva
23 April - 28 June 1957
(GAOR, Sess.XII, Suppl.9 (A/3623))

Tenth session, Geneva
28 April - 4 July 1958
(GAOR, Sess.XIII, Suppl.9 (A/3859))

11th session, ILO Headquarters, Geneva
20 April - 26 June 1959
(GAOR, Sess.XIV, Suppl.9 (A/4169))

12th session, Geneva
25 April - 1 July 1960
(GAOR, Sess.XV, Suppl.9 (A/4425))

13th session, Geneva
1 May - 7 July 1961
(GAOR, Sess.XVI, Suppl.9 (A/4843))

14th session, Geneva
24 April - 29 June 1962
(GAOR, Sess. XVII, Suppl.9 (A/5209))

15th session, Geneva
6 May - 12 July 1963
(GAOR, Sess. XVIII, Suppl.9 (A/5509))

16th session, Geneva
11 May-24 July 1964
(GAOR, Sess. XIX, Suppl.9 (A/5809))

17th session, (Part 1), Geneva
3 May - 9 July 1965
(GAOR, Sess.XX, Suppl.9 (A/6009))

17th session (Part 2), Monaco
3 - 28 January 1966
          and
18th session, Geneva
4 May - 19 July 1966
(GAOR, Sess.XXI, Suppl.9 (A/6309/Rev.1))

19th session, Geneva
8 May - 14 July 1967
(GAOR, XXII, Suppl.9 (A/6709/Rev.1))

20th session, Geneva
27 May - 2 August 1968
(GAOR, Sess.XXIII, Suppl.9 (A/7209/Rev.1))

21st session, Geneva
2 June - 8 August 1969
(GAOR, Sess.XXIV, Suppl.10 (A/7610/Rev.1))

22nd session, Geneva
4 May - 10 July 1970
(GAOR, Sess.XXV, Suppl.10 (A/8010/Rev.1))

23rd session, Geneva
26 April - 30 July 1971
(GAOR, Sess.XXVI, Suppl.10 (A/8410/Rev.1))

24th session, Geneva
2 May - 7 July 1972
(GAOR, Sess.XXVII, Suppl.10 (A/8710/Rev.1))

25th session, Geneva
7 May - 13 July 1973
(GAOR, Sess.XXVIII, Suppl.10 (A/9010/Rev.1))

Officers of the sessions were as follows:

First Session, 1949: Chairman: Manley O. Hudson
    (USA); First Vice-Chairman: Vladimir M.
    Koretsky (USSR); Second Vice-Chairman: Sir
    Benegal N. Rau (India); Rapporteur: Gilberto
    Amado (Brazil).
Second Session, 1950: Chairman: Georges Scelle
    (France); First Vice-Chairman: A.E.F. Sand-
    ström (Sweden); Second Vice-Chairman: Faris
    Bey el-Khoury (Syria); Rapporteur: Ricardo
    J. Alfaro (Panama).
Third Session, 1951: Chairman: James L. Brierly
    (UK); First Vice-Chairman: Shuhsi Hsu(China);
    Second Vice-Chairman: J.M. Yepes (Colombia);
    Rapporteur: Roberto Córdova (Mexico).
Fourth session, 1952: Chairman: Ricardo J. Al-
    faro (Mexico); First Vice-Chairman: J.P.A.
    François (Netherlands); Second Vice-Chair-
    man: Gilberto Amado (Brazil); Rapporteur:
    Jean Spiropoulos (Greece).
Fifth Session, 1953: Chairman: J.P.A. François
    (Netherlands); First Vice-Chairman: Gilberto
    Amado (Brazil); Second Vice-Chairman: F.I.
    Kozhevnikov (USSR); Rapporteur: E. Lauter-
    pacht (UK).

Sixth Session, 1954: Chairman: A.E.F. Sandström (Sweden); First Vice-Chairman: Roberto Córdova (Mexico); Second Vice-Chairman: Radhabinod Pal (India); Rapporteur: J.P.A. Francois (Netherlands).

Seventh Session, 1955: Chairman: Jean Spiropoulos (Greece); First Vice-Chairman: S.B. Krylov (USSR); Second Vice-Chairman: F.V. Garcia-Amador (Cuba); Rapporteur: J.P.A. François (Netherlands).

Eighth Session, 1956: Chairman: F.V. Garcia-Amador (Cuba); First Vice-Chairman: Jaroslav Zourek (Czech); Second Vice-Chairman: Douglas L. Edmonds (USA); Rapporteur: J.P.A. François (Netherlands).

Ninth Session, 1957: Chairman: Jaroslav Zourek (Czech); First Vice-Chairman: Radhabinod Pal (India); Second Vice-Chairman: Luis Padilla Nervo (Mexico); Rapporteur: Sir Gerald Fitzmaurice (UK).

Tenth Session, 1958: Chairman: Radhabinod Pal (India); First Vice-Chairman: Gilberto Amado (Brazil); Second Vice-Chairman: Grigory I. Tunkin (USSR); Rapporteur: Sir Gerald Fitzmaurice (UK).

11th Session, 1959: Chairman: Sir Gerald Fitzmaurice(UK); First Vice-Chairman: Shuhsi Hsu (China); Second Vice-Chairman: Ricardo J. Alfaro (Panama); Rapporteur: J.P.A. François (Netherlands).

12th Session, 1960: Chairman: Luis Padillo Nervo (Mexico); First Vice-Chairman: Kisaburo Yokota (Japan); Second Vice-Chairman: Milan Bartoš (Yugoslavia); Rapporteur: Sir Gerald Fitzmaurice (UK).

13th Session, 1961: Chairman: Grigory I. Tunkin (USSR); First Vice-Chairman: Roberto Ago (Italy); Second Vice-Chairman: Eduardo Jiménez de Aréchaga (Uruguay); Rapporteur: Ahmed Matine-Daftary (Iran).

14th Session, 1962: Chairman: Radhabinod Pal
(India); First Vice-Chairman: André Gros
(France); Second Vice-Chairman: Gilberto
Amado (Brazil); Rapporteur: Manfred Lachs
(Poland).

15th Session, 1963: Chairman: Eduardo Jiménez
de Aréchaga (Uruguay); First Vice-Chairman:
Milan Bartoš (Yugoslavia); Second Vice-
Chairman: Senjin Tsuruoka (Japan); Rapporteur: Sir Humphrey Waldock (UK).

16th Session, 1964: Chairman: Roberto Ago (Italy)
First Vice-Chairman: Herbert W. Briggs (USA);
Second Vice-Chairman: Grigory L. Tunkin
(USSR); Rapporteur: Mustafa K. Yasseen
(Iraq).

17th Session, 1965: Chairman: Milan Bartoš
(Yugoslavia); First Vice-Chairman: Eduardo
Jiménez de Aréchaga (Uruguay); Second Vice-
Chairman: Paul Reuter (France); Rapporteur:
Taslim O. Elias (Nigeria).

18th Session 1966: Chairman: Mustafa K. Yasseen
(Iraq); First Vice-Chairman: Herbert W.
Briggs (USA); Second Vice- Chairman; Manfred
Lachs (Poland); Rapporteur: Antonio de Luna
(Spain).

19th Session, 1967: Chairman: Sir Humphrey
Waldock (UK); First Vice-Chairman: José
María Ruda (Argentina); Second Vice-Chair-
man: Endre Ustor (Hungary); Rapporteur:
Abdullah El-Erian (UAR).

20th Session, 1968: Chairman: José María Ruda
(Argentina); First Vice-Chairman: Erik
Castrén (Finland); Second Vice-Chairman:
Nikolai Ushakov (USSR); Rapporteur: Abdul
Hakim Tabibi (Afghanistan).

21st Session, 1969: Chairman: Nikolai Ushakov
(USSR); First Vice-Chairman: Jorge Castañeda
(Mexico); Second Vice-Chairman: Nagendra
Singh (India); Rapporteur: Constantin Th.
Eustathi ades (Greece).

22nd Session, 1970: Chairman: Taslim O. Elias
(Nigeria); First Vice-Chairman: Richard D.
Kearney (USA); Second Vice-Chairman: Fern-
ando Albonico (Chile); Rapporteur: Milan
Bartoš (Yugoslavia).

23rd Session, 1971: Chairman: Senjin Tsuruoka
(Japan); First Vice-Chairman: Roberto Ago
(Italy); Second Vice-Chairman: Milan Bartoš
(Yugoslavia); Rapporteur: José Sette Câmara
(Brazil).

24th Session, 1972: Chairman: Richard D. Kearney
(USA); First Vice-Chairman: Endre Ustor
(Hungary); Second Vice-Chairman: Alfred
Ramangasoavina (Madagascar); Rapporteur:
Gonzalo Alcívar (Ecuador).

25th Session, 1973: Chairman: Jorge Castañeda
(Mexico); First Vice-Chairman: Mustafa K.
Yasseen (Iraq); Second Vice-Chairman: Milan
Bartoš (Yugoslavia); Rapporteur: Arnold J.P.
Tammes (Netherlands).

Selected Bibliography on Legal Matters

Yearbook of the International Law Commission (A/CN.4/SER.A/(Year))

Following a request of the International Law
Commission, the General Assembly, on 3 December
1955, adopted resolution 987 (X), requesting the
Secretary-General to arrange for the printing of
(a) the principal documents (namely, studies,
reports, principal draft resolutions and amendments presented to the Commission) relating to
the first seven sessions, in their original
languages, and the summary records of these sessions, initially in English; and (b) the principal documents and summary records relating to
the subsequent sessions, in English, French and
Spanish. Since 1969, it has also been published
in Russian. As a result, an annual publication

(starting in 1957), entitled <u>Yearbook of the</u>
<u>International Law Commission,</u> which are in ef-
fect the "Official Records" of the ILC, has
been printed in two volumes (except for the
<u>Yearbook</u> for 1949 published in one volume).
Volume I contains the summary records of the
meetings of the Commission, a list of its members and officers; and volume II reproduces all
principal documents, including the Commission's
annual report to the General Assembly. It also
contains a check list of documents referred to
in the volume, and a check list of documents of
the Commission's session which are not reproduced in the volume.

The <u>Yearbooks</u> are published as United Nations
sales publications, as follows:

Yearbook		UN Publication Sales No.
1949	Summary records and documents of the first session	57.V.1
1950,I	Summary records of the second session	57.V.3,vol.I
1950,II	Documents of the second session	57.V.3,vol.II
1951,I	Summary records of the third session	57.V.6,vol.I
1951,II	Documents - third sess.	57.V.6,vol.II
1952,I	Summary records of the fourth session	58.V.5,vol.I
1952,II	Documents - fourth sess.	58.V.5,vol.II
1953,I	Summary records of the fifth session	59.V.4,vol.I
1953,II	Documents - fifth sess.	59.V.4,vol.II
1954,I	Summary records of the sixth session	59.V.7,vol.I
1954,II	Documents - sixth sess.	59.V.7,vol.II
1955,I	Summary records of the seventh session	60.V.3,vol.I
1955,II	Documents - seventh sess.	60.V.3,vol.II

Yearbook		UN Publication Sales No.
1956,I	Summary records of the eighth session	56.V.3,vol.I
1956,II	Documents - eighth sess.	56.V.3,vol.II
1957,I	Summary records of the ninth session	57.V.5,vol.I
1957,II	Documents - ninth sess.	57.V.5,vol.II
1958,I	Summary records of the tenth session	58.V.1,vol.I
1958,II	Documents - tenth sess.	58.V.1,vol.II
1959,I	Summary records of the eleventh session	59.V.1,vol.I
1959,II	Documents - 11th sess.	59.V.1,vol.II
1960,I	Summary records of the twelfth session	60.V.1,vol.I
1960,II	Documents - 12th sess.	60.V.1,vol.II
1961,I	Summary records of the thirteenth session	61.V.1,vol.I
1961,II	Documents - 13th sess.	61.V.1,vol.II
1962,I	Summary records of the fourteenth session	62.V.4
1962,II	Documents - 14th sess.	62.V.5
1963,I	Summary records of the fifteenth session	63.V.1
1963,II	Documents - 15th sess.	63.V.2
1964,I	Summary records of the sixteenth session	65.V.1
1964,II	Documents - 16th sess.	65.V.2
1965,I	Summary records of the first part of the 17th session	66.V.1
1965,II	Documents - first part of 17th session	66.V.2
1966,I	Part 1 - Summary records of 2nd part of 17th sess.	67.V.1 (Pt 1)
1966,I	Part 2 - Summary records of 18th session	67.V.5
1966,II	Documents - second part of 17th session and of the 18th session	67.V.2

Yearbook		UN Publication Sales No.
1967,I	Summary records of the nineteenth session	E.68.V.1
1967,II	Documents - 19th sess.	E.68.V.2
1968,I	Summary records of the twentieth session	E.69.V.3
1968,II	Documents - 20th sess.	E.69.V.4
1969,I	Summary records of the twenty-first session	E.70.V.7
1969,II	Documents - 21st sess.	E.70.V.8
1970,I	Summary records of the twenty-second session	E.71.V.6
1970,II	Documents - 22nd sess.	E.71.V.7
1971,I	Summary records of the twenty-third session	E.72.V.5
1971,II	Documents - 23rd sess. Parts one and two	E.72.V.6 Pt I E.72.V.6 PtII
1972,I	Summary records of the twenty-fourth session	E.73.V.4
1972,II	Documents - 24th sess.	E.73.V.5
1973,I	Summary records of the twenty-fifth session	E.74.V.4
1973,II	Documents - 25th sess.	E.74.V.5
1974,I	Summary records of the twenty-sixth session	E.75.V.6
1974,II	Documents - 26th sess. Parts one and two	E.75.V.7 Pt I E.75.V.7 PtII

The Work of the International Law Commission, revised edition, (Sales no.:E.72.I.17) has a selected bibliography.

International Law Commission -- A Guide to the Documents 1949-1969 (United Nations Library at Geneva publication, ST/GENEVA/LIB/SER.B/Ref.2).

The Practice of the United Nations, the Specialized Agencies and the International Atomic

Special Committee on Technical Assistance to Promote the Teaching, Study, Dissemination and Wider Appreciation of International Law (A/AC. 117/-)

Established by Assembly resolution 1968 (XVIII), of 16 December 1963.

Terms of Reference

Having considered the report of the Sixth Committee (GAOR, Sess. XVIII, Annexes, vol. 3, agenda item 72, A/5672), and the report of the Secretary-General (Ibid., A/5585), containing practical suggestions relating to the proclamation of a United Nations Decade of International Law and to an initial program of assistance and exchange in the field of international law, the Committee was established for the purpose of drawing up a practical plan and proposals, which it was to present to the nineteenth session of the General Assembly.

Membership

The resolution nominated the following States as members, listed below with their representatives:

Afghanistan	Dr. Abdul Hakim Tabibi, Vice-Chairman, and Farouk Farhang
Belgium	Erik Bal, Rapporteur
Ecuador	Dr. Gonzalo Alcívar
Ghana	E.K. Dadzie, Chairman, and D.R. Vanderpuije
Hungary	Dr. Arpad Prandler
Ireland	J. Shields

Action

The Committee met informally on 31 March and 9 April 1964, having decided at a first meeting on 16 December 1963 to hold a series of preparatory and informal meetings early in 1964 and to convene its formal session about a week before the opening of the nineteenth session of the General Assembly. The formal session took place between 25 November 1964 and 29 January 1965. Its report (GAOR, Sess. XX, Annexes, vol.3, agenda item 89, A/5887) was issued on 17 February 1965.

The report, in four parts, included a practical plan and proposals for a program of assistance and exchange in the field of international law and for a United Nations "decade" of international law; methods of financing the program; a plan of activities to be undertaken in 1965-1967; machinery for implementing and supervising the program. The Committee also recommended that an advisory committee be established by the General Assembly to consist of not more than ten representatives of Member States, initially appointed by the General Assembly for a period of not more than three years. This committee would meet as appropriate to advise the Secretary-General on the substantive aspects of the program approved and to report to the General Assembly on its work.

Advisory Committee on the United Nations
Programme of Assistance in the Teaching, Study,
Dissemination and Wider Appreciation of Inter-
national Law (A/AC.123/-)

Established by Assembly resolution 2099 (XX),
of 20 December 1965, as the Advisory Committee
on Technical Assistance to Promote the Teaching,
Study, Dissemination and Wider Appreciation of
International Law (resolution 2204 (XXI), of 16
December 1966, changed the name to the Advisory
Committee on the United Nations Programme of
Assistance, as above), after consideration of
the report of the Special Committee on Technical Assistance to Promote the Teaching, Study,
Dissemination and Wider Appreciation of International Law (GAOR, Sess.XX, Annexes, vol. 3,
agenda item 89, A/5887).

The Advisory Committee was continued by the
General Assembly under resolutions 2313 (XXII),
of 14 December 1967; 2464 (XXIII), of 20 December 1968; 2550 (XXIV) of 12 December 1969; 2698
(XXV), of 11 December 1970; 2838 (XXVI), of
18 December 1971; and 3106 (XXVIII), of 12 December 1973.

Terms of Reference

The Advisory Committee was to meet, at the request of either the Secretary-General or a
majority of its members, to advise the Secretary-
General on the substantive aspects of the programs contained in the report of the Special Committee and on the implementation of the present
resolution, and was to report, as appropriate,
to the General Assembly. Representatives of
UNESCO and the United Nations Institute for
Training and Research (UNITAR) would be invited,
whenever necessary, to the meetings of the Advisory Committee.

Resolution 2204 (XXI) authorized the Secretary-General to carry out in 1967 the activities specified in his report on the program (<u>GAOR</u>, Sess.XXI, <u>Annexes</u>, vol.3, agenda item 86, A/6492, and Add.1), including the items of direct assistance as specified in the resolution.

In the Secretary-General's report to the twenty-sixth session of the Assembly (<u>GAOR</u>, Sess.XXVI, <u>Annexes</u>, agenda item 91, A/8508, and Corr.1), it was suggested that the program should in future be conducted on a two-year basis, with reports being submitted to the General Assembly in alternate years. This would make it desirable that members of the Advisory Committee be appointed for a period of four years.

Membership

The establishing resolution 2099 (XX) provided that the Advisory Committee should be composed of ten members to be elected every three years. At its 1404th plenary meeting, on 20 December 1965, the General Assembly appointed, on the proposal of the Sixth Committee (A/6136, mimeographed), the following ten members:
Afghanistan, Belgium, Ecuador, France, Ghana, Hungary, Tanzania, USSR, United Kingdom, and United States of America.

At the 1751st plenary meeting, on 20 December 1968, the same membership was reelected, except for Afghanistan which was replaced by Iraq.

Assembly resolution 2838 (XXVI), of 18 December 1971, increased the membership to 13 and the term of office from three to four years. The same resolution appointed the following membership, for a period of four years, from 1 January 1972 to 31 December 1975:

Barbados, Belgium, Cyprus, El Salvador, France, Ghana, Hungary, Iraq, Mali, Tanzania, USSR, United Kingdom, and United States of America.

Action

The Advisory Committee held five meetings in a first session from 19 to 26 September 1965. At its first meeting, W.B. Van Lara (Ghana) was elected as Chairman/Rapporteur. The Advisory Committee's recommendations were contained in chapter IV of the report of the Secretary-General (GAOR, Sess. XXI, Annexes, vol.3, agenda item 86, A/6492, and Add.1), of 1 November 1966.

The second session of the Advisory Committee was convened by the Secretary-General on 3 October 1967; six meetings were held up to 20 October. The Advisory Committee's recommendations were included in chapter III of the Secretary-General's report (GAOR, Sess.XXII, Annexes, vol.3, agenda item 90, A/6816), of 28 October 1967.

In its third session, the Advisory Committee held three meetings on 7, 9 and 14 October 1968. Its report was included in chapter IV of the Secretary-General's report (GAOR, Sess. XXIII, Annexes, vol.2, agenda item 89, A/7305), of 15 November 1968.

The fourth session, held from 6 to 7 October 1969, was covered in chapter IV of the Secretary-General's report (GAOR, Sess. XXIV, Annexes, vol.2, agenda item 91, A/7740), of 12 November 1969. The fifth session, held on 6 October 1970, was included in chapter IV of the Secretary-General's report (GAOR, Sess.XXV, Annexes, vol. 2, agenda item 90, A/8130, and Corr.1), of

24 November 1970. At the fifth session the Committee agreed to dispense with summary records. The sixth session of the Advisory Committee was convened by the Secretary-General on 12 October 1971. It endorsed the recommendations of the Secretary-General with respect to the execution of the program in 1972 and 1973, contained in paragraphs 51, 52, 59 and 62 of the report, and recommended that he submit them to the General Assembly for approval. The Secretary-General's report covering the session (A/8508, and Corr.1, chapter IV, offset) was issued on 17 November 1971. The report of the Sixth Committee to the General Assembly on the subject (GAOR, Sess.XXVI, Annexes, agenda item 91, A/8570) was issued on 15 December 1971.

The seventh session of the Advisory Committee was held on 20 November 1972. Although in previous years the Secretary-General had reported annually to the General Assembly on the activities of the program, he did not do so for 1972 since the Assembly had requested him, in resolution 2838 (XXVI), to report to the twenty-eighth session in 1973.

The eighth session was held on 8 to 9 November 1973, and the Advisory Committee's report was covered in chapter V of the report of the Secretary-General (A/9242, and Corr.1, offset) of 26 November 1973, which also included a report on the seventh session of the Advisory Committee in the same chapter. The report of the Sixth Committee on the subject (GAOR, Sess. XXVIII, Annexes, agenda item 98, A/9414) was issued on 7 December 1973.

Officers: - A representative of Ghana served as Chairman at all the sessions: W.B. Van Lare at the first; G.O. Lamptey at the second and third

sessions; D.F.H. Vanderpuije at the fourth
and fifth sessions; the representative of Ghana
(name not given) at the sixth; and F.E. Boaten
at the seventh and eighth sessions.

Commission on International Trade Law
(UNCITRAL) United Nations (A/CN.9/-)

Established by Assembly resolution 2205 (XXI),
of 17 December 1966, generally referred to herein as UNCITRAL, or as "the Commission".

Terms of Reference

The Commission was created to further progressive harmonization and unification of the law of
international trade by:

a) coordinating the work of organizations
active in this field and encouraging cooperation
among them;

b) promoting wider participation in existing international conventions and wider acceptance of existing model and uniform laws;

c) preparing or promoting the adoption of
new international conventions, model laws and
uniform laws and promoting the codification and
wider acceptance of international trade terms,
provisions, customs and practices, in collaboration, where appropriate, with the organizations
operating in this field;

d) promoting ways and means of ensuring a
uniform interpretation and application of international conventions and uniform laws in the
field of the law of international trade;

e) collecting and disseminating information on national legislation and modern legal
developments, including case law, in the field
of the law of international trade;

f) establishing and maintaining a close
collaboration with the United Nations Conference on Trade and Development (UNCTAD);

g) maintaining liaison with other United
Nations organs and specialized agencies concerned with international trade;

h) taking any other action it might deem useful to fulfill its functions.

Resolution 2421 (XXIII), paragraph 6, of 18 December 1968, extended the Commission's terms of reference as follows:

a) to continue its work on the topics to which it decided to give priority, that is, the international sale of goods, international payments and international commercial arbitration;

b) to consider the inclusion of international shipping legislation among the priority topics in its work program;

c) to consider opportunities for training and assistance in the field of international trade law, in the light of relevant reports of the Secretary-General;

d) to keep its program of work under constant review, bearing in mind the interests of all peoples, and particularly those of the developing countries, in the extensive development of international trade;

e) to consider at its second session ways and means of promoting coordination of the work or organizations active in the progressive harmonization and unification of international trade law and of encouraging cooperation among them;

f) to consider, when appropriate, the possibility of issuing a yearbook which would make its work more readily available.

The Commission normally holds one regular session a year and may meet alternately at United Nations Headquarters and the United Nations office at Geneva.

Resolution 2766 (XXVI), of 17 November 1971, further recommended that UNCITRAL should, inter alia. continue to give special consideration to

the interests of developing countries and to
bear in mind the special problems of land-locked
countries; and to keep its program of work under constant review.

Resolution 3108 (XXVIII), of 12 December 1973,
requested UNCITRAL to incorporate the reports
or summaries of the reports of working groups
in the reports of the work of the future sessions. It recommended further that UNCITRAL
should continue to consider the legal problems
presented by different kinds of multinational
(transnational) enterprises, in accordance with
the decision thereon adopted by the Commission
at its sixth session.

The resolution also invited UNCITRAL to consider
the advisability of preparing uniform rules on
the civil liability of producers for damage
caused by their products intended for or involved in international sale or distribution.

The Commission submits an annual report to the
General Assembly and simultaneously to UNCTAD
for comment.

Membership

The establishing resolution stipulated that the
Commission should consist of 29 States, elected
by the General Assembly, for a term of six
years, following a prescribed distribution:
    a) Seven from African States
    b) Five from Asian States
    c) Four from Eastern European States
    d) Five from Latin American States
    e) Eight from Western European and Other
                States

The General Assembly would also have due regard to the adequate representation of the principal economic and legal systems of the world, and of the developed and developing countries.

At the first election, the President of the Assembly, by drawing lots, selected the fourteen members who would serve for three years within each of the groups of States. Members elected at the first election took office on 1 January 1968, and thereafter, would take office on 1 January of the year following their election.

On 30 October 1967, at its twenty-second session, the General Assembly elected the following 29 States as members of the Commission:

Argentina	Hungary	Spain
Australia	India	Syria
Belgium	Iran	Tanzania*
Brazil	Italy*	Thailand*
Chile*	Japan*	Tunisia
Colombia*	Kenya	USSR*
Congo (Dem.Rep.of)	Mexico	UAR*
Czechoslovakia*	Nigeria*	United
France *	Norway*	Kingdom*
Ghana*	Romania	USA

The fourteen members indicated by asterisks were selected by the President of the General Assembly to serve for a term of three years ending on 31 December 1970. The other 15 members would serve for the full term of six years ending 31 December 1973.

At its 1903rd meeting, 12 November 1970, the General Assembly elected the following 14 members to succeed those whose terms of office expired on 31 December 1970:

Group A (African States):
    Ghana, Nigeria, Tanzania, UAR;
Group B (Asian States):
    Japan, Singapore;
Group C (East European States):
    Poland, USSR;
Group D (Latin American States):
    Chile, Guyana;
Group E (West European and Other States):
    Austria, France, Norway, United
    Kingdom.

At the sixth session of the Commission in 1973, the Secretary-General advised that the term of 15 of its members would end on 31 December 1973 and that the election to be held at the twenty-eighth session of the Assembly might affect the present membership of working groups. In order to ensure the proper functioning of the working groups, he proposed that, after the election of the 15 members, representatives of the Member States of the Commission should meet to decide, if necessary, on the replacement of outgoing members of the Commission in any working group that would meet prior to the seventh session of the Commission. The Commission approved of and accepted the proposal (GAOR, Sess. XXVIII, Suppl.17 (A/9017, paragraph 136)).

At the 2201st plenary meeting of the Assembly, on 14 December 1973, the following Member States were elected to serve for a period of six years, commencing 1 January 1974:
    Argentina, Belgium, Brazil, Bulgaria,
    Czechoslovakia, Germany (Fed.Rep.),
    Greece, India, Kenya, Mexico, Philippines,
    Sierra Leone, Syria, USA, and Zaire.

Membership was increased from 29 to 36 members by Assembly resolution 3108 (XXVIII), operative

paragraph 8, with the following distribution
of seats:
a) Two from African States
b) Two from Asian States
c) One from East European States
d) One from Latin American States
e) One from West European and Other States

Of the additional members, the terms of three
would expire at the end of three years, and
would be selected by the President of the General Assembly by drawing lots, as follows: one
from African States; one from Asian States; one
from those elected from other regions. The
seven would take office on 1 January 1974.

At the 2201st plenary meeting, on 14 December
1973, the following were elected: for three
years: Somalia, Nepal, Australia; and for six
years: Gabon, Cyprus, Barbados, Hungary.

Membership of the Commission from 1 January
1974 to 31 December 1979, (except for those
whose terms expired on 31 December 1976, indicated by an asterisk) was as follows:

Argentina	Gabon	Norway*
Australia*	Germany (Fed.Rep.)	Philippines
Austria*	Ghana*	Poland*
Barbados	Greece	Sierra
Belgium	Guyana*	Leone
Brazil	Hungary	Singapore*
Bulgaria	India	Somalia*
Chile*	Japan*	Syria
Cyprus	Kenya	Tanzania*
Czechoslovakia	Mexico	USSR*
Egypt*	Nepal*	United
France *	Nigeria*	Kingdom *
		USA
		Zaire

The representatives of the Members were listed
in an annex to each report of the Commission
from the first to the fourth sessions. From
the fifth session in 1972 to the present, the
lists of representatives of participants and
observers appear in the information series, as
follows: A/CN.9/INF,4, fifth session; INF.5,
sixth session; INF.6, seventh session; INF.7,
eighth session; INF.8 and Corr.1, ninth session.

Action in 1968

The Commission met at United Nations Headquarters in its first session from 29 January to 26
February 1968. At its 21st meeting, on 23 February 1968, the Commission decided to establish
a Working Group composed of 14 Member States,
to be appointed by the Chairman in consultation
with the various groups concerned. The Secretary-General was to arrange for a meeting of
the Working Group one week before the opening
of the second session of UNCITRAL, if, in the
light of the comments, reports and studies on
the priority topics received pursuant to the
proposals in a working paper (A/CN.9/L.3), the
Secretary-General believed it would be of assistance to the Commission's future to arrange
such a meeting. A letter of 24 January 1969
from the Secretary-General informed the members
of UNCITRAL that in his opinion the task of the
Working Group, as outlined by the Commission,
could be carried out by sessional working groups
which the Commission would wish to appoint at
the beginning of its second session, and that a
meeting of the Working Group was therefore not
necessary.

The report of the Commission on its first session (GAOR, Sess.XXIII, Suppl.16 (A/7216)) was
issued in April 1968. The UNICTRAL Yearbooks

republish the reports of the sessions of the
Commission and of its subsidiary bodies.

Action in 1969

The second session of UNCITRAL took place in
Geneva from 3 to 31 March 1969. At its 27th
meeting, the Commission established two committees of the whole which would meet simultaneously to consider the agenda items referred to
them. Committee I dealt with agenda items 4 on
international sale of goods, and 6 on international commercial arbitration. It met from 6
to 24 March, holding 15 meetings, and elected
Nagendra Singh (India) as Chairman, and Shinichiro Michida (Japan) and Ion Nestor (Romania)
as Rapporteurs. Following the departure from
Geneva of the Chairman, Gervasio Colombres
(Argentina) was elected to replace him.

Committee II dealt with agenda items 5 on international payments; 8 on registers of organizations and texts, and bibliography; 9 on consideration of ways and means of promoting co-
ordination of the work of the organizations
active in the progressive harmonization and unification of international trade law and of encouraging cooperation among them; and 12 on
publication of a yearbook. Committee II met
from 6 to 20 March, holding 12 meetings, and
elected Nehemias Gueiros (Brazil) as Chairman,
and Kevin W. Ryan (Australia) as Rapporteur.
The substance of the reports of both Committees
·was included in the chapters of the UNCITRAL report dealing with the items.

The Commission also established the following
three inter-sessional subsidiary bodies (see
"Working Groups" below for details):

(1)   Working Group on uniform rules governing the international sale of goods and the law
applicable thereto;

(2)   Working Group on time-limits and limitations (prescription) in the international sale
of goods;

(3)   Working Group on international legislation on shipping.

At its 45th meeting, on 26 March 1969, the Commission decided that the term "Working Group"
would be used for the present for all inter-
sessional bodies set up at its second session
on the understanding that the adoption of this
term would in no way prevent the organ from
having summary records of its discussions and
other services necessary for its work. This
decision was taken after receiving an opinion
from the Legal Counsel of the United Nations that
it was the decision of a particular organ and
not its name which determined whether summary
records should be issued, and that full assur-
ances could therefore be given that the question
of summary records and other services would not
be prejudiced if the subsidiary body was called
a working group rather than a committee or sub-
committee.

On 26 March 1969, the Commission decided to appoint Ion Nestor (Romania) as Special Rapporteur
on the most important problem concerning the application and interpretation of existing conventions and other problems related to international commercial arbitration. Mr. Nestor
presented a preliminary report (A/CN.9/42) on
18 February 1970, and a final report, "International Commercial Arbitration", on 1 March
1972 (A/CN.9/64, republished in chapter III of
the UNCITRAL Yearbook, vol. III, 1972).

The report of the second session (<u>GAOR</u>, Sess.
XXIV, <u>Suppl.18</u> (A/7618)) was issued in July
1969.

Action in 1970

The third session was held at United Nations
Headquarters from 6 to 30 April, holding 12
plenary sessions. At its 51st meeting, on 7
April, the Commission established two committees
of the whole. Committee I dealt with item 4 on
international sale of goods; and Committee II
dealt with items 5 on international payments;
7 on international legislation on shipping; 8
on register of organizations, register of texts,
bibliography; and 11 on publication of a yearbook. Committee I met from 7 to 27 April, holding 22 meetings, and elected Jorge Barrera Graf
(Mexico) as Chairman, and Emmanuel Sam (Ghana)
as Rapporteur. Committee II met from 8 to 27
April, and elected Iván Meznerics (Hungary) as
Chairman, and Stephen F. Parsons (Australia) as
Rapporteur. The substance of their reports was
included in the annual report of the Commission
in the chapters dealing with the items.

The report of the third session (<u>GAOR</u>, Sess.
XXV, <u>Suppl.17</u> (A/8017)) was issued in August
1970.

Action in 1971

The fourth session of UNCITRAL was held in
Geneva from 29 March to 20 April 1971. At the
66th meeting, on 30 March 1971, the Chairman
recalled that at its first session, the Commission had agreed that its decisions should, as
far as possible, be reached by consensus, and
that it was only in the absence of concensus
that decisions should be taken by a vote as provided for in the rules of procedure relating to

the procedure of Committees of the General Assembly. In all its sessions to date, all decisions have been reached by consensus. During the session the Commission dealt with international legislation on shipping, international payments, international sale of goods, the yearbook, register of texts, bibliography, training and assistance in the field of international trade law, and promotion of ratification of conventions prepared by the Commission.

The report (GAOR, Sess. XXVI, Suppl.17 (A/8417)) was issued in July 1971.

Action in 1972

The fifth session was held at United Nations Headquarters from 10 April to 5 May 1972. At its 93rd meeting, on 10 April, the Commission established a committee of the whole to deal with items 6 on international payments, 7 on international commercial arbitration, 8 on training and assistance in the field of international trade law, and 9 on the yearbook of the Commission. Its officers were: Chairman: Shinichiro Michida (Japan), and Rapporteur: Emmanuel Sam (Ghana). The substance of the report was included in the report of the work of the session.

At its 124th meeting, on 4 May 1972, the Commission established a Working Group on international negotiable instruments (see "Working Groups" below), pursuant to the report of the Secretary-General, of 31 March 1972 (A/CN.9/67, republished in chapter II of the UNCITRAL Yearbook, vol. III: 1972).

The annual report of UNCITRAL (GAOR, Sess.XXVII, Suppl.17 (A/8717)) appeared in July 1972.

Action in 1973

The sixth session of UNCITRAL was held at Geneva from 2 to 13 April 1973. Additional items considered by the Commission were (1) multinational (transnational) enterprises, pursuant to Assembly resolution 2928 (XXVII), of 28 November 1972, which in paragraph 5 invited the Commission to seek from Governments and interested international organizations information relating to legal problems presented by the different kinds of multinational enterprises; and (2) establishment of a union of "jus commune" in matters of international trade (chapter VIII of the Commission's report, A/9017).

The report of the session (GAOR, Sess. XXVIII, Suppl.17 (A/9017)) was issued in June 1973.

Officers

First session, 1968
During the first session, the Commission decided that it should have three Vice-Chairmen as it deemed it desirable that each of the five groups of States listed in paragraph 1 of section II of resolution 2205 (XXI) should be represented on the bureau of the Commission.

The officers elected at the first session were: Chairman: Emmanual K. Dadzie (Ghana); Vice-Chairmen: Anthony Mason (Australia), László Réczei (Hungary), Shinichiro Michida (Japan); Rapporteur: Jorge Barrera Graf (Mexico).

Second session, 1969
Chairman: László Réczei (Hungary); Vice-Chairmen: Gervasio Ramon Carlos Colombres (Argentina), Nagendra Singh (India), Mohsen Chafik (UAR); Rapporteur: Stein Rognlien (Norway).

Third session, 1970
Chairman: Albert Lilar (Belgium); Vice-Chairmen: Eugenio Cornejo Fuller (Chile), Abdelmajid Ben Messaouda (Tunisia), Ion Nestor (Romania); Rapporteur: Shinichiro Michida (Japan).

Fourth session, 1971
Chairman: Nagendra Singh (India); Vice-Chairmen: Nehemias Gueiros (Brazil), Joaquín Garrigues Diaz-Cañabate (Spain), Jerzy Jakubowski (Poland); Rapporteur: Joseph Diekola Ogundere (Nigeria).

Fifth session, 1972
Chairman: Jorge Barrera Graf (Mexico); Vice-Chairmen: L.H. Khoo (Singapore), Roland Loewe (Austria), Bernard A.N. Mudho (Kenya); Rapporteur: Jerzy Jakubowski (Poland).

Sixth session, 1973
Chairman: Mohsen Chafik (Egypt); Vice-Chairmen: László Réczei (Hungary), Akira Takakuwa (Japan), Paul R. Jenard (Belgium); Rapporteur: Nehemias Gueiros (Brazil).

Working Groups of the Commission on International Trade Law

I. - Working Group on Time-Limits and Limitations (Prescription) in the International Sale of Goods (A/CN.9/WG.1/WP.-)

Established on 26 March 1969, by a decision of UNCITRAL at its 44th meeting, second session, on recommendation of its Committee I established at the second session (A/7618, para. 45).

Terms of Reference

The Working Group should:
 a) study the topic of time-limits and limitations (prescription) in the field of international sale of goods with a view to the preparation of a preliminary draft of an international convention;
 b) confine its work to consideration of the formulation of a general period of extinctive prescription by virtue of which the rights of a buyer or seller would be extinguished or become barren.

The Working Group should not consider special time-limits by virtue of which particular rights of the buyer or seller might be abrogated, since these could most conveniently be dealt with by the Working Group on the international sale of goods.

The Working Group should, in its work, pay special attention, inter alia, to the following points:
 a) the moment from which time begins to run;
 b) the duration of the period of prescription;
 c) the circumstances in which the period may be suspended or interrupted;

d)   the circumstances in which the period may be terminated;

e)   to what extent, if any, the prescription period should be capable of variation by agreement of the parties;

f)   whether the issue of prescription should be raised by the court suo officio or only at the instance of the parties;

g)   whether the preliminary draft convention should take the form of a uniform or a model law;

h)   whether it would be necessary to state that the rules of the preliminary draft convention would take effect as rules of substance or procedure;

i)   to what extent it would still be necessary to have regard to the rules of conflict of laws.

Membership

The establishing decision listed the following seven members of the Commission as members of the Working Group:

Argentina, Belgium, Czechoslovakia, Japan, Norway, UAR, and United Kingdom.

Czechoslovakia's membership in the Commission having expired on 31 December 1970, Poland was unanimously appointed to replace it on the Working Group (A/8417, para.119).

Action

The Working Group met in Geneva from 18 to 22 August 1969. Its report (A/CN.9/30, republished in UNCITRAL Yearbook, vol. I:1968-1970, part three, I,D), issued on 3 November 1969, listed the participants in annex I. The second session, held in Geneva from 10 to 21 August 1970, issued its report (A/CN.9/50, Ibid., vol.II:

1971, part two, I,C) on 1 February 1971. During
this session the Working Group prepared a pre-
liminary draft of Uniform Law on Prescription
(Limitation) in International Sale of Goods,
text of which appeared in annex I of the report.
A list of participants appeared in annex IV.
Officers of the two sessions were: Chairman:
Stein Rognlien (Norway); Rapporteur: Ludvik
Kopac (Czech).

The third session was held in New York from 30
August to 10 September 1971, to prepare a final
draft of the Uniform Law on Prescription (Limit-
ation) for submission to the Commission at its
fifth session. Its officers were: Chairman:
Stein Rognlien (Norway); and Rapporteur: Paul R.
Jenard (Belgium). The report of the session
(A/CN.9/70, Ibid., vol. III, 1972, part two, I,
B.2) was issued on 21 September 1971. Annex I
contained text of a Draft Convention (Limitation) in the field of International Sale of
Goods, Annex II a list of participants, and
III list of documents and working papers before
the Working Group were not included in the Yearbook. Addendum 1 to the report (A/CN.9/70/Add.
1), of 14 January 1972, contained annex IV, a
"Commentary on the Draft Convention", which was
superseded by a report of 6 November 1972 (A/CN.
9/73, Ibid., vol. III: 1972, part two,I,B.3).
Addendum 2, annex V, (Ibid., part two, I,B.1),
issued on 24 February 1972, contained "Studies
and Proposals considered by the Working Group
on Prescription at the third session, and other
Comments by Governments on the Preliminary Draft
Uniform Law on Prescription (Limitation)" (August 1970).

At its 125th meeting, on 5 May 1972, fifth session, the Commission adopted unanimously a decision approving the text of the draft Convention on Prescription (Limitation) in the Inter-

national Sale of Goods, as set out in paragraph
21 of the report of UNCITRAL (A/8717), noting
that no consensus was reached with respect to
those provisions appearing within square brack-
ets; and recommended that the General Assembly
convene an international conference of plenipotentiaries to conclude, on the basis of the
draft adopted by the Commission, a Convention
on Prescription (Limitation) in the International Sale of Goods.

United Nations Conference on Prescription (Limitation) in the International Sale of Goods, New York, 20 May - 14 June 1974 (A/CONF.63/-)

The General Assembly, having considered chapter
II of the UNCITRAL report of the work of its
fifth session (A/8717), decided, in resolution
2929 (XXVII), of 28 November 1972, that an international conference of plenipotentiaries
should be convened in 1974, and in resolution
3104 (XXVIII), of 12 December 1973, requested
the Secretary-General to convene the Conference
at United Nations Headquarters. The Final Act
(A/CONF.63/14 and Corr.1) and a Convention on
the Limitation Period in the International Sale
of Goods (A/CONF.63/15) were published in the
UNCITRAL Yearbook. vol.V:1974, part three, annex I. A Supplement to the Yearbook published
the records of discussion on the item at the
fifth session of UNCITRAL.

II. - Working Group on the International Sale of Goods (A/CN.9/WG.2/WP.-)

Established on 26 March 1969, by a decision of UNCITRAL at the 44th meeting, second session, on recommendation of its Committee I established at the second session (A/7618, para.38).

Terms of Reference

Recalling Assembly resolution 2421 (XXIII), of 18 December 1968, and considering views expressed by a number of Governments that the Hague Conventions in their present text were not suitable for world-wide acceptance, the Commission requested the Secretary-General:

1) to complete the analysis of replies received from States regarding the Hague Conventions of 1964 (A/CN.9/17), and to submit the analysis to the Working Group; and

2) to prepare an analysis of the replies received from States regarding the Hague Convention of 1955 as well as comments of the members of the Commission during its second session, and to submit the analysis to the Working Group;

Further, the Working Group should:

3) - a. consider the comments and suggestions by States as analyzed in the documents to be prepared by the Secretary-General, in order to ascertain which modifications of the existing texts might render them capable of wider acceptance by countries of different legal, social, and economic systems, or whether it would be necessary to elaborate a new text for the same purpose, or what other steps might be taken to further the harmonization or unification of the law of the international sale of goods;

b. consider ways and means by which a more widely acceptable text might best be prepared and promoted, taking also into consideration the possibility of ascertaining whether

States would be prepared to participate in a Conference;

      c. submit a progress report to the third session of UNCITRAL.

At its third session, UNCITRAL decided (A/8017, para.72); *inter alia*, that instead of considering selected items, the Working Group should consider the Uniform Law on the International Sale of Goods (ULIS) systematically, chapter by chapter, giving priority to articles 1-17, taking into consideration the relevant suggestions of Governments, the documents mentioned in the report of the Commission on the work of its third session, and the decisions taken at that session as well as the practices of international trade.

At its fourth session, UNCITRAL decided (A/8417, para.92) that until the text of a uniform law or revised text of ULIS had been completed, the Working Group should submit a progress report on its work; and in preparing its final draft, the Working Group should take into consideration the comments and opinions voiced by representatives in connection with the items considered at the fourth session of UNCITRAL.

Membership

The decision of the Commission stipulated that the Working Group should be composed of 14 members, whose representatives would be especially qualified in the law of the international sale of goods. Membership was as follows:

    Brazil, France, Ghana, Hungary, India, Iran, Japan, Kenya, Mexico, Norway, Tunisia, USSR, United Kingdom, and United States of America.

Austria was appointed by the Commission at its fourth session following relinquishment by Norway of its membership in order to accomodate the inclusion of a new member of the Commission.

Action

The first session of the Working Group, held at United Nations Headquarters in New York from 5 to 16 January 1970, submitted its report (A/CN. 9/35, UNCITRAL Yearbook, vol.I:1968-1970, part three, I,A,2) on 27 January 1970. Annex I contained the list of participants. Its officers were: Chairman: Jorge Barrera Graf (Mexico); Rapporteur: Emmanuel Sam (Ghana). Mr. Barrera Graf continued to serve as Chairman at all the sessions.

The second session was held at the United Nations Office in Geneva from 7 to 18 December 1970. The Rapporteur of the session was Dileep Anant Kamat (India). The report (A/CN.9/52, Ibid., vol.II:1971, part two, I,A,2), was issued on 5 January 1971. Annex I contained a list of participants, and II the text of revised articles 1-17 of the Uniform Law (ULIS).

A progress report of the Working Group on the work of its third session, held in Geneva from 17 to 28 January 1972 (A/CN.9/62, and Add. 1-2, Ibid., vol. III:1972, part two, I,A,5) was issued on 24 February 1972. Its officers were the same as those who had served at the second session. Annex I and Add.1 (annex II), of 21 March 1972, dealt with the Working Group's conclusions with respect to articles 1-6 and 18-55 of the ULIS; and Add.2 (annex III), of 3 March 1972, contained the text of articles 1-55 as adopted or as deferred for further consideration.

The progress report on the work of the fourth session (A/CN.9/75, _Ibid._, vol. IV:1973, part two, I,A,3), held at United Nations Headquarters in New York from 22 January to 2 February 1973, was issued on 20 February 1973. The Rapporteur for the session was Roland Loewe (Austria). Annex I of the report contained the revised text of articles 18-70 of the ULIS; annex II contained a report of the Secretary-General on obligations of the seller in an international sale of goods; consolidation of work done by the Working Group and suggested solutions for unresolved problems (A/CN.9/WG.2/WP.16).

The fifth session would be held in Geneva from 21 January to 1 February 1974.

III. - Working Group on International Legislation on Shipping (A/CN.9/WG.III/WP.-)

Established on 27 March 1969 by a decision of UNCITRAL, at the 46th meeting, second session, recalling General Assembly resolution 2421 (XXIII), by which the Assembly recommended the Commission consider adding international legislation on shipping to its list of priority topics (A/7618, para.133).

At its fourth session in 1971, the Commission established a new and enlarged Working Group consisting of 21 Member States.

Terms of Reference

The Commission set up the Working Group to be convened by the Secretary-General, either on his own initiative or at the request of the Chairman, to meet sometime before, and preferably shortly before, the commencement of the third session of the Commission to indicate the topics and method of work on the subject, taking into consideration the study prepared by the Secretary-General, if it was ready, and giving full regard to the recommendations of UNCTAD and any of its organs, and to submit its report to the Commission at its third session.

At its 59th meeting, on 29 April 1970, the Commission adopted a decision (A/8017, para.166), inter alia, to request the Chairman of the Working Group on International Legislation on Shipping, as Special Representative of the Commission, to attend the session of the Working Group on Shipping Legislation of UNCTAD, to be held in Geneva in December 1970 or February 1971, in order to express the Commission's desire to avoid duplication of work, and to submit a report on that session. The Commission also decided that

a meeting of its Working Group should be held in
Geneva, after the session of the UNCTAD Working
Group and before the fourth session of UNCITRAL,
and set forth its composition, if the Working
Group met after 1 January 1971, and its terms of
reference.

At its fourth session, UNCITRAL, having considered a draft resolution submitted by India, and
having heard a statement on financial implications by the representative of the Secretary-
General, adopted a resolution (A/8417,para.19)
which decided that within the priority topic of
international legislation on shipping, the subject for consideration for the time being should
be bills of lading, a subject which should include the topics indicated in paragraphs 1 and 2
of the resolution adopted by the UNCTAD Working
Group (TD/B/C.4/86, annex I). The Commission
requested the Working Group to meet during the
fourth session of the Commission to consider the
organization of the work; to hold a further meeting in advance of the fifth session of the Commission and to report on the progress of its work.

Membership

The establishing decision designated the following Members of the Commission as members of the
Working Group:
> Chile, Ghana, India, Italy, UAR, USSR,
> United Kingdom.

At the 1903rd meeting, on 12 November 1970, the
United States of America was elected to replace
Italy, which had not been reelected to the Com-
mission. At the same meeting, the Commission
reelected those members of the Working Group
whose terms had expired, with the exception of
Italy, in the interests of continuity of the work
(A/8017, paras. 165-166 (5)).

At the Commission's third session, in April 1970, alternates were appointed for those whose terms were to expire in December 1970 as follows: Kenya as an alternate for the UAR; Congo (K), as an alternate for Ghana; Australia as an alternate for the United Kingdom; Mexico as an alternate for Chile; Hungary as an alternate for the USSR.

The Commission decided at the same session (A/8017, para.166 (9)) that the term of the Working Group would expire after it had submitted its report to the fourth session of the Commission, in view of the fact that a new and larger group would be set up at the fourth session.

At its fourth session in 1971, the Commission established a Working Group (A/8417, para.19 (2)) consisting of the following 21 Member States of the Commission:

> Argentina, Australia, Belgium, Brazil, Chile, Congo (K), France, Ghana, Hungary, India, Japan, Nigeria, Norway, Poland, Singapore, Spain, Tanzania, USSR, UAR, United Kingdom, and United States of America.

Action

A meeting of the Working Group was held during the third session of the Commission in 1970. The Chairman of the Working Group, E. Cornejo Fuller (Chile), reported to the Commission that the Group had agreed that its Chairman would represent UNCITRAL at the UNCTAD Working Group, even if Chile were not reelected to the Commission, and that an alternate Chairman would be elected from among the permanent missions of the members of the Working Group (A/8017, para. 164).

The Working Group held its second session in Geneva at the headquarters of the WHO, from 22 to 26

March 1971, and issued its report (A/CN.9/55,
UNCITRAL Yearbook, vol. II:1971, part two, III).
Its officers were: Chairman: Rafael Lasalvia
(Chile); Rapporteur: Dileep A. Kamat (India).
Annex I of the report listed the participants
and observers; and annex II contained a resolu-
tion on bills of lading (TD/B/C.4/86, annex I)
adopted at the second session of the UNCTAD
Working Group on International Shipping Legisla-
tion, in February 1971. The report by the Chair-
man of the first session of the UNCITRAL Working
Group on his participation as special representative at the session of the UNCTAD Working Group
(A/CN.9/WG.III/WP.3)was considered at the session.

An oral report was presented to the Commission at
its 77th meeting, on 7 April 1971, concerning a
sessional meeting of the new Working Group on International Legislation in Shipping held on 6
April 1971 to consider the organization of its
work. Nagendra Singh (India) had been elected as
Chairman, and Gervasio Colombres (Argentina) as
Vice-Chairman; their terms of office would continue through the first regular session of the enlarged Working Group. The Chairman stated that
after a full discussion of the agenda, and the
annotations to the agenda submitted by the Secretariat, the Working Group unanimously adopted a
decision providing for positive and specific
steps to carry the work forward (A/8417, para.
20-21).

The third session (and first for the enlarged
Working Group) was held in Geneva from 31 January
to 11 February 1972. The Vice-Chairman was unable to attend the session, and the following officers were elected: Second Vice-Chairman: Stanislaw Suchorzewski (Poland); Rapporteur: Richard St.
John (Australia). Its report (A/CN.9/63 and Add.
1, Ibid., vol.III:1972, part two, IV) was issued

on 29 February 1972. On 17 March 1972, a report
by the Secretary-General on "Responsibility of
Ocean Carriers for Cargo: Bills of Lading" (A/CN.
9/WG.III/WP.4, vols.I-III) was issued as an addendum to the report (A/CN.9/63/Add.1, Ibid.)

At the fifth session of UNCITRAL, April-May 1972,
the Secretary-General was requested to convene a
special session of the Working Group in Geneva
for two weeks for completion of its work on areas
left unfinished at its third session. Accordingly, the Working Group held its fourth (special)
session in Geneva from 25 September to 6 October
1972. Its officers were: Chairman: José Domingo
Ray (Argentina); Vice-Chairman: Stanislaw Suchorzewski (Poland); Rapporteur: Mohsen Chafik (UAR).
The report of the session (A/CN.9/74, Ibid., vol.
IV:1973, part two, IV, 1) was issued on 12 October 1972. Annexes I and II of the report contained Secretariat working papers on approaches
to basic policy decisions concerning allocation
of risks between the cargo owner and carrier,
and on arbitration clauses in bills of lading.

The fifth session of the Working Group was held
in New York from 5 to 16 February 1973. Its
elected officers were: Chairman: José Domingo
Ray (Argentina); Vice-Chairman: Stanislaw Suchorzewski (Poland); Rapporteur: L.H. Khoo (Singapore).
Its report (A/CN.9/76, Ibid., vol.IV:1973, part
two, IV,5) was issued on 28 February 1973. An
addendum to the report (A/CN.9/76/Add.1, Ibid.,
part two, IV,4), issued on 21 March 1973, contained the second report of the Secretary-General on
"Responsibility of Ocean Carriers for Cargo:
Bills of Lading" (A/CN.9/WG.III/WP.10, vols.I-
III).

A sixth session was to be held in Geneva from 4
to 20 February 1974.

IV. - Working Group on International Negotiable Instruments (A/CN.9/WG.IV/WP.-)

Established on 4 May 1972, by a decision of UNCITRAL at its 124th meeting, fifth session (A/8717, para.61), after taking note of the report of the Secretary-General setting forth a draft uniform law on international bills (A/CN. 9/67), UNCITRAL Yearbook, vol.III:1972, part two, II,1), in pursuance of the Commission's request at its fourth session (A/8417, para.35).

Terms of Reference

Under the Commission's decision, the Working Group was requested to:
  1) prepare a final draft uniform law on international bills of exchange and promissory notes;
  2) consider the desirability of preparing uniform rules applicable to international cheques and the question whether this can best be achieved by extending the application of the draft uniform law to international cheques or by drawing up a separate uniform law on international cheques, and to report its conclusions on these questions to the Commission at a future session.

The Secretary-General was requested to modify the draft uniform law on international bills of exchange with a view to extending its application to international promissory notes, and to submit the draft uniform law so modified to the Working Group at its first session; to consider the proposal made by the International Institute for the Unification of Private Law that the draft uniform law provide uniform rules in respect of the means by which the execution of obligations embodied in an international bill of exchange could be obtained, and to report to the Working Group; to carry out further work in connection with the draft uniform law after consultation with the Commission's Study Group of International Payments composed of experts provided by interested international organizations and banking and trade institutions, and for these purposes to convene meetings as required.

Membership

The Working Group consisted of representatives of Egypt, France, India, Mexico, Nigeria, USSR, United Kingdom, and United States of America. The Secretary-General was requested to invite members of the Working Group to appoint as their representatives persons especially qualified in the law of negotiable instruments and in banking practices.

Action

The Working Group held its first session at the United Nations Office at Geneva from 8 to 19 January 1973. The elected officers were: Chairman: Moshen Chafik (Egypt); Rapporteur: Roberto Luis Montilla-Molina (Mexico). The Working Group had before it the Secretary-General's report entitled "Draft Uniform Law on International Bills of Exchange and International Promissory Notes, and Commentary" (A/CN.9/WG.IV/WP.2, Ibid., vol.IV:1973, part two, II,2). The report of the Working Group on its first session (A/CN.9/77, Ibid., vol.IV:1973, part two,II,1) was issued on 30 January 1973.

The second session would be held in New York, from 7 to 18 January 1974.

Documents

The documents issued under the Commission's document series symbol (A/CN.9/-) were issued in mimeographed form, unless otherwise indicated. Many of the important documents of the series are republished in the UNCITRAL Yearbook.

Yearbook of the United Nations Commission on International Trade Law

Assembly resolution 2502 (XXIV), of 12 November 1969, having considered a note of the Secretary-General (A/CN.9/28), of 6 March 1969, on the possibility of issuing a yearbook, and his report (A/CN.9/32 and Add.1) of 17 September 1969 and 25 March 1970, concerning the financial implications of alternative proposals, approved in principle the establishment of the UNCITRAL Yearbook.

Paragraph 7 of the resolution requested the Commission at its third session to consider the timing and content of the Yearbook in the light of the report of the Secretary-General, and authorized the la tter, in paragraph 8, to establish the Yearbook in accordance with the decisions and recommendations to be adopted by UNCITRAL at its third session.

At its third session, held in April 1970, the Commission requested the Secretary-General (a) to publish in 1970 a first volume of the Yearbook which would contain the materials relating to its first three sessions, and in general to follow the arrangements set out in annex I of the report of the Secretary-General; (b) to submit to the Commission at its fourth session a report on the publication of a second volume and the financial implications thereof.

At its fourth session, held in March-April 1971, the Commission adopted a decision which requested the Secretary-General to include in the second

volume of the Yearbook the material on the work
of the fourth session of the Commission; to publish a second volume as soon as practicable in
English, French, Russian and Spanish...and approved the guidelines for the contents of future
volumes of the Yearbook as set fourth in the
Secretary-General's report (A/CN.9/57 and Corr.1)
of 10 February 1971. A second report of the
Secretary-General on the "Timing and Contents of
the UNCITRAL Yearbook" (A/CN.9/66) was issued
on 20 March 1972.

The publication of the Yearbook was intended to
serve the purpose of making the work of the
Commission more widely known and more readily
available beyond the forum of the United Nations.
To aid in the intensive examination and evaluation of the developing measures for the unification and harmonization of international trade
law, the Yearbook includes, in so far as possible,
the studies which provide the basis for the Commission's work.

The first volume, 1968-1970, is divided into
three main parts, covering the period from the
creation of UNCITRAL to the end of the third session of the Commission, in April 1970. The first
part provides the essential background on the
creation of UNCITRAL, the second presents the
documents reflecting the work of the first three
sessions, including the reports of the Commission
on the sessions, the third is concerned primarily
with the work done on each of the four priority
subjects selected by the Commission.

Each issue of the Yearbook thereafter is divided
into two parts: the first contains the report of
the Commission on its annual session for the period covered, the comments of UNCTAD, report of
the Sixth Committee, and resolutions of the General Assembly concerning the report. Part two

contains studies and reports on specific subjects, including the reports of the Working
Groups. Each issue also contains lists of relevant documents not reproduced in the volume,
a check list of UNCITRAL documents presented to
the session, and a bibliography on UNCITRAL and
related subjects.

The following issues of the <u>Yearbook</u> have been
published:
     Volume I: <u>1968-1970</u>, New York, 1970 (A/CN.
9/SER.A/1970;Sales no.:E.71.V.1)
     Volume II: <u>1971</u>.New York, 1972 (A/CN.9/SER.
A/1971; Sales no.: E.72.V.4)
     Volume III: <u>1972</u>, New York, 1973 (A/CN.9/
SER.A/1972;Sales no.:E.73.V.6)
     Volume III: <u>1972</u>, <u>Supplement</u>, New York, 1973
(A/CN.9/SER.A/1972/Add.1;Sales no.:E.73.V.9)
     Volume IV: <u>1973</u>, New York, 1974 (A/CN.9/SER.
A/1973;Sales no.:E.74.V.3)
     Volume V: <u>1974</u>, New York, 1975 (A/CN.9/SER.
A/1974;Sales no.:E.75.V.2)

B. Question of Defining Aggression

Special Committee on the Question of Defining Aggression (A/AC.66/-)

Established by Assembly resolution 688 (VII), of 20 December 1952, in conformity with resolution 599 (VI), of 31 January 1952, and with the report of the Secretary-General (GAOR, Sess. VII, Annexes, agenda item 54, A/2211) concerning the inclusion of the items on the question of defining aggression in the agenda of the seventh session of the General Assembly.

Terms of Reference

The Committee was to study the various forms of aggression, the connection between a definition of aggression and the maintenance of international peace and security, the problem raised by the inclusion of a definition of aggression in the Code of Offenses against the Peace and Security of Mankind and by its application within the framework of the international criminal jurisdiction, the effect of a definition of aggression on the exercise of the jurisdiction of the various organs of the United Nations, and any other problems referred to above on the assumption of a definition being adopted by a resolution of the General Assembly.

The Special Committee was to submit a draft definition of aggression or draft statements of the notion of aggression at the ninth session of the General Assembly.

The resolution also requested the Secretary-General to communicate the Special Committee's report to Member States for their comments and to place the question on the provisional agenda of the ninth session of the General Assembly.

Membership

The resolution adopted a membership of 15 listed as follows, with their representatives and alternates:

Bolivia: Gaston Araoz
Brazil: Gilberto Amado
China: Shushi Hsu
Dominican Republic: Tulio Franco y Franco,
                     Enrique de Marchena
France: Charles Chaumont
Iran: Fereydoun Adamiyat
Mexico: Jorge Castañeda
Netherlands: Bernard V.A. Röling
Norway: Hans Engen, Erik Dons, Rasmus S.
         Gundersen
Pakistan: A.H.B. Tyabji
Poland: Josef Winiewicz
Syria: Salasheddine Tarazi
USSR: Platon D. Morozov
United Kingdom: Francis A. Vallat
United States of America: John Maktos

Action

The Special Committee met at United Nations Headquarters from 24 August to 21 September 1953, and elected the following officers: Chairman: Enrique de Marchena (Dom.Rep.); Vice-Chairman: B.V. A. Röling (Netherlands); Rapporteur: S. Tarazi (Syria). Its report (GAOR, Sess.IX, Suppl.11 (A/2638)) of 14 October 1953, covered the background of the question of defining aggression, and the problems set out in its mandate. The Special Committee agreed that any definition of aggression would merely have the status of a recommendation and would not have a binding character, but some members felt such a definition would exercise great moral authority.

The comments of Governments were issued on 6 August 1954 (Ibid., Annexes, agenda item 51, A/2689, Corr.1 and Add.1).

General Assembly resolution 895 (IX), of 4 December 1954, decided to place the question of the definition of a ggression on the provisional agenda of the eleventh session, and to establish a new special committee of 19 to report to that session.

1956 Special Committee on the Question of Defining Aggression (A/AC.77/-)

Established by resolution 895 (IX), of 4 December 1954.

Terms of Reference

The resolution requested the Special Committee to submit to the General Assembly at its eleventh session a detailed report followed by a draft definition of aggression, having regard to the ideas expressed at the ninth session of the General Assembly and to the draft resolutions and amendments submitted.

Membership

The resolution designated 19 members listed below with their representatives and alternates:

China: Yu-Chi Hsueh
Czechoslovakia: Karel Petrželka, Dusan Spáčil
Dominican Rep.: Enrique de Marchena, Ambrosio Alvarez Aybar
France: Charles Chaumont
Iraq: Hassen al Chalabi
Israel: Jacob Robinson, Arthur C. Liveran
Mexico: Rafael de la Colina, Enrique Bravo Caro
Netherlands: Bernard V.A. Röling
Norway: Per Vennemoe
Paraguay: Pacífico Montero de Vargas
Peru: Manuel F. Maúrtua
Philippines: Felixberto M. Serrano
Poland: Jerzy Michalowski
Syria: Rafik Asha, Jawdat Mufti
USSR: Platon D. Morozov
United Kingdom: Patrick L. Bushe-Fox
United States of America: William Sanders
Yugoslavia: Djura Ninčić, Aleksandar Božović

Action

The Special Committee met at United Nations Headquarters from 8 October to 9 November 1956, and
elected as officers: Chairman: Enrique de Marchena (Dom.Rep.); Vice-Chairman: Karel Petrželka
(Czech); and Rapporteur: Bernard V.A. Röling
(Netherlands).

The General Assembly, at its 577th plenary meeting, on 15 November 1956, on the report of the
General Committee (A/3350, mimeographed) decided
to postpone until the twelfth session its consideration of the question of aggression and of
the two related items concerning the draft Code
of Offenses against the Peace and Security of
Mankind and international criminal jurisdiction.
The report of the Special Committee (GAOR, Sess.
XII, Suppl.16 (A/3674)), was issued on 18 January 1957. The report gave the views of the members on the legal and moral value of a General
Assembly resolution defining aggression among
other considerations, and published selected
texts of definitions and draft definitions of
aggression prepared by the Secretariat, and draft
definitions submitted to the 1956 Special Committee.

Special Committee on the Question of Defining Aggression (A/AC.91/-)

Established by resolution 1181 (XII), of 29 November 1957.

Terms of Reference

Noting the report of the 1956 Special Committee (GAOR, Sess.XII, Suppl.16 (A/3574)), the General Assembly requested the Secretary-General to ascertain the views of Members, in view of 22 new States having joined the United Nations, and to refer replies to a committee composed of Member States whose representatives had served on the General Committee at the most recent regular session of the General Assembly.

Membership

The membership of 21 at the first session in 1959 was as follows:
Australia, Ceylon, China, Czechoslovakia, Ecuador, El Salvador, France, Greece, Indonesia, Ireland, Japan, Lebanon, Mexico, Nepal, Netherlands, Pakistan, Romania, USSR, United Kingdom, United States of America, and Uruguay.

Membership at the second session in 1962 was as follows:
Argentina, Bulgaria, China, Costa Rica, Cyprus, Czechoslovakia, Denmark, France, Ghana, Greece, Italy, Liberia, Mexico, Netherlands, Niger, Panama, Philippines, Tunisia, USSR, United Kingdom, and United States of America.

At the first meeting of the third session, in 1965, the Acting Chairman noted that the establishing resolution's requirements concerning membership could not be met, since at the 19th session of the Assembly only a President was elected and no other members of the General Committee, and therefore the Secretary-General had extended invitations on the basis of the composition of the General Committee at the 18th session of the Assembly. Since one member of the General Committee, the President, had been elected, the Secretary-General invited Ghana, whose representative had been elected President of the 19th session, to send a representative to the Committee.

Membership at the third session was as follows:
Argentina, Bulgaria, Cameroon, Canada, Chile, China, Cyprus, El Salvador, France, Ghana, Guinea, Iceland, Netherlands, Romania, Somalia, Syria, Turkey, USSR, United Kingdom, United States of America, and Venezuela.

Membership at the fourth session in 1967 was as follows:
Afghanistan, Austria, Bolivia, China, Congo (Kinshasa), Costa Rica, Cyprus, Czechoslovakia, Ecuador, Finland, France, Gabon, Greece, Hungary, Iraq, Jordan, Morocco, Rwanda, Senegal, Sudan, Trinidad and Tobago, Turkey, USSR, United Kingdom, and United States of America.

Representatives of members were listed in the reports of the Special Committee.

Action

The Committee met in April 1959 and April 1962, at which time it was decided to defer until April 1965 further discussion of when the Assembly might again take up the question of defining aggression, but would meet at an earlier date if an absolute majority so decided.

The first session took place at United Nations Headquarters from 14 to 24 April 1959. Its officers were: Chairman: Ali Sastroamidjojo (Indonesia); Vice-Chairman: José A. Correa (Ecuador); Rapporteur: Basile Vitsaxis (Greece). The report of the Special Committee (A/AC.91/ 2) was issued on 24 April 1959. The participants of the session were listed in paragraph 5 of the report.

The Special Committee was reconvened and held five meetings between 2 and 9 April 1962, with the following officers: Chairman: Nathan Barnes (Liberia); Vice-Chairman: Dmitri Bitsios (Greece); Rapporteur: Gonzalo Ortiz (Costa Rica). The report (A/AC.91/3) was issued on 13 April 1962. The participants of the session were listed in paragraph 4 of the report.

On 5 April 1965 the Special Committee held a third session at United Nations Headquarters with the following officers: Chairman: A. A. Vidaurre (El Salvador);Vice-Chairman: Z.Rossides (Cyprus);Rapporteur: Rafik Asha (Syria). The Special Committee held ten meetings up to 16 April, and adopted a resolution which decided to reconvene the Special Committee in April 1967, unless a majority of the members, who would be consulted in writing in January 1966 by the Secretary-General, considered it desirable for the Special Committee to meet in April 1966. The report of the session (A/AC. 91/5) was issued on 16 April 1965. A list of participants appeared in paragraph 5 of the report.

A Secretary-General note (A/AC.91/L.10) of 3 March 1965, gave a historical summary of the various efforts made to define aggression from the time of the League of Nations to date. An earlier report of the Secretary-General (GAOR, Sess.VII, Annexes, agenda item 54,A/2211) had been issued on 3 October 1952.

A Secretary-General note of 17 March 1966 (A/AC.91/6) transmitted communications from Governments of States Members of the Special Committee regarding the question of whether it was desirable for it to meet in April 1956. As a meeting was not requested by a majority of the members, it was decided to convene in April 1967, in accordance with the resolution adopted at the third session of the Special Committee.

The fourth session of the Special Committee was held in New York from 3 April to 28 May 1967. Its officers were: Chairman: Kurt Waldheim (Austria); Vice-Chairman: Eugenio Jimenez (Costa Rica); Rapporteur: Dr. Arpad Prandler (Hungary). The list of representatives attending the session was issued on 14 April 1967 (A/AC.91/INF.4).

The Special Committee took no decision on the various proposals submitted to it, and issued no report. Its meeting, on 26 May, (A/AC.91/SR.29) was the last one to be documented.

Under agenda item 95, the General Assembly considered the report of the Sixth Committee (GAOR, Sess.XXII, Annexes, agenda item 95, A/6988), and approved the draft resolution to establish a special committee of 30 to expedite the definition of aggression (resolution 2330 (XXII), 18 December 1967.

Documents issued under the Special Committee's document series symbol (A/AC.91/-) were issued in mimeographed form.

Special Committee on the Question of Defining Aggression (A/AC.134/-)

Established by Assembly resolution 2330 (XXII), of 18 December 1967, under agenda item 95, "Need to expedite the drafting of a definition of aggression in the light of the present international situation". The resolution noted that there was still no generally recognized definition of aggression, and recognized that there was a widespread conviction of the need to expedite the definition of aggression.

Terms of Reference

The resolution instructed the Special Committee, having regard to the present resolution and the international legal instruments relating to the matter as well as relevant precedents, methods, practices, criteria and the debates of the question in the Sixth Committee and in plenary meetings, to consider all its aspects in order that an adequate definition of aggression may be prepared, and to submit to the twenty-third General Assembly a report which would reflect all the views expressed and the proposals made.

Assembly resolution 2549 (XXIV), of 12 December 1969, considering the urgency of defining aggression and the desirability of achieving this objective, if possible, by the twenty-fifth anniversary of the United Nations, decided that the Special Committee should resume its work at Geneva in the second half of 1970; resolution 2644 (XXV), of 25 November 1970, decided the Special Committee should resume its work as early as possible in 1971; resolution 2967 (XXVII) of 14 December 1972, requested the Special Committee to resume its work as early as possible in 1972; and resolution

3105 (XXVIII), of 12 December 1973, decided it should resume its work early in 1974 in New York, with a view to completing its task and to submitting to the General Assembly at its twenty-ninth session a draft definition of aggression.

Membership

The Special Committee was composed of 35 members appointed by the President of the General Assembly, taking into consideration the principles of equitable geographic representation and the necessity that the principal legal systems of the world should be represented.

In a note (A/7061, mimeographed), of 19 March 1968, the Secretary-General stated that he had been informed by the President of the twenty-second session of the Assembly that he had appointed the following Member States to serve on the Committee:

Algeria, Australia, Bulgaria, Canada, Colombia, Congo (K), Cyprus, Czechoslovakia, Ecuador, Finland, France, Ghana, Guyana, Haiti, Indonesia, Iran, Italy, Japan, Jordan, Madagascar, Mexico, Norway, Romania, Sierra Leone, Spain, Sudan, Syria, Turkey, Uganda, USSR, UAR, United Kingdom, USA, Uruguay, Yugoslavia.

In a note (A/7061/Add.1, mimeographed), of 17 May 1968, the Secretary-General advised he had been informed by the President of the Assembly that Jordan would be unable to attend the meetings of the Special Committee and was not in a position to accept membership. The President, after appropriate consultations, appointed Iraq to replace Jordan. (Congo (K), later listed as Congo (Democratic Rep·), and, as of 1 January 1972, as Zaire; UAR, as of 1 September 1971, is listed as Egypt).

Action

A Secretariat memorandum (A/AC.134, and Add.1), of 24 March 1968, contained a survey of previous United Nations action on the question of defining aggression; an annex contained a list of United Nations documents which had a bearing on the question of defining aggression.

The Committee met in Geneva between 4 June and 6 July 1968, holding 24 meetings, and with the exception of Haiti and Sierra Leone, all members participated in its work. Its elected officers were: Chairman: Mustafa Kamil Yasseen (Iraq); Vice-Chairmen: Milko Harizanov (Bulgaria), José R. Martínez Cobo (Ecuador), Francesco Caportorti (Italy); Rapporteur: George O. Lamptey (Ghana). The report of the Special Committee (GAOR, Sess.XXIII, agenda item 86, A/7185/Rev.1) was published as a separate document in November 1968. It contained the texts of a number of draft proposals and amendments, a summary of the debate, and a draft resolution to be adopted by the General Assembly (see resolution 2420 (XXIII)). The annex of the report listed the members and their representatives.

The Special Committee met again at United Nations Headquarters in New York where it held 27 meetings between 24 February and 3 April 1969. The following officers were elected: Chairman: Fakhreddine Mohamed (Sudan); Vice-Chairmen: Leopoldo Benites (Ecuador), Roeslan Abdulgani (Indonesia), Mrs. Elena Gavrilova (Bulgaria); Rapporteur: Matti Cawén (Finland). Its report (GAOR, Sess.XXIV, Suppl.20 (A/7620)), May 1969, contained in annex 1 a report of the Working Group of the Whole which the Special Committee had established at its 37th meeting, on 18 March 1969, concerning the method of work; annex II contained a list of members and their representatives. Its recommendation was adopted by the General Assembly in resolution 2549 (XXIV).

The third session of the Special Committee was held in Geneva from 13 July to 14 August 1970. Its elected officers were as follows: Chairman: Fakhreddine Mohamed (Sudan); Vice-Chairmen: Zenon Rossides (Cyprus), Gonzalo Alcívar (Ecuador), G. Badesco (Romania); Rapporteur: E.F. Ofstad (Norway). At its meeting on 7 August, the Special Committee established a Working Group of eight members representing the sponsors of the three draft proposals in proportion to their number, that is, one representative for the Soviet draft, five for the 13-Power draft, and two for the six-power draft. The Working Group was requested to help the Committee by formulating an agreed or generally accepted definition of aggression and, in case it was unable to reach such a definition, to report to the Committee its assessment of the progress made during the session. The report of the Working Group was annexed to the Committee report. The report of the third session (GAOR, Sess. XXV, Suppl. 19 (A/8019)), issued in October 1970, contained in annex I the draft proposals before the Special Committee; II the report of the Working Group; III, the list of participants to the session.

In 1971, the Special Committee met from 1 February to 5 March. Its officers were: Chairman: Augusto Legnani (Uruguay); Vice-Chairmen: Matti Cawén (Finland), Vincent Mutuale (Congo (K)), Dr. Ilja Hulinský (Czech); Rapporteur: Riyadh Al-Qaysi (Iraq). At its 88th meeting, on 12 February. a Working Group was established, on recommendation of the Chairman, to consist of the same eight members as served in the 1970

Working Group, plus the Rapporteur of the Committee (Iraq). Its mandate was to help the Committee in the fulfillment of its task by formulating an agreed or generally accepted definition, and to inform the Committee of the progress made. The Working Group issued two reports (A/AC.134/L.30, and Corr.1), on 19 February, and (A/AC.134/L.35), on 4 March, which were annexed to the report of the Committee. The report of the fourth session (GAOR, Sess. XXVI, Suppl.19 (A/8419)), issued in July 1971, contained the following annexes: I and II - Draft proposals before the Special Committee; III - Report of the Working Group; IV - Working Paper submitted by Mexico (A/AC.134/L.28); V - list of members and their representatives.

The Special Committee held its fifth session at United Nations Headquarters in New York from 31 January to 31 March 1972. The following officers were elected: Chairman: Zenon Rossides (Cyprus); Vice-Chairmen: Ion Datcu (Romania), Gonzalo Alcívar (Ecuador), Erik B. Want (Canada); Rapporteur: Aly Ismail Teymour (Egypt). At its 94th meeting, the Special Committee reestablished a Working Group, enlarged from eight to thirteen members, as follows:

Cyprus, Czechoslovakia, Ecuador, France, Ghana, Italy, Mexico, Spain, Syria, USSR, United Kingdom, United States of America, and the Committee's Rapporteur (Egypt).

The mandate was the same as had been given it in the two previous sessions. Its report (A/AC.134/L.37, and Add.1-2) was annexed to the Committee report. The report of the Special Committee (GAOR, Sess.XXVII, Suppl.19 (A/8719)), was issued in April 1972. Its annexes included I - Draft proposals before the Special Committee; II - Report of the Working Group with two appendices:

A. Summary of the report of the informal negotiating group established by the Working Group;

B. Proposals submitted to the Working Group.

At its 99th meeting, on 3 March 1972, the Special Committee recommended, at the suggestion of the Chairman, that, in the period between March 1972 and the 27th session of the General Assembly, the members of the Special Committee carry on informal consultations with a view to overcoming existing differences and difficulties, and devote their utmost efforts to ensuring the success of their common task.

The Special Committee held its sixth session in Geneva from 25 April to 30 May 1973. Its officers were: Chairman: Dragutin Todoric (Yugoslavia); Vice-Chairmen: Luigi Ferrari-Bravo (Italy), Teodoro Bustamente Muñoz (Ecuador), Riyadh Al-Adhami (Iraq); Rapporteur: Matey Karassimeonov (Bulgaria). The Committee also elected Bengt H.G.A. Bro ms (Finland) as one of the Committee's officers and as Chairman of the Working Group.

At its 103rd meeting, on 30 April 1972, the Special Committee established a Working Group open to all delegations with the same rights of participation and decision. It was requested to attempt to prepare and submit a draft definition of aggression, taking as the basis of its work the report of the informal negotiating group in the previous report of the Special Committee (A/8719). The Chairman of the Working Group was requested to report periodically to the Special Committee, either orally or in writing. At its 106th meeting, on 28 May, the Working Group submitted a report (A/AC.134/L. 42, and Corr.1, and Add.1), which was included as an annex in the Committee report.

The report of the Special Committee (GAOR,Sess. XXVIII, Suppl. 19 (A/9019)) was issued in August 1973. Its annexes included: I - Draft proposals before the Special Committee; II - Report of the Working Group, with two appendices: A. Consolidated text of the reports of the contact groups and of the drafting group; B. Proposals submitted to the Working Group. General Assembly resolution 3105 (XXVIII), of 12 December 1973, decided the Special Committee should resume its work early in 1974, and submit a draft definition of aggression to the twenty-ninth session of the Assembly.

In accordance with this resolution, the Special Committee met at United Nations Headquarters in New York from 11 March to 12 April 1974. Its officers were: Chairman: Bengt H.G.A. Broms (Finland); Vice-Chairmen: Dinos Moushoutas (Cyprus), Moise Rakotosihanaka (Madagascar),Jan Azud (Czech); Rapporteur; Joseph Sanders (Guyana). At its 110th meeting, on 11 March 1974, the Special Committee established an open-ended Working Group which would be chaired by the Chairman of the Special Committee and would use as the basis of its work the consolidated text contained in appendix A of annex II to the report of the Special Committee on its 1973 session (A/9019).

The report of the Special Committee on its seventh session (GAOR, Sess. XXIX, Suppl. 19 (A/9619, and Corr.1)), issued in June 1974, contained in chapter II the report of the Working Group; two annexes contained the views expressed by members of the Special Committee at the concluding stage of its session; and a list of members and representatives. The recommendation to the General Assembly which contained a draft definition was approved by the Assembly in resolution 3314 (XXIX), of 14 December 1974, annex of which contained the text of the definition of aggression. The resolution also expressed the appreciation of the Assembly to the Special Committee for its work which resulted in the elaboration of the definition of aggression.

Documents of the Special Committee issued under the Committee's document series symbol (A/AC.134/-) were issued in mimeographed form.

C. Special Legal Problems

Committee on International Criminal Jurisdiction (A/AC.48/-)

Established by Assembly resolution 489 (V), of
12 December 1950, which referred to resolution
260 B (III), of 9 December 1948, to part IV of
the report of the International Law Commission
(GAOR, Sess. V, Suppl. 12 (A/1316), and to the
fact that a final decision regarding the setting up of such an international penal tribunal could not be taken except on the basis
of concrete proposals.

Terms of Reference

The General Assembly decided that a committee,
composed of representatives of 17 Member States,
should meet in Geneva on 1 August 1951, for
the purpose of preparing one or more preliminary draft conventions and proposals relating
to the establishment of an international criminal court. It was to report to the seventh
session of the General Assembly.

Membership

The resolution designated the following seventeen Member States as members of the Committee,
listed below with their representatives as follows:

Australia: William Anstey Wynes
Brazil: Gilberto Amado
China: Hua-Cheng Wang
Cuba: Luis del Valle, Luis Valdés Roig
Denmark: Max Sörensen
Egypt: Abdel Monem Mostafa Bey
France: René de Lacharrière, Roger Pinto

Iran: Khosro Khosrovani
Israel: Jacob Robinson, Haim Cohn
Netherlands: Bernard Victor A. Roling
Pakistan: Muhammad Munir
Syria: Abdul Wahab Homad, Salah el dine
              Tarazi
United Kingdom: Sir Frank Soskice, Lionel
                I. Gordon, E.C. Jones,
                Ian D. Turner
United States of America: George Maurice
                Morris, John Maktos
Uruguay: Luis E. Pineyro Chain

India and Peru, although designated as Members
of the Committee, did not send any representatives.

Action

The Committee consulted, _inter alia_, a memorandum entitled _Historical Survey of the Question of International Criminal Jurisdiction_
(A/CN.47/Rev.1, Sales no.:1949.V.8), September
1949, originally prepared by the Secretary-
General for the International Law Commission:
and a memorandum (A/AC.48/1, mimeographed), of
2 July 1951, on "The Creation of an International Criminal Court", submitted by the Secretary-General.

The Committee met from 1 to 31 August 1951, in
Geneva, and at its first and second meetings
elected the following officers: Chairman:
George M. Morris (USA); First Vice-Chairman:
Muhammad Munir (Pakistan); Second Vice-Chair-
man: Gilberto Amado (Brazil); and Rapporteur:
Max Sörensen (Denmark).

Its report (_GAOR_, Sess.VII, _Suppl. 11_ (A/2136)),
July 1952, contained chapters on general prin-

ciples concerning the establishment of such a
court, organization and jurisdiction of the
court, committing authority and prosecution,
procedure, final provisions and jurisdiction
in respect of genocide. Annex I contained a
draft statute for an international criminal
court, and II, a Voeu that along with the in-
strument establishing the International Criminal Court a protocol should be drawn up confer-
ring jurisdiction on that Court in respect of
the crime of genocide.

General Assembly resolution 687 (VII), of 5
December 1952, established a second Committee
on International Criminal Jurisdiction to explore the question further.

1953 Committee on International Criminal Jurisdiction (A/AC.65/-)

Established by Assembly resolution 687 (VII), of 5 December 1952, after discussion of annex I of the report of the 1951 Committee on International Criminal Jurisdiction (<u>GAOR</u>, Sess. VII, <u>Suppl.11</u> (A/2136)).

Terms of Reference

In the light of comments and suggestions on the draft statute submitted by Governments, as well as those made during the debates in the Sixth Committee, the Assembly asked the Committee to explore the implications and consequences of establishing an international criminal court and of the various methods by which this might be done; and to study the relationship between such a court and the United Nations and its organs; to reexamine the draft statute and to submit a report to the ninth session of the General Assembly.

Membership

The resolution called for a Committee composed of one representative each of seventeen Member States, designated by the President of the Assembly in consultation with the Chairman of the Sixth Committee. The President announced at the 407th plenary meeting, on 19 December 1952, the following Member States would comprise the Committee, listed below with their representatives:

Argentina: Fernando García Olano, Raúl A. Laurel
Australia: Allan H. Loomes
Belgium: J. Y. Dautricourt

China: Hua-Cheng Wang
Denmark: Birger Dons-Moeller
Egypt: Yehia Sami
France: Marcel Merle
Israel: Jacob Robinson, David I. Marmor
Netherlands: B.V.A. Röling
Panama: Ernesto de la Ossa
Peru: Manuel Feliz Maúrtua
Philippines: Mauro Méndez
United Kingdom: Francis A. Vallat
United States of America: George Maurice
      Morris, John Maktos
Venezuela: Victor M. Pérez Perozo
Yugoslavia: Djuro Nincić, Aleksander
           Božović

Pakistan was also designated but did not send
a representative.

Action

The Committee met in New York from 27 July to
20 August 1953, holding 23 meetings during
that period. At its first meeting it elected
the following officers: Chairman: George M.
Morris (USA); Vice-Chairman: Victor M. Pérez
Peroso (Venezuela); Rapporteur: B.V.A. Röling
(Netherlands).

The report (GAOR, Sess.IX, Suppl. 12 (A/2645)),
April 1954, contained in an annex a revised
draft statute for an international criminal
court, and an index to the report and draft
statute.

The General Assembly, in resolution 897 (IX),
of 4 December 1954, decided to postpone further
consideration of the draft Code of Offences
against the Peace and Security of Mankind until the Special Committee on the Question of

Defining Aggression (resolution 895 (IX), 4 December 1954) had submitted its report. By resolution 898 (IX), of 14 December 1954, the Assembly decided to postpone consideration of the question of an international criminal jurisdiction until the Assembly had taken up the report of the Special Committee on the Question of Defining Aggression, and had again considered the Draft Code of Offences against the Peace and Security of Mankind.

A Secretary-General's note (A/3649, mimeographed), of 28 August 1957, gave background on the subject from the third session of the General Assembly in 1948; and a note of the same date (GAOR, Sess.XII, Annexes, agenda item 55, A/3650), traced the history of action on the Code referred to above up to the eleventh session of the General Assembly.

At the twelfth session of the General Assembly, it was decided (resolution 1186 (XII), 11 December 1957) on the recommendation of the Sixth Committee (Ibid., A/3770) to defer the question of the international criminal jurisdiction until such time as the General Assembly again took up the question of defining aggression and the question of a draft Code of Offences against the Peace and Security of Mankind.

Related Document

Memorandum prepared by the Secretariat "Tribunals created by the General Assembly of the United Nations" (A/AC.65/2, mimeographed), of 29 July 1953. The memorandum was submitted pursuant to a request by the 1953 Committee on International Criminal Jurisdiction, and attempted to give a brief factual account of the United Nations Administrative Tribunal, the United Nations Tribunal for Libya and the United Nations Tribunal for Eritrea, with special refer-

ence to the method and the juridical basis
of their creation, their jurisdiction and
their judicial independence.

Preparatory Group of Experts to Advise the Secretary-General on Preparation of a Conference on the Law of the Sea

Established by Assembly resolution 1105 (XI), of 21 February 1957, which requested the Secretary-General to invite appropriate experts to advise and assist the Secretariat in preparing for the international conference of plenipotentiaries to examine the law of the sea.

Terms of Reference

The expert group was to obtain comments from Governments on the report of the International Law Commission (ILC) (GAOR, Sess.XI, Suppl. 9 (A/3159)), on its eighth session containing draft articles and commentaries on the law of the sea; to make recommendations regarding the method of work and procedures of the conference; to prepare working documents of a legal, technical, scientific or economic nature in order to facilitate the work of the conference.

Membership

The ten experts invited by the Secretary-General to advise and assist the Secretariat were the following:

Kenneth H. Bailey (Australia), Solicitor-General of Australia

Jorge Castañeda (Mexico), Legal Adviser, Mexican Delegation to the United Nations

B. N. Chopra (India), former Adviser to the Government of India on Fisheries Development

W. V. J. Evans (UK), Counselor and Legal Adviser, United Kingdom Mission to the United Nations

J.P.A. François (Netherlands), Rapporteur of the International Law Commission on the Law of the Sea

F.V. Garcia Amador (Cuba), member of the International Law Commission

Hamed Abdul Fattah Gohar (Egypt), Director of the Institute of Oceanography, University of Cairo

Luis Melo Lecaros (Chile), member of the Delegation of Chile to the General Assembly

Karel Petrželka (Czech), member of the Czechoslovakian Delegation to the General Assembly

William Sanders (USA), Special Assistant to the Secretary of State, USA.

Action

Ten meetings were held from 25 February to 6 March 1957, and eight meetings between 7 and 16 October 1957. In consultation with the experts, a letter was sent to the Governments invited to the conference requesting them to send to the Secretary-General further provisional comments they might wish to make on the ILC report and related matters. The Governments' replies were issued in documents A/CONF. 13/5 and Adds.1-4. A complete guide to these and earlier comments was issued in document A/CONF.13/30. The result of the work and procedures of the conference were included in the provisional agenda of the conference (A/CONF. 13/9), the provisional rules of procedure (A/CONF.13/10), and the memorandum concerning the method of work and procedure of the conference (A/CONF.13/11). The Secretary-General's report on the Preparation of the Conference (A/CONF.13/20) as well as those cited above, were issued in volume I: Preparatory Documents of

the Official Records of the United Nations
Conference on the Law of the Sea.

The United Nations Conference on the Law of
the Sea took place in Geneva from 24 February
to 27 April 1958. Its Official Records were
published in seven volumes (A/CONF.13/37-43;
Sales no.:58.V.4, Vols. I-VII) published in
1959.

<u>Special Committee on Principles of Internation-
al Law concerning Friendly Relations and
Cooperation among States (A/AC.119/- and
A/AC.125/-)</u>

Established by Assembly resolution 1966 (XVIII)
of 16 December 1963.

Assembly resolution 2103 (XX), of 20 December
1965, decided to reconstitute the Special Committee, with four additional members, in order
to complete the consideration and elaboration
of the seven principles set forth in paragraph
1 of resolution 1815 (XVII), of 18 December
1962; and to report to the twenty-first session
of the General Assembly.

Terms of Reference

The Special Committee was requested to draw
up a report containing -- for the purpose of
the progressive development and codification
of the four principles set forth in paragraph
3 of resolution 1815 (XVII), so as to secure
their more effective application -- the conclusions of its study and its recommendations,
taking into account:

(a) the practice of the United Nations
and of States in the application of the principles established in the United Nations Charter;

(b) comments submitted by Governments in
accordance with paragraph 4 of resolution 1815
(XVII);

(c) views and suggestions advanced by the
representatives of Member States during the
seventeenth and eighteenth sessions of the General Assembly.

The Special Committee was requested to report
to the nineteenth session of the General Assembly.

Resolution 2103 (XX) requested the Special Committee to continue consideration of the four principles set forth in paragraph 3 of resolution 1815 (XVII), having full regard to matters on which the previous Special Committee was unable to reach agreement; to consider the three principles set forth in paragraph 5 of resolution 1966 (XVIII); to submit a comprehensive report on the results of its study of the seven principles set forth in resolution 1815 (XVII), including its conclusions and recommendations with a view to enabling the General Assembly to adopt a declaration containing an enunciation of these principles.

Assembly resolution 2533 (XXIV), of 8 December 1969, further defined the terms of reference.

Membership

The establishing resolution requested the President of the General Assembly to appoint the members of the Special Committee, and recommended that the Governments of States designated as members appoint jurists as their representatives, in view of the general importance and technical aspect of the item. The President appointed (A/5689, mimeographed) the following 27 States to serve:

Afghanistan*	Guatemala	Poland
Argentina	India	Romania
Australia	Italy	Sweden
Cameroon	Japan	USSR
Canada	Lebanon	UAR
Czechoslovakia	Madagascar	United
Dahomey	Mexico	Kingdom
France	Netherlands	USA
Ghana	Nigeria	Venezuela
		Yugoslavia

*Afghanistan resigned in view of the fact that it was unable to attend the Committee's first session, and Burma was appointed in its place (A/5727-A/AC.119/2, mimeographed), 26 August 1964.

Resolution 2103 (XX), of 20 December 1965, de-
signated the following additional four Member
States to serve on the reconstituted Committee:
  Algeria, Chile, Kenya, Syria.

Annexes to the reports of the Special Committee
contained a list of Member States and their representatives.

Action

The Special Committee met in Mexico City for a
five-week session from 27 August to 1 October
1964, during which time it held 43 meetings,
under the Chairmanship of A. García Robles
(Mexico). Other officers elected were: Vice-
Chairmen: Vratislav Pĕchota (Czech), and K.
Krishna Rao (India); Rapporteur: Hans Blix
(Sweden). The Special Committee's report (GAOR,
Sess.XX.Annexes, vol.3, agenda item 90 (a), A/
5746), of 16 November 1964, contained in chapter IX a summary of general remarks made in the
Special Committee concerning the four principles
of international law referred to it by the General Assembly; and chapters III, IV, V, and VI
dealt separately with the four principles; chapter VII dealt with the question of methods of
fact-finding, referred to the Special Committee
by Assembly resolution 1967 (XVIII), of 16 December 1963.

In 1966, the reconstituted Special Committee
held 52 meetings during a seven-week session
from 8 March to 25 April. Its elected officers
were: Chairman: K. Krishna Rao (India); Vice-
Chairmen: Vratislav Pĕchota (Czech), and Armando
Molina Landaeta (Venezuela); Rapporteur: W. Riphagen (Netherlands). Its report (GAOR, Sess.
XXI, Annexes, vol. 3, agenda item 87 (a), A/
6230) was issued on 27 June 1966. It contained

nine chapters and two annexes which described
the composition, organization and terms of reference of the Special Committee, dealt with the
seven principles of international law referred
to the Special Committee by the General Assembly
and reported its conclusions on its work with
respect to those principles on which it was unable to arrive at any agreed formulations. Annex II listed the background documentation.

The Special Committee held 28 public and 5 private meetings at its second session at the United Nations Office at Geneva from 17 July to 19
August 1967, in accordance with operative paragraph 9 of resolution 2181 (XXI), of 12 December 1966. Its officers were: Chairman: Paul
Bamela Engo (Cameroon); Vice-Chairmen: Souheil
Chammas (Lebanon), and Ernesto de la Guardia
(Argentina); Rapporteur: Milan Sahović (Yugoslavia). The report (GAOR, Sess. XXII, Annexes,
vol.3, agenda item 87, A/6799), was issued on
26 September 1967. It was divided into six
chapters, the last chapter dealing with the concluding stage of the Special Committee's session,
including the decisions and the adoption of its
report to the Assembly.

In 1968, the Special Committee met at United
Nations Headquarters in New York, and held 16
meetings in the course of a three-week session
from 9 to 30 September. Its elected officers
were: Chairman: Willem Riphagen (Netherlands);
Vice-Chairmen: M. Kestler (Guatemala), and W.B.
Van Lare (Ghana); Rapporteur: D.A. Kamat (India).
Its report (GAOR, Sess.XXIII, Annexes,agenda
item 87, A/7326, issued as a separate document),
was published in November 1968. The introduction to the report briefly recalled the background of the work of the Special Committee.
Chapter II of the report was divided into two
sections, and dealt with the consideration of

the two principles of international law referred
to in paragraph 4 of resolution 2327 (XXII),
with a view to completing their formulation.
Chapter III recorded the Special Committee's
decision regarding the third principle referred
to it by paragraph 5 of resolution 2327 (XXII).

In 1969, the Special Committee met at United Nations Headquarters, and held 13 meetings in the
course of a five-week session from 18 August to
19 September. Its elected officers were: Chairman: Milan Sahović (Yugoslavia); Vice-Chairmen:
S.P. Jagota (India), and A.W. Robertson (Canada);
Rapporteur: E. Sam (Ghana). Its report of October 1969 (GAOR, Sess. XXIV, Suppl.19 (A/7619))
reported in chapter I on the work of the fourth
session, and in chapter II on the completion of
its work in the light of the debate which took
place in the Sixth Committee during the twenty-
third and preceding sessions of the General Assembly and in the 1964, 1966, 1967 and 1968 sessions of the Special Committee, by endeavoring
to resolve, pursuant to General Assembly resolution 2327 (XXII), all relevant questions relating to the formulation of the seven principles.

The Special Committee's fifth session took place
at the United Nations Office at Geneva in the
course of a five-week session from 31 March to
1 May 1970. Its elected officers were: Chairman: Sergio González Gálvez (Mexico); Vice-
Chairmen: Aurel Cristescu (Romania), and El
Sayed Abdel Raouf El-Reedy (UAR); Rapporteur:
Gaetano Arangio-Ruiz (Italy). The report (GAOR,
Sess. XXV, Suppl. 18 (A/8018)) appeared in September 1970. Chapter II of the report, which was
divided into four sections, dealt with the completion at the present session of the Special
Committee's work on the remaining questions relating to the formulation of the seven principles

of international law concerning friendly relations and cooperation among States. At the last
meeting of the session, the 114th, on 1 May
1970, the Special Committee adopted without objection the draft report presented by its Rapporteur in the understanding that the final
version would be rearranged in the light of the
outcome of the session and would include the report of the drafting committee, the summary of
the statements made by members of the Special
Committee at the concluding stage of the session, and the decisions taken by the Special
Committee.

Assembly resolution 2625 (XXV), of 24 October
1970, approved the Declaration on Principles of
International Law concerning Friendly Relations
and Cooperation among States in accordance with
the Charter of the United Nations, text of which
was annexed to the resolution, and expressed
its appreciation to the Special Committee for
its work resulting in the elaboration of the
Declaration.

Register of Experts on Methods of Fact-Finding

Established by Assembly resolution 2329 (XXII), of 18 December 1967, recalling resolution 1967 (XVIII), 16 December 1963; 2104 (XX), 20 December 1965; 2182 (XXI), 12 December 1966, on the question of methods of fact-finding, and two reports submitted by the Secretary-General in pursuance of these resolutions (GAOR, Sess. XX, Annexes, vol.3, agenda item 90 (c)), on 1 May 1964, and (GAOR, Sess.XXI, Annexes, vol.3, agenda item 87 (b)), on 22 April 1968.

Terms of Reference

Recognizing the usefulness of impartial fact-finding as a means towards the settlement of disputes, believing that an important contribution to the peaceful settlement and prevention of disputes could be made by providing for impartial fact-finding within the framework of international organizations and in bilateral and multilateral conventions or through other appropriate arrangements; reaffirming the importance of impartial fact-finding, in appropriate cases, for the settlement and prevention of disputes, the Assembly requested the Secretary-General to prepare a register of experts in legal and other fields, whose services the States parties to a dispute may use by agreement for fact-finding in relation to the dispute.

Membership

Paragraph 3 of the resolution requested Member States to nominate up to five of their nationals to be included in the register of experts.

Action

The Secretary-General issued a preliminary list (A/7240, mimeographed) on 24 September 1968; and

a revised version (A/7751, mimeographed) on 7
November 1969, bringing the list up to 30 September 1969, 42 States having responded to the
Secretary-General's request up to that date.
The revised version contained biographies of
the experts listed. The Secretary-General issued changes and additions to the list which
Member States wished to make in the revised
version (A/8108, offset), on 18 November 1970.

Ad Hoc Committee on International Terrorism (A/AC.160/-)

Established by Assembly resolution 3034 (XXVII), of 18 December 1972, after consideration of the report of the Sixth Committee (GAOR, Sess.XXVII, Annexes, agenda item 92, A/8969), of 16 December 1972, and the Secretary-General's request for inclusion of the item on the agenda of the General Assembly (Ibid., A/8791, and Add.1), of 8 September 1972.

Terms of Reference

The Ad Hoc Committee was requested to consider the observations of States under paragraph 7 (which invited States to consider the subject matter urgently and to submit observations to the Secretary-General by 10 April 1973, including concrete proposals for finding an effective solution to the problem), and to submit its report to the General Assembly at its twenty-eighth session, with recommendations for possible cooperation for the speedy elimination of the problem, bearing in mind the provisions of paragraph 3 (the inalienable right to self-determination and independence of all peoples under colonial and racist regimes and other forms of alien domination, and the legitimacy of their struggle, in particular the struggle of national liberation movements, in accordance with the purposes and principles of the Charter and the relevant resolutions of the organs of the United Nations).

Membership

The resolution decided that the Ad Hoc Committee should consist of 35 members, to be appointed by the President of the General Assembly, bearing in mind the principle of equitable geographical representation.

In a letter of 20 April 1973 (A/8993, mimeographed), the President informed the Secretary-General that, after consultations with all the regional groups, he had appointed the following Member States:

Algeria	Hungary	Tanzania
Austria	India	Tunisia
Barbados	Iran	Turkey
Canada	Italy	Ukrainian SSR
Congo	Japan	USSR
Czechoslovakia	Mauretania	United Kingdom
Democratic	Nicaragua	United States
Yemen	Nigeria	of America
France	Panama	Uruguay
Greece	Sweden	Venezuela
Guinea	Syria	Yemen
Haiti		Yugoslavia
		Zaire
		Zambia

Action

The Ad Hoc Committee met at United Nations Headquarters from 16 July to 11 August 1973. The following officers were elected: Chairman: Aquilino Boyd (Panama); Vice-Chairmen: Erik B. Wang (Canada), Gyula Jelenik (Hungary); Rapporteur: Mukuna Kabongo (Zaire). The Committee decided at its 17th meeting, on 31 July 1973, to set up three sub-committees of the whole to study, respectively, the definition of international terrorism, its underlying causes, and measures for the prevention of international terrorism. Reports of the work of the three sub-committees were included in chapters III, IV and V of the report of the Com-

mittee (<u>GAOR</u>, Sess. XXVIII, <u>Suppl. 28</u> (A/9028)),
issued in September 1973.

At the 1458th meeting, on 7 December 1973, of
the Sixth Committee, it was decided to recommend
that, because of the lack of time, consideration
of the question should be deferred until the
twenty-ninth session (<u>GAOR</u>, Sess. XXVIII, <u>An-
nexes</u>, agenda item 94, A/9410, paragraph 4). At
the 2197th plenary meeting, on 12 December 1973,
the General Assembly approved the recommendation.

Related Document

<u>International Terrorism</u>: A Select Bibliography
(ST/LIB/31), 26 September 1973.

ANNEXES

ANNEX I - A

Membership in the United Nations
(as of 31 December 1976)

The original Members of the United Nations (51)
are those which participated in the United Nations Conference on International Organization
at San Francisco or had previously signed the
United Nations Declaration of 1 January 1942,
and which signed and ratified the Charter.

The [145] Member States of the United Nations,
with dates on which they became Members, are
listed below; the asterisk indicates the original Members and the numbers indicate the notes
that follow:

Member	Date of Admission
Afghanistan	19 Nov. 1946
Albania	14 Dec. 1955
Algeria	8 Oct. 1962
*Argentina	24 Oct. 1945
*Australia	1 Nov. 1945
Austria	14 Dec. 1955
Bahamas	18 Sept. 1973
Bahrain	21 Sept. 1971
Bangladesh	17 Sept. 1974
Barbados	9 Dec. 1966
*Belgium	27 Dec. 1945
Benin[1]	20 Sept. 1960
Bhutan	21 Sept. 1971
*Bolivia	14 Nov. 1945
Botswana	17 Oct. 1966
*Brazil	24 Oct. 1945
Bulgaria	14 Dec. 1955
Burma	19 Apr. 1948
Burundi	18 Sept. 1962
*Byelorussia	24 Oct. 1945

Member	Date of Admission
Cambodia[2]	14 Dec. 1955
*Canada	9 Nov. 1945
Cape Verde	16 Sept. 1975
Central African Republic	20 Sept. 1960
Chad	20 Sept. 1960
*Chile	24 Oct. 1945
*China[3]	24 Oct. 1945
*Colombia	5 Nov. 1945
Comoros	12 Nov. 1975
Congo[4]	20 Sept. 1960
*Costa Rica	2 Nov. 1945
*Cuba	24 Oct. 1945
Cyprus	20 Sept. 1960
*Czechoslovakia	24 Oct. 1945
Democratic Yemen[5]	14 Dec. 1967
*Denmark	24 Oct. 1945
*Dominican Republic	24 Oct. 1945
*Ecuador	21 Dec. 1945
*Egypt[6]	24 Oct. 1945
*El Salvador	24 Oct. 1945
Equatorial Guinea	12 Nov. 1968
*Ethiopia	13 Nov. 1945
Fiji	13 Oct. 1970
Finland	14 Dec. 1955
*France	24 Oct. 1945
Gabon	20 Sept. 1960
Gambia	21 Sept. 1965
German Democratic Republic	18 Sept. 1973
Germany, Federal Republic of	18 Sept. 1973
Ghana	8 Mar. 1957
*Greece	25 Oct. 1945
Grenada	17 Sept. 1974
*Guatemala	21 Nov. 1945
Guinea	12 Dec. 1958
Guinea-Bissau	17 Sept. 1974
Guyana	20 Sept. 1966
*Haiti	24 Oct. 1945
*Honduras	17 Dec. 1945

Member	Date of Admission
Hungary	14 Dec. 1955
Iceland	19 Dec. 1946
*India	30 Oct. 1945
Indonesia[7]	28 Sept. 1950
*Iran	24 Oct. 1945
*Iraq	21 Dec. 1945
Ireland	14 Dec. 1955
Israel	11 May 1949
Italy	14 Dec. 1955
Ivory Coast	20 Sept. 1960
Jamaica	18 Sept. 1962
Japan	18 Dec. 1956
Jordan	14 Dec. 1955
Kenya	16 Dec. 1963
Kuwait	14 May 1963
Laos[15]	14 Dec. 1955
*Lebanon	24 Oct. 1945
Lesotho	17 Oct. 1966
*Liberia	2 Nov. 1945
Libya	14 Dec. 1955
*Luxembourg	24 Oct. 1945
Madagascar	20 Sept. 1960
Malawi	1 Dec. 1964
Malaysia[8]	17 Sept. 1957
Maldives	21 Sept. 1965
Mali	28 Sept. 1960
Malta	1 Dec. 1964
Mauritania	27 Oct. 1961
Mauritius	24 Apr. 1968
*Mexico	7 Nov. 1945
Mongolia	27 Oct. 1961
Morocco	12 Nov. 1956
Mozambique	16 Sept. 1975
Nepal	14 Dec. 1955
*Netherlands	10 Dec. 1945
*New Zealand	24 Oct. 1945
*Nicaragua	24 Oct. 1945
Niger	20 Sept. 1960

Member	Date of Admission
Nigeria	7 Oct. 1960
*Norway	27 Nov. 1945
Oma n	7 Oct. 1971
Pakistan	30 Sept. 1947
*Panama	13 Nov. 1945
Papua New Guinea	10 Oct. 1975
*Paraguay	24 Oct. 1945
*Peru	31 Oct. 1945
*Philippines	24 Oct. 1945
*Poland[9]	24 Oct. 1945
Portugal	14 Dec. 1955
Qatar	21 Sept. 1971
Romania	14 Dec. 1955
Rwanda	18 Sept. 1962
São Tomé and Príncipe	16 Sept. 1975
*Saudi Arabia	24 Oct. 1945
Senegal	28 Sept. 1960
Seychelles	21 Sept. 1976
Sierra Leone	27 Sept. 1961
Singapore[8]	21 Sept. 1965
Somalia	20 Sept. 1960
*South Africa	7 Nov. 1945
Spain	14 Dec. 1955
Sri Lanka[10]	14 Dec. 1955
Sudan	12 Nov. 1956
Surinam	4 Dec. 1975
Swaziland	24 Sept. 1968
Sweden	19 Nov. 1946
*Syria[6]	24 Oct. 1945
	(resumed 13 Oct. 1961)
Thailand[11]	16 Dec. 1946
Togo	20 Sept. 1960
Trinidad and Tobago	18 Sept. 1962
Tunisia	12 Nov. 1956
*Turkey	24 Oct. 1945
Uganda	25 Oct. 1962
*Ukraine	24 Oct. 1945
*Union of Soviet Socialist Republics	24 Oct. 1945

1374

Member	Date of Admission
United Arab Emirates	9 Dec. 1971
*United Kingdom	24 Oct. 1945
United Republic of Cameroon	20 Sept. 1960
United Republic of Tanzania[12]	14 Dec. 1961
*United States of America	24 Oct. 1945
Upper Volta	20 Sept. 1960
*Uruguay	18 Dec. 1945
*Venezuela	15 Nov. 1945
Yemen[13]	30 Sept. 1947
*Yugoslavia	24 Oct. 1945
Zaire[14]	20 Sept. 1960
Zambia	1 Dec. 1964

Notes pertaining to the country listing:

1) Benin was listed as Dahomey from 1960 until 1975. It was proclaimed as the People's Republic of Benin as of 30 November 1975, and listed at the United Nations as Benin in December 1975.

2) Cambodia was listed as Cambodia from 1955 to 1970. It was proclaimed the Khmer Republic on 9 October 1970, and listed under that name in January 1971. It reverted to the name of Cambodia (Kingdom of Cambodia (Kampuchea)) in April 1975. From September 1976, has been listed as Democratic Kampuchea.

3) By resolution 2758 (XXVI), of 25 October 1971, the General Assembly decided "to restore all its rights to the People's Republic of China and to recognize the representatives of its Government as the only legitimate representatives of China

in the United Nations, and to expel
forthwith the representatives of Chiang
Kai-shek from the place which they un-
lawfully occupy at the United Nations
and to all the organizations related to
it". After October 1971, the China listing has represented the People's Republic of China (mainland China).

The China listing at the United Nations
from 1946 to 1949 represented mainland
China. After January 1949 to October
1971, the China listing represented the
Republic of China in Taiwan.

4) Congo, formerly the French Congo, was
    listed as Congo (Brazzaville) from 1960.
    It became the People's Republic of the
    Congo in May 1971, and has been listed
    as Congo at the United Nations as of
    January 1972.

5) Yemen (capital Aden) was admitted to
    membership on 14 December 1967 and listed
    as Southern Yemen from 1968 to 1970;
    from 1971 to 1972, it was listed as the
    People's Democratic Republic of Yemen
    (PDRY). As of 1973, it has been listed
    as Democratic Yemen, although its of-
    ficial name has not changed.

6) Egypt and Syria were original Members of
    the United Nations from 24 October 1945.
    Following a plebiscite on 21 February
    1958, the United Arab Republic was estab-
    lished by a union of Egypt and Syria and
    continued as a single Member (UAR) until
    13 October 1961, when Syria resumed its
    status as an independent State and simul-
    taneously its United Nations membership.

On 2 September 1971, the United Arab
Republic changed its name to the Arab
Republic of Egypt, and is listed as
Egypt.

7) Indonesia, by letter of 20 January 1965,
    announced its decision to withdraw from
    the United Nations "at this stage and
    under the present circumstances". By
    telegram of 19 September 1966, it an-
    nounced its decision "to resume full
    participation in its (UN) activities".
    On 28 September 1966, the General Assem-
    bly took note of this decision and the
    President invited the representatives of
    Indonesia to take seats in the Assembly.

8) The Federation of Malaya joined the Uni-
    ted Nations on 17 September 1957. On
    16 September 1965, its name was changed
    to Malaysia, following the admission to
    the new federation of Singapore, Sabah
    (North Borneo) and Sarawak. Singapore
    became an independent State on 9 August
    1965 and a Member of the United Nations
    on 21 September 1965.

9) Although Poland was not represented at
    San Francisco, it was agreed that it
    should sign the Charter subsequently as
    an original member.

10) Sri Lanka was formerly listed as Ceylon
    from 1955 up to May 1972.

11) Thailand was formerly listed as Siam
    from 1947-1949.

12) Tanganyika was a Member of the United
    Nations from 14 December 1961 and
    Zanzibar was a Member from 16 December

1963. Following ratification on 26 April 1964 of Articles of Union between Tanganyika and Zanzibar, the United Republic of Tanganyika and Zanzibar continued as a single Member, changing its name to the United Republic of Tanzania on 1 November 1964.

13) The United Nations listing of Yemen represented Yemen (Sanaa) from September 1947 to 1970, when it became the Yemen Arab Republic as of January 1971, and retained its listing as Yemen.

14) Zaire, formerly the Belgian Congo, became the Democratic Republic of the Congo and listed as Congo (Leopoldville) from 20 September 1960 to July 1967, when it was listed as Congo (Kinshasa). Its name was changed to Zaire and so listed at the United Nations as of January 1972.

15) As of 16 December 1975, Laos is listed as the Lao People's Democratic Republic.

Abbreviations of country names used in the text
to save space when identifying the nationality
of persons named as members of General Assembly
bodies

United Nations documents in general use the
short form to identify countries, instead of
the long form, such as People's Republic of,
Democratic Republic of, Republic of, United
Republic of, etc. The short form is further
abbreviated in this book in some cases as listed
below:

Name	Abbreviation
Central African Republic	CAR
Congo (Brazzaville)	Congo (Brazza)
Congo (Kinshasa)	Congo (K)
Congo (Leopoldville)	Congo (L)
Czechoslovakia	Czech
Democratic Yemen	Dem. Yemen
Dominican Republic	Dominican Rep.
Equatorial Guinea	Equat. Guinea
German Democratic Republic	German Dem. Rep.
(East)	GDR
Germany, Federal Republic	Germany (Fed.Rep.)
of (West)	FRG
Khmer Republic	Khmer
New Zealand	NZ
People's Republic of China	China
People's Democratic Republic	Yemen (PDRY)
of Yemen (Aden)	Dem. Yemen
Republic of China (Taiwan)	China (to Oct.1971)
Republic of South Africa	South Africa
Saudia Arabia	S. Arabia
Sierra Leone	S. Leone
Southern Yemen	So. Yemen

Name	Abbreviation
Union of South Africa	South Africa
Union of Soviet Socialist Republics	USSR
United Arab Emirates	UAE
United Arab Republic	UAR
United Kingdom	UK
United Republic of Cameroon	Cameroon
United Republic of Tanzania	Tanzania
United States of America	USA
Yemen Arab Republic	Yemen

ANNEX II

Resolutions and Other Decisions of the General Assembly

1946 -- 1975

To facilitate reference, each resolution of the General Assembly has been given a serial number, beginning with the resolution adopted at the first part of the first session (document A/64). There is no break in the continuity of numbering from session to session.

The resolutions are therefore referred to by quoting the following two numbers:
      (a) their serial number:1, 2, 3, etc.;
      (b) the number of the session during which they were adopted: I, II, etc.

The resolutions adopted at the first part of the first session of the General Assembly have been numbered by the Secretariat in accordance with the above method in the order of their appearance in document A/64. A complete list of the titles of these resolutions, together with their numbers, is published at the end of volume 2 of resolutions adopted by the General Assembly during the second part of its first session (GAOR, Sess.I, A/64/Add.1).

The special and emergency special sessions are indicated as follows: resolution 184 (S-II), the second special session; and resolution 1004 (ES-II), the second emergency special session.

The first four sessions and the first special session were published as separate documents in the Official Records of the General Assembly.

Starting with the second special and the fifth regular sessions, the resolutions have been issued as supplements to the Official Records of each session.

The session, supplement number and document symbol are indicated in the following list.

Year	Resolutions	Sessions	GAOR
1946	1(I) -- 34 (I)	1st sess., part 1	(A/64)
1946	35(I) -- 103(I)	1st sess., part 2	(A/64/Add.1)
1947	104(S-I)--107(S-I)	1st special session	(A/310)
1947	108(II)--184(II)	2nd session	(A/519)
1948	185(S-II)--189(S-II)	2nd special session	Suppl.2(A/555)
1948	190(III)--264(III)	3rd sess., part 1	(A/810 and Corr.1)
1948	265(III)--306(III)	3rd sess., part 2	(A/900)
1949	307(IV)--375(IV)	4th session	(A/1251 and Corrs.1 and 2)
1950	376(V)--497(V)	5th sess., part 1	Suppl.20(A/1775)
1950/51	498(V)--501(V)	5th sess., part 2	Suppl.20A(A/1775/Add.2)
1951/52	502(VI)--608(VI)	6th session	Suppl.20(A/2119)
1952	609(VII)--699(VII)	7th sess., part 1	Suppl.20(A/2361)
1952/53	700(VII)--709(VII)	7th sess., part 2	Suppl.20A(A/2361/Add.1)
1953	710(VII)--712(VII)	7th sess., part 3	Suppl.20B(A/2361/Add.2)
1953	713(VIII)--806(VIII)	8th session	Suppl.17(A/2630)
1954	807(IX)--907(IX)	9th session	Suppl.21(A/2890)
1955	908(X)--995(X)	10th session	Suppl.19(A/3116)
1956	996(ES-I)--1003(ES-I)	1st emergency spec. session	Suppl.1(A/3354)
1956	1004(ES-II)--1008 (ES-II)	2nd emergency spec. session	Suppl.1(A/3355)
1956	1009(XI)--1132(XI)	11th sess., part 1	Suppl.17(A/3572)

Year	Resolutions	Sessions	GAOR
1957	1133(XI)	11th sess., part 2	Suppl.17A(A/3572/Add.1)
1957	1134(XII)--1236(XII)	12th session	Suppl.18(A/3805)
1958	1237(ES-III)--1238 (ES-III)	3rd emergency spec. session	Suppl.1(A/3905)
1958	1239(XIII)--1348(XIII)	13th sess., part 1	Suppl.18(A/4090)
1959	1349(XIII)--1350(XIII)	13th sess., part 2	Suppl.18A(4090/Add.1)
1959	1351(XIV)--1473(XIV)	14th session	Suppl.16(A/4354)
1960	1474(ES-IV)--1475 (ES-IV)	4th emergency spec. session	Suppl.1(A/4510)
1960	1476(XV)--1592(XV)	15th sess., part 1	Suppl.16(A/4684)
1961	1593(XV)--1620(XV)	15th sess., part 2	Suppl.16A(A/4684/Add.1)
1961	1621(S-III)--1622(S-III)	3rd special session	Suppl.1(A/4860)
1961/62	1623(XVI)--1745(XVI)	16th sess., part 1	Suppl.17(A/5100)
1962	1746(XVI)--1747(XVI)	16th sess., part 2	Suppl.17A(A/5100/Add.1)
1962	1748(XVII)--1871(XVII)	17th session	Suppl.17(A/5217)
1963	1872(S-IV)--1880(S-IV)	4th special session	Suppl.1(A/5441)
1963	1881(XVIII)--1993 (XVIII)	18th session	Suppl.15(A/5515)
1964/65	1994(XIX)--2007(XIX)	19th session	Suppl.15(A/5815)
1965	2008(XX)--2132(XX)	20th session	Suppl.14(A/6014)
1966	2133(XXI)--2247(XXI)	21st session	Suppl.16(A/6316)
1967	2248(S-V)--2251(S-V)	5th special session	Suppl.1(A/6657)
1967	2252(ES-V)--2257(ES-V)	5th emergency spec. session	Suppl.1(A/6798)

Year	Resolutions	Sessions	GAOR
1967	2258(XXII)--2370(XXII)	22nd sess., part 1	Suppl.16(A/6716)
1968	2371(XXII)--2375(XXII)	22nd sess., part 2	Suppl.16A(A/6716/Add.1)
1968	2376(XXIII)--2492(XXIII)	23rd session	Suppl.18(A/7218)
1969	2493(XXIV)--2619(XXIV)	24th session	Suppl.30(A/7630)
1970	2620(XXV)--3750(XXV)	25th session	Suppl.28(A/8028)
1971	3751(XXVI)--2903(XXVI)	26th session	Suppl.29(A/8429)
1972	2904(XXVII)--3049(XXVII)	27th session	Suppl.30(A/8730)
1973	3050(XXVIII)-- 3199(XXVIII)	28th sess., part 1	Suppl.30(A/9030)
1973	Decisions	28th sess., part 2	Suppl.30A(A/9030/Add.1)
1974	3200(S-VI)--3202(S-VI)	6th special session	Suppl.1(A/9559)
1974	3203(XXIX)--3360(XXIX)	29th sess., part 1	Suppl.31(A/9631) and Corr.1)
1974	Decisions	29th sess., part 2	Suppl.31A(A/9631/Add.1)
1975	3361(S-VII)--3372(S-VII)	7th special session	Suppl.1(A/10301)
1975	3373(XXX)--3541(XXX)	30th session	Suppl.34(A/10034)

Related Publications

There is an Index to Resolutions of the General
Assembly, 1946-1970:Part I, Numerical list, arranged by resolution number and containing the
number of the resolution, title, date of adoption and document in which the text is found;
covers numbered resolutions only (ST/LIB/SER.H/
1, Part I, Sales no.:E.72.I.3); and Part II,
Subject Index, arranged alphabetically and containing an analytical description of the substantive contents of the resolutions; also
covers decisions taken by the General Assembly
on important matters (ST/LIB/SER.H/1, Part II,
Sales no.:E.72.I.14). The Index covers the
first to the 25th sessions of the General Assembly.

United Nations Resolutions, Series I, General
Assembly, are being republished by Oceana Publications, Dobbs Ferry, N.Y. 10522. Compiled
and edited by D.J. Djonovich, there have been
twelve volumes issued as of 1975, covering the
first to the 24th sessions, 1946 to 1969. Each
volume covers two sessions and any special sessions which have taken place within the two
years covered; and contains, besides the texts
of the resolutions, a voting record for every
resolution and, if voted in parts, the exact
voting record for each part, and date of adoption. When roll-calls were taken, a special
voting record is supplied indicating how each
country voted, or whether it abstained or was
absent. A topical index pulls together all
resolutions dealing with the same matter.

United Nations on Record: United Nations Gen-
Assembly Roll-Call Votes (1946-1973), by Lynn
Schopen, Hanna Newcombe, Chris Young, James
Wert. Published by the Canadian Peace Research

Institute, Oakville-Dundas, Ontario, Canada.
The material was taken from General Assembly
Official Records, and covers only roll-call
votes taken in plenary meetings of the General
Assembly.

Index to Proceedings of the General Assembly,
covering the year 1975 (ST/LIB/SER.B/A.26),
contains in an annex, for the first time, a
voting chart of resolutions adopted by recorded
or roll-call vote at the 30th session of the
General Assembly.

ANNEX III

The membership of the General Committee from 1946 to 1973 was as follows:

First session, 1946
President: Paul-Henri Spaak (Belgium)
Vice-Presidents(7): China, France, South Africa, USSR, United Kingdom, USA, Venezuela
Chairmen of Main Committees(6):
    1st: Dr. Dmitro Z. Manuilsky (Ukraine)
    2nd: Waclaw Konderski (part 1) and Oscar Lange (Poland) (part 2)
    3rd: Peter Fraser (part 1) and Sir Carl Berendsen (part 2) (New Zealand)
    4th: Dr. Roberto F. MachEachen (Uruguay)
    5th: Faris Al-Khoury (Syria)
    6th: Dr. Roberto Jiménez (Panama)

First special session, April-May 1947
President: Dr. Oswaldo Aranha (Brazil)
Vice-Presidents(7): China, Ecuador, France, India, USSR, United Kingdom, USA
Chairmen of Main Committees(6):
    1st: Lester B. Pearson (Canada)
    2nd: Jan Papanek (Czech)
    3rd: Mahmoud Hassan Pasha (Egypt)
    4th: Hernán G. Erikson (Sweden)
    5th: Josef Winiewicz (Poland)
    6th: Tiburcio Carias (Honduras)

Second session, 1947
President: Dr. Oswaldo Aranha (Brazil)
Vice-Presidents (7): China, Cuba, France, Mexico, USSR, United Kingdom, USA
Chairmen of Main Committees (6):
    1st: Joseph Bech (Luxembourg)
    2nd: Herman Santa Cruz (Chile)
    3rd: Oscar Lange (Poland)
    4th: Sir Carl Berendsen (New Zealand)
    5th: Sir Fazl Ali (India)
    6th: Faris El-Khouri (Syria)

Second special session, April-May 1948
    President: Dr. José Arce (Argentina)
    Vice-Presidents (7): France, Peru, Sweden,
Turkey, USSR, United Kingdom, USA
    Chairmen of Main Committees (6):
        1st: Dr. Ting-Fu Tsiang (China)
        2nd: Eduardo Anze Matienzo (Bolivia)
        3rd: Dr. Carlos García Bauer (Guatemala)
        4th: Sir Carl Berendsen (NZ)
        5th: Dr. Joza Vilfan (Yugoslavia)
        6th: Nasrollah Entezam (Iran)

Third session, 1948
    President: Dr. H.V. Evatt (Australia)
    Vice-Presidents (7): China, France, Mexico,
Poland, USSR, United Kingdom, USA
    Chairmen of Main Committees (6):
        1st: Paul-Henri Spaak (part 1) and F. van
Langenhove (part 2) (Belgium)
        2nd: Hernán Santa Cruz (Chile)
        3rd: Dr. Charles Malik (Lebanon)
        4th: Nasrollah Entezam (Iran)
        5th: L. Dana Wilgress (part 1) and George
Ignatieff (part 2) (Canada)
        6th: Ricardo J. Alfaro (Panama)

Fourth session, 1949
    President: Brigadier General Carlos P.
Romulo (Philippines)
    Vice-Presidents (7): Brazil, China, France,
Pakistan, USSR, United Kingdom, USA
    Chairmen of Main Committees (6):
        1st: Lester B. Pearson (Canada)
        2nd: Hernán Santa Cruz (Chile)
        3rd: Dr. Carlos Eduardo Stolk (Venezuela)
        4th: Hermod Lannung (Denmark)
        5th: Alexis Kyrou (Greece)
        6th: Manfred Lachs (Poland)

Fifth session, 1950
    President: Nasrollah Entezam (Iran)
    Vice-Presidents (7): Australia, China,
France, USSR, United Kingdom, USA, Venezuela
    Chairmen of Main Committees (6):
        1st: R. Urdaneta Arbelaez (Colombia)
        2nd: G. Gutiérrez (Cuba)
        3rd: G.J. van Heuven Goedhart (Nether-
lands)
        4th: Prince Wan Waithayakon (Thailand)
        5th: The Maharaja Jan Saheb of
Nawanagar (India)
        6th: V. Outrata (Czech)

Sixth session, 1951
    President: Luis Padilla Nervo (Mexico)
    Vice-Presidents (7): China, France, Iraq,
USSR, United Kingdom, USA, Yugoslavia
    Chairmen of Main Committees (6):
        1st: Finn Moe (Norway)
        2nd: Prince Wan Waithayakon (Thailand)
        3rd: Mrs. Ana Figueroa (Chile)
        4th: Max Henriquez Urena (Dom.Rep.)
        5th: T. A. Stone (Canada)
        6th: Manfred Lachs (Poland)

Seventh session, 1952
    President: Lester B. Pearson (Canada)
    Vice-Presidents (7): China, Egypt, France,
Honduras, USSR, United Kingdom, USA
    Chairmen of Main Committees (6) and Ad Hoc
Political Committee:
        1st: João Carlos Muniz (Brazil)
        2nd: Jiři Nosek (Czech)
        3rd: Amjad Ali (Pakistan)
        4th: Rodolfo Muñoz (Argentina)
        5th: Brig. General Carlos P. Romulo
(Philippines)
        6th: Prince Wan Waithayakon (Thailand)
        Ad Hoc Political Committee: Alexis Kyrou
(Greece)

Eighth session, 1953
President: Mrs. Vijaya Lakahmi Pandit
(India)
Vice-Presidents (7): China, France, Israel,
Mexico, USSR, United Kingdom, USA
Chairmen of Main Committees (6) and Ad Hoc
Political Committee:
  1st: Fernand van Langenhove (Belgium)
  2nd: Leo Mates (Yugoslavia)
  3rd: G. F. Davidson (Canada)
  4th: Santiago Pérez-Pérez (Venezuela)
  5th: Awni Khalidy (Iraq)
  6th: Juliusz Katz-Suchy (Poland)
  Ad Hoc Political Committee: Miguel Rafael
Urquía (El Salvador)

Ninth session, 1954
President: Eelco N. van Kleffens
(Netherlands)
Vice-Presidents (7): Burma, China, Ecuador,
France, USSR, United Kingdom, USA
Chairmen of Main Committees (6) and Ad Hoc
Political Committee:
  1st: Francisco Urrutia (Colombia)
  2nd: Sir Douglas Copland (Australia)
  3rd: Jiři Nosek (Czech)
  4th: Rafik Asha (Syria)
  5th: Pote Sarasin (Thailand)
  6th: Francisco García Amador (Cuba)
  Ad Hoc Political Committee: Thors Thors
(Iceland)

Tenth session, 1955
President: José Maza (Chile)
Vice-Presidents (7): China, Ethiopia, France,
Luxembourg, USSR, United Kingdom, USA
Chairmen of Main Committees (6) and Ad Hoc
Political Committee:
  1st: Sir Leslie Munro (New Zealand)
  2nd: Ernest Chauvet (Haiti)
  3rd: Omar Loutfi (Egypt)
  4th: Luciano Joublanc Rivas (Mexico)

5th: Hans Engen (Norway)
6th: Manfred Lachs (Poland)
<u>Ad Hoc</u> Political Committee: Prince Wan
Waithayakon (Thailand)

11th session, 1956/1957
<u>President</u>: Prince Wan Waithayakon (Thailand)
<u>Vice-Presidents</u> (8): China, El Salvador,
France, India, Italy, USSR, United Kingdom,
USA
Chairmen of Main Committees (7):
1st: Victor A. Belaunde (Peru)
Special Political Committee: Selim
Sarper (Turkey)
2nd: Mohammad Mir Khan (Pakistan)
3rd: Hermod Lannung (Denmark)
4th: Enrique de Marchena (Dom.Rep.)
5th: Omar Loutfi (Egypt)
6th: Karel Petrželka (Czech)

12th session, 1957
<u>President</u>: Sir Leslie Munro (New Zealand)
<u>Vice-Presidents</u> (9): Ceylon, China, France,
Paraguay, Spain, Tunisia, USSR, United Kingdom,
USA
Chairmen of Main Committees: (7)
1st: Djalal Abdoh (Iran)
Special Political Committee: Emilio
Arenales (Guatemala)
2nd: Jiři Nosek (Czech)
3rd: Mrs. Aase Lionaes (Norway)
4th: Thanat Khoman (Thailand)
5th: W.H.J. van Asch van Wijck (Netherlands)
6th: Santiago Pérez-Pérez (Venezuela)

13th session, 1958/1959
<u>President</u>: Charles Malik (Lebanon)
<u>Vice-Presidents</u> (13): Australia, China,
Czechoslovakia, Ecuador, France, Indonesia,
Nepal, Netherlands, Pakistan, USSR, United
Kingdom, USA, Uruguay

Chairmen of Main Committees (7):
   1st: Miguel Rafael Urquía (El Salvador)
   Special Political Committee: Mihai Magheru
(Romania)
   2nd: Toru Hagiwara (Japan)
   3rd: Mrs. Lina P. Tsaldaris (Greece)
   4th: Frederick H. Boland (Ireland)
   5th: Sir Claude Corea (Ceylon)
   6th: Jorge Castañeda (Mexico)

14th session, 1959

   President: Victor Belaunde (Peru)
   Vice-Presidents (13): Brazil, Burma, China,
France, Morocco, Philippines, Romania, Sweden,
Turkey, South Africa, USSR, United Kingdom, USA
   Chairmen of Main Committees (7):
   1st: Franz Matsch (Austria)
   Special Political Committee: Charles T.O.
King (Liberia)
   2nd: Marcial Tamayo (Bolivia)
   3rd: Mrs. Georgette Ciselet (Belgium)
   4th: Lambertus Nicodemus Palar (Indonesia)
   5th: Jiři Nosek (Czech)
   6th: Alberto Herrarte (Guatemala)

15th session, 1960

   President: Frederick H. Boland (Ireland)
   Vice-Presidents (13): Bulgaria, Canada,
China, France, Japan, Libya, Pakistan, Panama,
Sudan, USSR, United Kingdom, USA, Venezuela
   Chairmen of Main Committees (7):
   1st: Sir Claude Corea (Ceylon)
   Special Political Committee: Carlet
Auguste (Haiti)
   2nd: Janez Stanovnik (Yugoslavia)
   3rd: Eduard Mezincescu (Romania)
   4th: Adnan Pachachi (Iraq)
   5th: Mario Majoli (Italy)
   6th: Gonzalo Ortíz Martín (Costa Rica)

16th session, 1961

President: Mongi Slim (Tunisia)

Vice-Presidents (13): China, Costa Rica, Cyprus, Czechoslovakia, France, Ghana, Greece, Mexico, Netherlands, Niger, USSR, United Kingdom, USA

Chairmen of Main Committees (7):

1st: Mario Amadeo (Argentina)

Special Political Committee: Yordan Tc hobanov (Bulgaria)

2nd: Blasco Lanza d'Ajeta (Italy)

3rd: Salvador P. López (Philippines)

4th: Miss Angie Brooks (Liberia)

5th: Hermod Lannung (Denmark)

6th: César A. Quintero (Panama)

17th session, 1962

President: Muhammad Zafrulla Khan (Pakistan)

Vice-Presidents (13): Australia, Belgium, China, Colombia, France, Guinea, Haiti, Jordan, Madagascar, Romania, USSR, United Kingdom, USA

Chairmen of Main Committees (7):

1st: Omar Abdel Hamid Adeel (Sudan)

Special Political Committee: Leopoldo Benites (Ecuador)

2nd: Bohdan Lewandowski (Poland)

3rd: Nemi Chandra Kasliwal (India)

4th: Guillermo Flores Avedaño (Guatemala)

5th: Jan Paul Bannier (Netherlands)

6th: Constantine Th. Eustathiades(Greece)

Fourth special session, May-June 1963

The General Assembly decided that the President, Vice-Presidents and Chairmen of the Main Committees of the 17th session would serve in the same capacities at the fourth special session, except for the Chairmen of the Third and Sixth Committees. India and Greece appointed representatives to replace Mr. Kasliwal (India) and Mr. Eustathiades (Greece) who were absent by: A.B. Bhadkamkar (India) and Dimitri S. Bitsios (Greece).

18th session, 1963

President: Carlos Sosa Rodríguez (Venezuela)

Vice-Presidents (13): Bulgaria, Cameroon, China, Cyprus, El Salvador, France, Iceland, Somalia, Syria, Turkey, USSR, United Kingdom, USA

Chairmen of Main Committees (7):
1st: C.W.A. Schurmann (Netherlands)
Special Political Committee: Mihail Haseganu (Romania)
2nd: Ismael Thajeb (Indonesia)
3rd: Humberto Díaz Casanueva (Chile)
4th: Achkar Marof (Guinea)
5th: Milton Fowler Gregg (Canada)
6th: José María Ruda (Argentina)

19th session, 1964

President: Alex Quaison-Sackey (Ghana)

Elected by acclamation. No elections being held at the 19th session of the General Assembly, it was impossible to constitute the General Committee.

20th session, 1965

President: Amintore Fanfani (Italy)

Vice-Presidents (17): Burundi, Central African Republic, Chile, China, France, Guatemala, Kuwait, Laos, Malaysia, Morocco, Paraguay, Poland, Sierra Leone, Spain, USSR, United Kingdom, USA

Chairmen of Main Committees (7):
1st: Karoly Csatorday (Hungary)
Special Political Committee: Carlet Auguste (Haiti)
2nd: P.A. Forthomme (Belgium)
3rd: Francisco Cuevas Cancino (Mexico)
4th: Majid Rahnema (Iran)
5th: Nejib Bouziri (Tunisia)
6th: Abdullah El-Erian (UAR)

21st session, 1966
    President: Abdul Rahman Pazhwak (Afghanistan)
    Vice-Presidents (17): Austria, Bolivia,
China, Congo (K), Costa Rica, Cyprus, France,
Gabon, Greece, Hungary, Iraq, Rwanda, Senegal,
Trinidad and Tobago, USSR, United Kingdom, USA
    Chairmen of Main Committees (7):
        1st: Leopoldo Benites (Ecuador)
        Special Political Committee: Max Jakobsen
(Finland)
        2nd: Moraiwid M. Tell (Jordan)
        3rd: Mrs. Halima Warzazi (Morocco)
        4th: Fakhreddine Mohamed (Sudan)
        5th: Vahap Asiroglu (Turkey)
        6th: Vratislav Pechota (Czech)

Fifth special session, April-June 1967
    The General Assembly decided that the Presi-
dent, Vice-Presidents and Chairmen of the Main
Committees of the 21st session would serve in
the same capacities at the fifth special ses-
sion, except for the Chairmen of the Third,
Fifth and Sixth Committees, who were absent.
Morocco appointed Mohammed Tabiti to replace
Mrs. Warzazi as Chairman of the Third Committee;
Turkey appointed Nasif Cuhruk to replace Vahap
Asiroglu as Chairman of the Fifth Committee; and
Czechoslovakia appointed Zdenek Seiner to re-
place Vratislav Pechota as Chairman of the
Sixth Committee.

22nd session, 1967
    President: Corneliu Manescu (Romania)
    Vice-Presidents (17): Australia, China,
Dahomey, Dominican Republic, Ecuador, France,
Iceland, Jordan, Laos, Libya, Nepal, Nicaragua,
Sudan, Tanzania, USSR, United Kingdom, USA
    Chairmen of the Main Committees (7):
        1st: Ismail Fahmy (UAR)
        Special Political Committee: Humberto
López Villamil (Honduras)

2nd: Jorge Pablo Fernandini (Peru)
3rd: Mrs. Mara Radic (Yugoslavia)
4th: George J. Tomeh (Syria)
5th: Harry L. Morris (Liberia)
6th: Edvard Hambro (Norway)

23rd session, 1968
President: Emilio Arenales (Guatemala)
Vice-Presidents (17): Bulgaria, Canada, China, France, Guinea, Guyana, Iran, Lebanon, Mauritania, Peru, Philippines, Sweden, Yugoslavia, Uganda, USSR, United Kingdom, USA
Chairmen of Main Committees (7):
1st: Piero Vinci (Italy)
Special Political Committee: Abdulrahim Abby Farah (Somalia)
2nd: Richard M. Akwei (Ghana)
3rd: Erik Nettel (Austria)
4th: P.V.J. Solomon (Trinidad-Tobago)
5th: G.G. Tchernouchtchenko (Byelorussia)
6th: K. Krishna Rao (India)

24th session, 1969
President: Miss Angie E. Brooks (Liberia)
Vice-Presidents (17): Barbados, Chile, China, Denmark, France, Ghana, Indonesia, Jordan, Luxembourg, Malawi, Mongolia, Nigeria, Panama, USSR, United Kingdom, USA, Yugoslavia
Chairmen of Main Committees (7):
1st: Agha Shahi (Pakistan)
Special Political Committee: Eugeniusz Kulaga (Poland)
2nd: Costa P. Caranicas (Greece)
3rd: Mrs. Turkia Ould Daddah (Mauritania)
4th: Theodore Idzumbuir (Congo (K))
5th: David Silveira da Mota (Brazil)
6th: Gonzalo Alcívar (Ecuador)

25th session, 1970

President: Edward Hambro (Norway)

Vice-Presidents (17): Brazil, Chad, China, Ecuador, France, Iraq, Jamaica, Kenya, Malta, Mauritius, Nepal, Philippines, Senegal, USSR, Ukraine, United Kingdom, USA

Chairmen of Main Committees (7):

    1st: Dr. Andres Aguilar (Venezuela)

    Special Political Committee: Abdul Ramad Ghaus (Afghan)

    2nd: Dr. Walter Gueva Arze (Bolivia)

    3rd: Miss Maria Gross (Romania)

    4th: Vernon Johnson Mwaanga (Zambia)

    5th: Max Wershof (Canada)

    6th: Paul Ramela Engo (Cameroon)

26th session, 1971

President: Adam Malik (Indonesia)

Vice-Presidents (17): Belgium, Burundi, China, Costa Rica, France, Greece, Hungary, Japan, Peru, Sierra Leone, Sudan, USSR, United Kingdom, USA, Venezuela, Yemen (PDRY), Zambia

Chairmen of Main Committees (7):

    1st: Milko Tarabanov (Bulgaria)

    Special Political Committee: Cornelius C. Cremin (Ireland)

    2nd: Narciso G. Reyes (Philippines)

    3rd: Mrs. Helvi Sipila (Finland)

    4th: Keith Johnson (Jamaica)

    5th: Olu Sanu (Nigeria)

    6th: Zenon Rossides (Cyprus)

27th session, 1972

President: Stanislaw Trepczynski (Poland)

Vice-Presidents (17): China, Colombia, Cyprus, Ethiopia, France, Haiti, Iceland, Libya, Mauritania, New Zealand, Paraguay, Philippines, Rwanda, Syria, USSR, United Kingdom, USA

Chairmen of Main Committees (7):

    1st: R. K. Ramphul (Mauritius)

    Special Political Committee: Hady Touré (Guinea)

2nd: Bruce Rankin (Canada)
3rd: Carlos Giambruni (Uruguay)
4th: Zdenek Cernik (Czech)
5th: Motoo Ogiso (Japan)
6th: Eric Suy (Belgium)

28th session, 1973

President: Leopoldo Benites (Ecuador)

Vice-Presidents (17): Cameroon, China, Czechoslovakia, Fiji, France, Ghana, Guyana, Honduras, Netherlands, Spain, Sri Lanka, Tunisia, Uganda, USSR, United Arab Emirates, United Kingdom, USA

Chairmen of Main Committees (7):
1st: Otto R. Borch (Denmark)
Special Political Committee: Karoly Szarka (Hungary)
2nd: Zewde Gabre-Sellassie (Ethiopia)
3rd: Yahya Mahmassani (Lebanon)
4th: Leonardo Díaz Gonzáles (Venezuela)
5th: Conrad S.M. Mselle (Tanzania)
6th: Sergio González Gálves (Mexico)

ANNEX IV

The Membership of the Credentials Committee from 1946 to 1973 was as follows:

First session, 1946
Byelorussia, China, Denmark, France, Haiti, Paraguay, Philippines, Saudi Arabia, Turkey

First special session, April-May 1947
Argentina, Australia, Denmark, Lebanon, Peru, Ukraine, USSR, USA, Yugoslavia

Second session, 1947
Chile (replaced by Bolivia at first meeting of the Credentials Committee), Czechoslovakia, Honduras, Iran, New Zealand, Norway, Poland, Siam, United Kingdom

Second special session, April-May 1948
Belgium, Dominican Republic, Egypt, India, Mexico, Netherlands, Pakistan, Ukraine, Uruguay.

Third session, 1948
Brazil, Burma, Canada, Ecuador, France, Iran, Sweden, Ukraine, Yemen

Fourth session, 1949
Belgium, Brazil, Byelorussia, Cuba, Iran, South Africa, USSR, USA, Uruguay

Fifth session, 1950
Belgium, Chile, India, Mexico, Thailand, Turkey, USSR, United Kingdom, USA

Sixth session, 1951
Bolivia, Byelorussia, Ethiopia, France, Haiti, Indonesia, Iraq, New Zealand, Norway

Seventh session, 1952
Belgium, Burma, Lebanon, New Zealand, Panama, Paraguay, Sweden, USSR, USA

Eighth session, 1953
Cuba, Iceland, Indonesia, New Zealand, Peru, Syria, USSR, United Kingdom, USA

Ninth session, 1954
Burma, El Salvador, France, Lebanon, New Zealand, Pakistan, USSR, USA, Uruguay

Tenth session, 1955
Afghanistan, Australia, Colombia, Dominican Republic, France, Indonesia, Iraq, USSR, USA

First emergency special session, 1-10 November 1956, and Second emergency special session, 4-10 November 1956, were served by the same membership as that of the tenth regular session.

11th session, 1956
Argentina, Brazil, Burma, Iraq, Netherlands, New Zealand, Spain, USSR, USA

12th session, 1957 and Third emergency special session, August 1958
Burma, Canada, Iceland, Liberia, Nicaragua, Panama, USSR, United Kingdom, USA

13th session, 1958
Argentina, Chile, France, Nepal, Tunisia, Turkey, Union of South Africa, USSR, USA

14th session, 1960 and Fourth emergency special session, September 1960
Afghanistan, Australia, Ecuador, France, Honduras, Italy, Pakistan, USSR, USA

15th session, 1960 and Third special session, August 1961
Costa Rica, Haiti, Morocco, New Zealand, Philippines, Spain, USSR, UAR, USA

16th session, 1961
Australia, Burma, Iceland, Italy, Mali, Nicaragua, Peru, USSR, USA

17th session, 1962 and Fourth special session, May 1963
Canada, El Salvador, Greece, Guinea, Indonesia, Mexico, Nigeria, USSR, USA

18th session, 1963
Algeria, Belgium, Ecuador, Iceland, Liberia, Nepal, Panama, USSR, USA

19th session, 1964
Australia, Cambodia, Costa Rica, Guatemala, Iceland, Madagascar, USSR, UAR, USA

20th session, 1965
Australia, Costa Rica, Guatemala, Iceland, Madagascar, Syria, USSR, UAR, USA

21st session, 1966 and Fifth special session, April 1967, and Fifth emergency special session, June 1967
Austria, El Salvador, Guinea, Ivory Coast, Japan, Nepal, Nicaragua, USSR, USA

22nd session, 1967
Ceylon, Ireland, Japan, Madagascar, Mali, Mexico, Paraguay, USSR, USA

23rd session, 1968
Austria, Brazil, Costa Rica, Liberia, Mongolia, New Zealand, Tanzania, USSR, USA

24th session, 1969
Bolivia, Iceland, Mongolia, Nicaragua, Sudan,
Thailand, Togo, USSR, USA

25th session, 1970
Australia, Ecuador, Greece, Ireland, Liberia,
Mauritania, Poland, USSR, USA

26th session, 1971
Australia, Colombia, France, Ireland, Liberia,
Mongolia, Somalia, USSR, USA

27th session, 1972
Belgium, China, Costa Rica, Japan, Senegal,
Tanzania, USSR, USA, Uruguay

28th session, 1973
China, Greece, Japan, Nicaragua, Senegal,
Tanzania, USSR, USA, Uruguay

ANNEX V

SELECTED SOURCES OF INFORMATION
ON THE GENERAL ASSEMBLY

A. United Nations Publications

Index to Proceedings of the General
Assembly (ST/LIB/SER.B/A/-)

This series of bibliographical guides to the
discussions and documentation of the sessions
of the General Assembly is the most useful tool
to the researcher as well as to official users
of United Nations documents. The Index appears
annually in the Bibliographical Series of the
United Nations Headquarters Library, and contain, inter alia, an index to speeches made by
representatives to the session, information as
to the republication of mimeographed documents
in the printed fascicles of Annexes to the Official Records, a subject index and a numerical
list of documents.

The first four sessions of the General Assembly
were covered by a series of mimeographed documents, containing checklists of documents issued for the sessions, under the document series
symbol A/INF/-. Beginning with the fifth session, in 1950, they are published in yearly volumes as sales publications. The Index to Proceedings (ST/LIB/SER.B/A.26), covering the 30th
regular session of the Assembly, for the first
time contained in an annex a voting chart of
resolutions adopted by recorded or roll-call
vote during the session.

Yearbook of the United Nations

Issued annually, as a United Nations sales publication, it covers the work of the General Assembly in detail with texts of resolutions

adopted and citations to relevant documents and references to previous Yearbook accounts; lists members of subsidiary organs appointed; has both a subject and name index. Its appendices include a roster of the United Nations, text of its Charter, and a list of UN Information Centres and Offices. The first volume of the Yearbook covered 1946/1947.

UN Monthly Chronicle, prepared by the United Nations Office of Public Information (OPI).

Presents every month an illustrated and summarized account of the activities of the United Nations and its specialized agencies. Available in English, French and Spanish.

Repertory of Practice of United Nations Organs

Useful when dealing with procedural matters. Issued irregularly since 1955, the Repertory treats the practice of the United Nations in a series of studies on the articles of the Charter or on parts of articles pertaining to the General Assembly (as well as other organs). From 1955 to 1973, there have been five volumes and supplements to some volumes.

Basic Facts, pamphlet prepared by OPI.

Provides a general introduction to the role and functions of the United Nations and its related agencies. Gives brief description of how the United Nations functions and its actions in various fields. Has a list of UN Information Centres and Services throughout the world. Is published irregularly, the latest in October 1972 (Sales no.:E.72.I.16).

<u>Everyman's United Nations</u>, prepared by
OPI.

This book contains a basic history of the United
Nations from 1945 to 1965. A five-year supplement brings it up to 1970.(Sales no.E.67.I.2
(cloth), 5 (paper); supplement, E.71.I.10
(cloth), 13 (paper). A ten-year supplement, now
in progress, will replace the first supplement
and bring the material up through 1975, thus
covering 30 years of United Nations history in
two volumes.

<u>List of Speeches and Visits made by</u>
<u>Heads of States and Dignitaries</u> (at
the United Nations) 1945-1972 (ST/OGS/
SER.F/4 and Add.1).

The addendum brings the information up to 1973-
1974. Prepared by the Sound Recording Unit of
the Telecommunication Section at the United Nations, it is a chronological listing of visits
by Heads of States and Dignitaries, and of their
speeches at the meetings of the United Nations
organs. From 1960, the speeches have been recorded in the original language, directly from
the floor. Prior to 1960, official sound records of proceedings were used in preparing the
tapes.

<u>Index to Resolutions of the General</u>
<u>Assembly</u> 1946-1970 (ST/LIB/SER.H/1,
Parts I and II, Sales no.E.72.I.14).

The resolutions supplements to the General Assembly (see Annex II) are useful as a guide to
the resolutions and decisions of the Assembly
for each session, and include its agenda, allocation of items, officers of the session,
elections to other bodies, texts of resolutions
and decisions adopted, with citations to reports
and draft resolutions, dates and numbers of the

plenary meetings adopting these texts, and an index. The end of each volume contains a list of subsidiary organs established by the Assembly whose composition may be found in the volumes of resolutions for the session indicated in roman figures, and a list providing a reference to the conventions and declarations, and to the agreements, covenants and treaties, the texts of which appear in the volumes of resolutions as indicated in the list.

B.   How to obtain United Nations documents

Catalogues and Price Lists of UN Publications

Prepared by the United Nations Publications, a yearly catalogue contains a limited list of material available, and should be supplemented by the more detailed lists in the Periodic Checklist and the United Nations Publications in Print.

A standing order service makes it possible, by ordering once, to receive all titles in any category, such as the General Assembly Official Records, plenary meetings, annexes, and committees. General Assembly mimeographed documents may be purchased on annual subscription.

General Assembly resolutions, plenary meetings, supplements and annexes are also available in microfiche. A microfiche price-list is available from the UN Publications service.

Publications and catalogues may be ordered from United Nations Publications, Room LX-2300, New York, N.Y. 10017, USA. In Europe, Africa and the Middle East, orders should be sent to the United Nations Publications, Palais des Nations, CH-1211, Geneva 10, Switzerland.

The Public Inquiries Unit of the Office of
Public Information at UN Headquarters responds
to requests for information on the activities
of the United Nations and its related agencies
by correspondence, telephone and personal visit.

United Nations documents and publications are
found in depository libraries and United Nations
Information Centers throughout the world, a list
of which is available in document ST/LIB/12/Rev.
5, of 1 January 1971.

United Nations reprints and microprint may be
obtained from the following private firms, which
have catalogues of their offerings:
    Kraus Reprint Corp., 16 E. 46th St., New
York, N. Y. 10017, or Route 100, Millwood, New
York 10546. Publishes Index to Proceedings of
the General Assembly, Sessions 1 to 15, 1946-
1961; UN Yearbook, 1946/47-1971; International
Law Commission Yearbook, 1949-1962.
    Oceana Publications, Dobbs Ferry, N.Y.10522.
Publishes General Assembly resolutions (see Annex II).
    Readex Microprint Publications, 101 Fifth
Ave., New York, N.Y. 10003. Reproduces almost
all General Assembly material, mimeographed and
printed, including the Official Records of the
General Assembly, as soon as it becomes available to be processed.

C. Guides on the Use of United Nations
              Documents

    United Nations Documentation: A brief guide
for official recipients. (ST/LIB/34), New York,
1974. Intended primarily for the staff of permanent missions accredited at UN Headquarters
and, more particularly, the staff in charge of
maintaining collections of United Nations docu-

ments and publications, it contains information of a practical nature and should be useful to the researcher who is not familiar with United Nations documentation.

List of United Nations Document Series Symbols (ST/LIB/SER.B/5/Rev.2, Sales no.:E.70. I.21), New York, 1970. Issued by the UN Dag Hammarskjold Library Bibliographical Series. The list is now being revised, bringing the material up through the end of 1975, and should be available early in 1977.

A Student's Guide to United Nations Documents and Their Use by John Bothwell McConaughy and Hazel Janet Blanks, with a preface by Joseph Groesbeck, Deputy Director, Dag Hammarskjold Library, United Nations, 1969. Published by the Council on International Relations and United Nations Affairs, the collegiate affiliate of the United Nations Association of the United States of America, 833 United Nations Plaza, New York, N.Y. 10017.

Citation Rules and Forms for United Nations Documents and Publications, by Marie H. Rothman, Long Island University Press, Brooklyn, N.Y., 1971. Discusses both United Nations mimeographed documents and printed publications, including legal materials and the documents of the San Francisco Conference and of the Preparatory Commission.

D.   Non-United Nations Publications

Issues before the (session number) General Assembly of the United Nations. Published by the Carnegie Endowment for International Peace, New York, N.Y. until the 25th session of the General Assembly in 1970, when UNA-USA (United Nations Association of the United States of America) assumed responsibility for publication of this annual survey of issues facing the General Assembly. Issued before the Assembly opens, its coverage is selective, concentrating on important issues in every category, and omitting some minor agenda items. To purchase copies, address GA ISSUES, UNA-USA, 345 East 46th St., New York, N.Y. 10017, USA.

United States Participation in the United Nations. An annual report by the President of the United States to the Congress. May be purchased from the Superintendent of Documents, US Government Printing Office, Washington, D.C. 20402, USA.

E. For Official Use at United Nations Headquarters

Journal of the United Nations

Issued at UN Headquarters on each working day; contains the program of meetings and agenda for each day of issue and the next day, a summary of scheduled meetings of the day previous to the day of issue (giving names of countries whose representative made statements but no summary of their remarks, briefly records the action taken -- election of officers, postponement of decisions, adoption of draft resolutions and draft reports --); both programs of meetings and summaries of meetings cite the number of the agenda item and the symbols of documents.

Supplementing the Journal is the Daily List of Documents, which appears in two parts during the sessions of the General Assembly. The second part lists only the documents relating to the

General Assembly session, and gives the agenda item numbers to which they relate, their symbols and titles, pagination, and language editions distributed on the day of issue or previously. The Journal and the Daily List are available only for official use at Headquarters.

General Assembly "Round-Up" Press Release

At the end of each General Assembly session the Press Section of the Office of Public Information issues a "round-up" press release containing the texts of all resolutions adopted and information on the votes thereon, with the number of the resolution, date and meeting when adopted. The round-up is prepared for the use of the information media and is not available externally.

Information for Delegations (ST/CS/-)

Issued annually by the Division of General Assembly Affairs of the Cffice of Conference Services. Contains information of a general nature about the United Nations Headquarters, and is applicable throughout the year, including information on documentation and other facilities available during sessions of the General Assembly.

SUBJECT INDEX

SUBJECT INDEX

Accounts (see Auditors, and UN Budget and
  Finances)
Ad Hoc Advisory Group on Youth, 673
Ad Hoc Commission on Prisoners of War, 696
Ad Hoc Committee for South West Africa, 781
Ad Hoc Committee of Experts to Examine the
  Finances of the UN and the Specialized
  Agencies, 1026
Ad Hoc Committee on Building (Geneva), 1240
Ad Hoc Committee on Cooperation between the UN
  Development Programme (UNDP) and the UN In-
  dustrial Development Organization (UNIDO),
  631
Ad Hoc Committees on Factors (NSGT), 818
Ad Hoc Committee on Headquarters, 1237
Ad Hoc Committee on Improvement of Methods of
  Work of the General Assembly, 1006
Ad Hoc Committee on the Indian Ocean, 129
Ad Hoc Committee on International Terrorism,
  1367
Ad Hoc Committee on Navigation Satellites
  (Outer Space Committee), 464
Ad Hoc Committee on Oman, 961
Ad Hoc Committee on the Palestinian Question,
  282
Ad Hoc Committee on the Peaceful Uses of Outer
  Space, 438
Ad Hoc Committee on the Question of the Estab-
  lishment of a Special UN Fund for Economic
  Development (SUNFED), 1065
Ad Hoc Committee on South West Africa, 759
Ad Hoc Committee on the Transmission of In-
  formation under Article 73 (e) of the
  Charter, 822
Ad Hoc Committee on the UN Organization for
  Industrial Development, 606
Ad Hoc Committee on the World Disarmament Con-
  ference, 182

Apartheid:
      International Conference of Experts for
        the Support of Victims of Colonialism
        and Apartheid in South Africa, 367
      Special Committee Against, 337
      UN Commission on the Racial Situation in
        South Africa, 332
      UN Good Offices Commission on Treatment
        of People of Indian Origin in the Un-
        ion of South Africa, 334
      Unit on Apartheid, 361
Arab Territories, occupied (see Palestine
   Question)
Arbitration:
      Italian-Libyan Mixed Arbitration Commis-
        sion, 243
Arms Control:
      Group of consultant Experts on the Econo-
        mic and Social Consequences of the
        Arms Race and Military Expenditures,
        192
      Group of Consultant Experts on the Effects
        of the Possible Use of Nuclear Weapons,
        and on the Security and Economic Impli-
        cations for States of the Acquisition
        and Further Development of These
        Weapons, 169
      Group of Consultant Experts on Napalm and
        other Incendiary Weapons, 176
      Group of Consultant Experts to Study the
        Effects of the Possible Use of Chemi-
        cal and Bacteriological Weapons, 172
Assessments, scale of (see Committee on Con-
   tributions)
Assistance to Developing Countries (see Dis-
   armament, economic consequences)
Atomic Energy, peaceful uses (see also Nuclear
Weapons):
      Advisory Committee on Peaceful Uses (see
        UN Scientific Advisory Committee), 414

Atomic Energy, peaceful uses:
    Atomic Energy Commission, 400
    Committee of Twelve (on international
        control), 412
    Consultations of Six Permanent Members
        of the Atomic Energy Commission, 408
    International Conferences on Peaceful
        Uses, 422
    UN Scientific Advisory Committee and
        Scientific Advisory Panel, 414
Atomic Energy, radiation, UN Scientific Com-
    mittee on Effects (UNSCEAR), 423
Atomic Energy Commission, 400
Auditors:
    Board of Auditors, 40
    Panel of External Auditors, 1089

Bacteriological (Biological) (see Chemical
    and Bacteriological)
Bacteriological Warfare, UN Commission of In-
    vestigation of charges of use by UN Forces,
    274
Balkans:
    Balkan Sub-Commission (POC), 121
    Standing Committee on the Repatriation of
        Greek Children, 376
    UN Special Committee, 113
Basutoland, Bechuanaland and Swaziland, Sub-
    Committee (Committee on Decolonization),
    936
Berlin, elections:
    UN Commission to Investigate Conditions
        for Free Elections in Germany, 379
Board of Auditors, 40
British Guiana (see Committee on Decoloniza-
tion):
    Sub-Committee, 934
    Sub-Committee of Good Offices, 935
Budget, UN (see UN Budget and Finances)

Protein Problem confronting Developing Countries, Panel of Experts, 629
Public Administration:
    Meetings of Experts on the UN Programme, 686
    Special Committee on Public Administration Problems, 681
    Working Party of Experts, 683
Public Information (see UN Public Information)

Racial Questions (see Apartheid, Discrimination, Human Rights)
Racial Discrimination, Committee on Elimination, 712
Radiation, atomic, effects (see Atomic Energy, radiation)
Refugees and Displaced Persons:
    Office of the UN High Commissioner for Refugees (UNHCR), and its subsidiary bodies (Advisory Committee, UN Refugee Fund Executive Committee, Executive Committee of the UNHCR), 543-578
    UN Relief and Works Agency for Palestine Refugees in the Near East (UNRWA), 522
Refugees, Financing:
    Negotiating Committee on Contributions to Programmes of Relief and Rehabilitation (in Korea), and Relief and Reintegration of Palestine Refugees, 1035
    Negotiating Committees for Extra-Budgetary Funds, 1039-1040
    Working Group on Financing of UN Relief and Works Agency for Palestine Refugees in Near East, 1057
Refugees, relief:
    Committee of Trustees for UN Trust Fund for South Africa, 363
    Committee on UN Relief and Rehabilitation Administration (UNRRA), 522

Secretariat, UN (see UN Secretariat)
Secretariat Study Group on the UN Emergency
    Force, 109
Security (see Peace and Security, Peace-keep-
    ing Activities)
Shipping, international:
        Preparatory Committee for UN Conference
            on Code of Conduct for Liner Confer-
            ences, 635
        UN Conference on Code of Conduct for
            Liner Conferences, 637
        Working Group on International Legis-
            lation (UNCITRAL), 1322
Somaliland, UN Advisory Council for Trust
    Territory under Italian Administration,
    726
South Africa (Union of, Republic of):
        Committee of Trustees of UN Trust Fund,
            363
        International Conference of Experts for
            Support of Victims of Colonialism and
            Apartheid, 367
        Special Committee against Apartheid, 337
        UN Commission on Racial Situation, 332
        UN Good Offices Commission on Treatment
            of People of Indian Origin, 334
South Viet-Nam, UN Fact-finding Mission, 388
South West Africa (see also Namibia):
        Ad Hoc Committees, 759, 781
        Committee of Investigation (on South West
            Africa), 178
        Committee on, 762
        Special Committee for, 773
        Sub-Committee on (Committee on Decolon-
            ization), 937
        UN Good Offices Committee, 770
Southern Africa (see Africa, Southern)
Southern Rhodesia, Sub-Committee (Committee
    on Decolonization), 925

1445

United Nations Conference on the Exploration
   of Peaceful Uses of Outer Space, Vienna,
   1968, and Panel of Experts for the Preparation, 482, 484
United Nations Conference on the Human Environment, Stockholm, 1972, and Preparatory Com-
   mittee, 640, 653
United Nations Conference on the Law of the
   Sea: First, Geneva (1958); Second, Geneva
   (1960); Third, New York and Caracas, Venezuela (1973 , 1974), 1356
United Nations Conference on Prescription
   (Limitation) in the International Sale of
   Goods, 1317
United Nations Conference on Trade and Develop-
   ment (UNCTAD), 638
United Nations Council for Libya, 234
United Nations Council for Namibia, and its
   subsidiary bodies (Ad Hoc Committees on
   Question of Travel Documents, on Reorgani-
   zation, Standing Committees I, II, III),
   784-808
United Nations Council for South West Africa
   (see UN Council for Namibia)
United Nations Development Decade, First, 621
United Nations Development Decade, Proposals,
   622
United Nations Development Programme (UNDP):
      Ad Hoc Committee on Cooperation between
         UNDP and UNIDO, 631
      Preparatory Committee for the Second
         UN Development Decade, 616
      UN Development Decade, first, 621
      UN Development Programme and Governing
         Council, 633
United Nations Educational and Training Pro-
   grammes(see Africa, Southern, education
   and training; and Education)

United Nations Emergency Force (UNEF):
    Advisory Committee (on a UN Emergency
       Force), 104
    Committee appointed under General As-
       sembly resolution 448 (on UNEF), 107
    Secretariat Study Group, 109
    Survey Team, 110
United Nations Environment Programme (UNEP)
  (see also Environment), 653
United Nations Fact-finding Mission to South
  Viet-Nam, 388
United Nations Field Service, 102
United Nations Finances (see UN Budget and
  Finances)
United Nations Forces:
    Special Committee on a UN Guard, 100
    UN Field Service, 102
United Nations Fund for Namibia, 812
United Nations Good Offices Commission on the
  Treatment of People of Indian Origin in the
  Union of South Africa, 334
United Nations Good Offices Committee on South
  West Africa, 770
United Nations Guard, Special Committee, 100
United Nations Headquarters and Offices:
    Ad Hoc Committee on Building (Geneva),
      1240
    Ad Hoc Committee on Headquarters, 1237
    Headquarters Advisory Committee, 1230
    Headquarters Commission, 1228
    Interim Committee for Selection of a De-
      finite Site for Permanent Headquarters
      of the UN, 1218
    Negotiations Committee on Negotiations
      with the Authorities of the USA con-
      cerning Arrangements required in the
      USA, 1221
    Permanent Headquarters Committee, 1224

United Nations High Commissioner for Refugees,
547
United Nations High Commissioner for Refugees,
Office: 543-578

Advisory Committee on Refugees, 552

Executive Committee of the High Commissioner's Programme, 565

UN Refugee Fund (UNREF) Executive Committee, 555

United Nations Host Country Relations:

Committee on Relations with Host Country,
1257

Informal Joint Committee, 1250

US Mission to the UN (USUN)-New York City
(NYC) Host Country Advisory Committee,
1245

United Nations Industrial Development Organization (UNIDO):

Ad Hoc Committee on the UN Organization
for Industrial Development, 606

Ad Hoc Committee on Cooperation between
the UNDP and UNIDO, 631

UN Industrial Development Organization
(UNIDO), and its Industrial Development Board (IDB), 607

United Nations International Children's Emergency Fund (UNICEF), 525

United Nations Joint Staff Pension Board, 1144

United Nations Joint Staff Pension Fund (see
UN Joint Staff Pension Board)

United Nations Korean Reconstruction Agency,
(UNKRA), 579

United Nations Malaysian Mission, 386

United Nations Mediator in Palestine, 291

United Nations Membership (Annex I), 1371 and
1379 (see also UN Admission of New Members)

United Nations Mission for the Supervision of
the Referendum and the Elections in Equator-
ial Guinea (Committee on Decolonization),
940